THE ART OF CRETE
AND EARLY GREECE

THE PRELUDE TO GREEK ART

BY FRIEDRICH MATZ

GREYSTONE PRESS/NEW YORK

Translated by Ann E. Keep

To
GEORG KARO
on his 90th birthday
11 January 1962

Frontispiece: 'The Pelasgian Wall': remains of a Mycenaean citadel on the Acropolis, Athens. 13th cent. B.C. *Cf. p. 9.*

The publishers and translator are grateful to Mr. R. A. Higgins, Deputy Keeper, Department of Greek and Roman Antiquities, British Museum, for reading the text and making many valuable suggestions.

CONTENTS

LIST OF PLATES

For black-and-white photographic illustrations see pp. 227ff.

CHRONOLOGICAL TABLE AND MAPS

ACKNOWLEDGEMENTS

The following museums allowed reproduction of the coloured plates listed below:

National Museum, Athens 1, 2, 5, 6, 7, 9, 12, 36, 37, 39, 41, 42, 43, 45, 46, 50, 54, 56

Archaeological Museum, Iraklion 8, 10, 11, 13, 14, 22, 25, 26, 27, 28, 29, 30, 31, 32, 33, 34, 35, 38, 40, 44

5

We take this opportunity of expressing our sincere thanks to M. Karouzos, Director of the National Museum, Athens and M. Platon, Director of the Archaeological Museum, Iraklion, Crete for permission to take photographs in their museums and their kind assistance.

Professor Bernabó Brea of Syracuse was kind enough to permit reproduction of the amphora on p. 39 and the jewellery on p. 61.

Dr. Theocharis of Athens allowed reproduction of the cup on p. 40 and Professor Blegen of Athens provided material for the plan on p. 202.

M. J. A. Lavaud of Paris was responsible for all the coloured plates.

LIST OF FIGURES

*All the figures were drawn by Heinz Prüstel, Mainz, as were the maps,
from data provided by the author.*

INTRODUCTION

As one climbs the Acropolis in Athens one's eye is at once caught by the little THE SETTING marble Temple of Athena Nike, which stands before the Propylaea. If one makes a detour for a few yards to the right, and stands on the bastion that supports this jewel of Greek architecture, one may enjoy a splendid view over Attica and the Saronic Gulf (Gulf of Aegina). On returning to his main path the visitor finds himself confronted by a curious and contradictory scene. Before him rises the western facade of the Parthenon, with the blue sky in the background, which dominates the entire Acropolis and the surrounding countryside. To the left the view is obscured by the marble south wall of the Propylaea, which abuts upon some masonry, consisting of crudely hewn blocks of limestone. Behind are the cliffs of the Acropolis, rising up to the Parthenon above. This juxtaposition of natural beauty and formal classicism is somewhat disconcerting. Most visitors pass by unseeing, all too keen to reach the classical splendour of the Acropolis. Yet this contrasting picture contains something that is fundamental to an understanding of Greek art. It links together in a single unity primitive beginnings and the peak of perfection. It illustrates the complexity of the problems that face us in the study of Greek classicism, the very foundation of Western art.

This 'Cyclopean' wall is a relic of a Mycenaean citadel. It was built not later FRONTIS-PIECE than the 13th century B.C., at a time when there were Greeks but not as yet Hellenes. For nearly one hundred years, since the days of Schliemann, scholars have been endeavouring to establish the relationship between the pre-Greek, Mycenaean culture of the Bronze Age and the classical culture of the Hellenes. In the following pages we shall attempt to show the contribution that our present knowledge of the pre-Greek era can make to the elucidation of this problem. We shall therefore not lead the reader over the threshold that he feels impelled to cross. Instead we shall seek to show how the forms of the future are contained in those of an earlier and more primitive phase of development. It is not our purpose to contrast the primitive and the perfect in order to demonstrate that progress took place, but to examine artistic creation in its infancy. Our frontispiece thus raises a question in our minds: Is it really possible to treat pre-Greek and Greek styles together? Or are the former simply an element in the historical development of the latter?

The complex character of our picture shows to what extent the Hellenes, even at the peak of their prowess, were influenced by their pre-Hellenic past, and how important our question therefore is.

When Pericles planned to reconstruct the Acropolis, an integral part of the design was the monumental gate of the Propylaea. But the architect Mnesicles was hindered in the execution of his plan by the fact that several ancient sanctuaries were situated around the entrance to the citadel. Among them were, in addition to the Temple of Athena Nike with its bastion, a part of the old Mycenaean fortress wall. On the strength of an utterance of the Delphic oracle, this 'Pelasgian Wall' was regarded as sacrosanct. The argument as to its fate was settled in favour of the more conservative element in Athenian society, and the death of Pericles, followed by the outbreak of the Peloponnesian War, made their victory a permanent one. The south wing of the Propylaea was not completed, and thus the Cyclopean wall that was to have been pulled down remained standing — to this day, as can be seen from the frontispiece.

This is just one example of the strength of tradition, the sources of which we shall be exploring in the pages of this volume. It will be obvious that tradition did not always act as an impediment, as it did in this instance.

GEOGRAPH-
ICAL
FACTORS

MAPS PP. 238-41

From historical we may turn to geographical factors. The title of this book relates only to the larger part of our subject. In reality the Aegean area formed a single unit, despite all the local differences that existed, as early as the 8th century B.C., when the first Greek colonies were founded. For this reason, in addition to mainland Greece, we shall consider Thrace and the coastlands of Asia Minor, and the archipelagos of the Aegean and Ionian Seas as well as Crete. The magic of this landscape is of course rooted in its unique natural beauty. Even where it is most grandiose, wild and elemental, one never loses the sense of being in a country that is civilized. But this term must be interpreted in its loftiest sense, to mean not simply that it abounds in works created by human hands, but that the whole countryside is steeped in history — that it is permeated with a kind of spiritual quality. To understand the emotional intensity with which it is charged, it is essential to perceive it *in continuo,* so to speak — in other words, to visualize the close connection that exists between the present and the past, a connection that extends back even to prehistoric times.

Already the fact that one can rapidly gain an impression of the principal geographical features illustrates the power of the Greek landscape to influence history and culture. It is characterized by an extremely high degree of plasticity. By this we mean not merely the rich beauty of mountains and valleys, bays and islands — what the geographer refers to as the relief — but also the suggestive contours of the barren mountain ranges, and the sharp contrast between light and shade, due to the unique transparency of the atmosphere. Then there is the variegated nature of the mountainous scenery, which accounts for the fact that already in prehistoric times each region was to a large extent able to develop along lines of its own. Even in the broad fertile plains of Thessaly and Boeotia the mountains that skirt them invariably form an integral part of the landscape, although they may be many miles distant from the place where one is standing. In general, however, one's view is limited, and one can encompass it at a glance. Typical in this respect is Attica, where the plain of Cephisus, bounded by mountains, can be seen in its entirety from the Acropolis, and one can also just make out the Mesogaea in the east and the Eleusinian Plain in the north-west.

One must also note the highly indented coastline. Deep inroads are made into the land mass by large bodies of water such as the Gulf of Corinth, the Saronic Gulf and the Pagasaean Gulf (Gulf of Volo) — as well as countless smaller bays and harbours, separated by numerous peninsulas and promontories. Even the centres of mainland Greece and the Peloponnese art not so far from the sea that it cannot be glimpsed from the mountain-tops. Similarly, there is nowhere in the Aegean whence, with good visibility, one cannot see some stretch of coastline or some island on the horizon.

This alternation of land and sea acquires a special quality where it is combined with an abundance of surface relief, as occurs where high mountains drop down steeply to the water's edge. For example, Mount Olympus in Thessaly (almost 3000 m. high) and Mount Ida in Crete (2500 m.) tower over the surrounding countryside and are a most impressive sight. The landscape is somewhat reminiscent of the Atlas Mountains, Etna, or the Lebanon. Here, too, dazzling white snow-capped peaks contrast with the deep blue of the sea. But a comparison shows what exceptional charm the Greek landscape acquires by virtue of its high degree of articulation. One must also mention the radiant translucent quality of the light in Greece, which gives colours a splendid depth and a soft shimmer.

The full significance of all these natural factors becomes apparent when one considers the geographical situation of the Aegean lands. They are separated by the Bosporus, Dardanelles and Aegean from the Anatolian peninsula, that western most promontory of Asia, yet historically there have been close links between these two regions. The chains of mountains that traverse Asia Minor from east to west are continued in Crete, the islands of the Aegean, and in Greece itself, where they merge into the ranges of the north-western Balkans — and so into the backbone of Europe. Crete and the other Aegean islands are relics of these ranges, much of which are beneath sea-level. In early times the sea acted as a bridge rather than a barrier. This meant that whereas Hellas was closed towards the west and north it was open towards the south and east. It is true that the western coastline of Greece is also highly indented, and that mariners could make their way northwards along it. But communication with the hinterland was barred by high mountains, and the overland connections to the north were more important than those by sea. This led to the peculiar situation that Hellas, although geographically an integral part of Europe, was open to traffic from the east and south, from Asia and Africa. Its prehistory and early history were characterized by the penetration of cultural influences from south-east to north-west, while corresponding counter-pressures were exerted in the reverse direction by 'under-developed' peoples — the latter being felt more strongly at some times than at others.

Yet despite these links the difference between the Aegean area and the Anatolian plateau is very clearly marked. The latter lies at the threshold of desert country which had a considerable influence upon the advanced cultures that developed in Mesopotamia and the Nile valley.

It is thus significant that Greece is the most highly articulated region of the Old World and stands in the same relationship to the rest of Europe as Europe itself (including Greece) does to the Near East. These geographical factors help to explain much in the art history of the Aegean lands. However, at this point we shall not explore this question further. It is enough to point to the tension that made itself felt between the various cultural influences present in the region. From this we can already deduce that the early art of the Aegean was concerned, first and foremost, with asserting its individuality among the competing trends that existed in the surrounding area.

We may now go on to consider the peoples that actually produced these works of art. We have seen that in this region, with its unique temperate climate, man experiences a correspondingly high degree of emotional tension. The prime task of students of early Aegean culture is to ascertain how far knowledge of the pre-Greek period can help us to understand the works of the Greeks themselves. This, as we have seen, was the question raised by the contrasting view before us as we ascended the Acropolis. It may also be considered from a broader angle, as relating to the incipient contrast between East and West.

DISCOVERY The source material for the art history of the Aegean has been brought to light gradually, piece by piece. The first stage in the process of discovery was the work of Schliemann, in the 1870s. He studied the culture of mainland Greece from approximately 1600 to 1100 B.C., which even today may still properly be called Mycenaean. When Sir Arthur Evans began his excavations at Knossos 30 years later we obtained the first glimpse of the sources of Mycenaean culture. Cretan culture is also known by the term 'Minoan culture'. This is derived from King Minos, the legendary builder of the labyrinth, which the later Greeks identified with the site of the palace subsequently excavated by Evans. The 'heroic age' of Minoan archaeology extends from 1900 to 1930. During these three decades the palaces of Phaestos, Hagia Triada and Mallia were excavated, as well as that of Knossos. Since then a number of significant, and even brilliant, results have also been recorded at various sites. But none of the discoveries made since 1930 have had the epoch-making effect of those in earlier years, which we shall now consider.

Aegean archaeology owes its inception to the zeal and energy of a dilettante. *First phase:* Schliemann began his excavations at Troy in 1871 and at Mycenae in 1874. *1870—1900* His achievements astonished the entire world of learning. True, he pursued a solitary path, and some time elapsed before he established contact with other scholars. But his motives were characteristic of the spirit of the age, a spirit which influenced archaeological research in other ways as well. Schliemann began his career as an impoverished and neglected youth. He worked as an apprentice, cabin-boy and messenger before, at the age of 41, when he had already become a wealthy man, he renounced his business interests to carry out the plans of his youth. As he wrote in 1868, during a journey to Greece: "At last I could realize the dream of my life, to visit the scene of events that had interested me so profoundly, the home of heroes whose adventures had delighted and comforted me in my childhood." In his autobiography he describes the dream he had as a ten-year-old boy, in the company of his childhood sweetheart, when he was living in his native village in Mecklenburg. He dreamed that he would make Homer's Troy rise once again from the earth by excavating its ruins. Schliemann is prone to emphatic language, but we can discern a romantic note in his words. He was born in 1822, and thus it is not surprising that the ideas of the later Romantics should find expression in the work of a scholar of his generation. Of greater significance is his unsophisticated, and essentially un-Romantic, belief in the historical reality of Homer's narrative. This was a naive reflection of — one could almost say, a layman's compliment to — the positivist conception of history fashionable at the time, which in classical scholarship had begun to displace the humanistic and romantic tradition. "From the very start the sole purpose of my excavations was to discover Troy, the site of which had been the subject of a hundred books by a hundred scholars, none of whom, however, had as yet tried to bring it to light by undertaking actual excavations. If I should fail, I would none the less be more than pleased to have been able to enrich the world of learning by discovering a few interesting pages from the ancient history of the great Hellenic people." These sentences, written in 1881, show clearly that in his enthusiasm for history Schliemann was a child of his time. More than a hundred years earlier, when Winckelmann, who was also ahead of his contemporaries, thought of carrying out excavations at Olympia, he wrote: "I am assured that a careful examination of this site will throw considerable light upon the history of art." In other words, Winckelmann was looking for works of art, Schliemann for historical documents. As well as the differences in the personalities of the two men evidenced by these remarks, they reveal a characteristic contrast between two ages.

To assess Schliemann's achievement in both its positive and negative aspects, one should not forget that in the same decade in which he set to work, major systematic excavations were undertaken by other scholars at Olympia, Pergamon, Samothrace and Delos. This again shows how Schliemann, contrary to his own intentions, was actually working within a wider framework. His merit lies in the healthy instinct that allowed him to approach a non-classical object, as yet still unclassified, with singular lack of prejudice. In the last instance the fact that Schliemann belonged to the category of great business entrepreneurs helps one to understand his motives, and so to assess this first period in the history of the discovery of Creto-Mycenaean culture. Schliemann embodies this type in one of its early forms, with all its pros and cons. He has become a cautionary example for later explorers in so far as matters of finance and organization are concerned.

From Troy Schliemann felt himself spontaneously drawn to Mycenae, and from there to nearby Tiryns. Here his success was no less than it had been at Troy. The precious objects found in the graves of Mycenaean princes surpassed the 'Treasure of Priam' in size and splendour. But the relationship between his finds remained unclear, and his attitude to the academic world was still ambiguous. Even where other scholars showed good will they found that Schliemann and they were speaking in different languages. The complex stratification of the 10 metre-high mound at Troy presented unfathomable difficulties, especially for a dilettante. Those who were opposed to Schliemann or who doubted his achievements were thereby given ample ammunition.

It stands to his credit, and testifies to his sense of realism, that he himself sought the aid of an architect. His choice could scarcely have been more fortunate. Wilhelm Dörpfeld had been associated with Schliemann since his expedition to Troy in 1882. He was then 29 years old, and had already won his spurs in the excavation of Olympia. He now succeeded in deciphering the stratigraphy of Troy. The importance of his discovery lay in his conclusion that the so-called 'burnt city', which yielded the treasure he discovered, was much more ancient than the stately citadel (Troy VI), which Dörpfeld was the first to identify, and that the latter could be assigned to the same period as the Mycenaean citadels in Hellas. Dörpfeld brought final proof of his hypothesis after Schliemann's death in 1890, through the results he obtained during his two 'heroic campaigns' in 1893 and 1894. These expeditions were made possible by a grant from the German Emperor, William II.

For this triumph Dörpfeld was greatly indebted to two archaeologists of his own age who succeeded in establishing a sound chronological basis for Schliemann's finds at Mycenae, thereby making them available to other scholars. In 1879 Adolf Furtwaengler and Georg Loeschcke, in their monumental work *Mycenaean Pottery,* gave a scientific description of the ceramic ware found in the shaft graves of Mycenae. In 1884 they produced a still more comprehensive work entitled *Mycenaean Vases,* in which they classified all the painted vases and sherds of this type known at the time. When arranged in orderly succession it became feasible for the first time to draw inferences from one object with regard to the others. An important aid to classification was the connection with datable objects from Egypt or Asia Minor. This made it possible to speak of a 'Mycenaean culture', which flourished between 1500 and 1200 B.C. The historical analysis of the Homeric epics that had been inaugurated by F. A. Wolf received a fresh impetus from the many subjects described by the poet depicted on monuments of Mycenaean culture. The argument that in this way one could distinguish between earlier and later material in the Iliad and the Odyssey was advanced by several leading scholars, and it obtained wide currency. The accepted view of Mycenaean history after these first thirty years, before any knowledge had been gained of the Minoan world, is set out in exemplary form in a chapter in the volume *Ancient Gems* (1900) by Adolf Furtwaengler, who studied Mycenaean sealstones. Even today it is still a standard work.

It was in the epoch-making year 1900, when Furtwaengler's work appeared, *Second phase:* that the first excavations were made at Knossos. These became possible, not *1900—1930* only as a result of the natural interest among scholars in Crete, but also by the fact that external obstacles to investigation, which had hitherto proved insuperable, were overcome at this time. In 1898 Crete was *de facto* incorporated into the kingdom of Greece, and the period of internecine strife on the island came to an end. Already Schliemann had deduced that evidence of Mycenaean culture was to be found in Crete. He had deferred his plan to carry out excavations at Knossos mainly because he had hoped that the exaggerated demands put forward by the proprietors of the site would become less of a problem at some future date. But he died before he could fulfil his wishes. Sir Arthur Evans, as he was later to become, was drawn to Crete from the 1880s onwards by remains of a pre-Greek script which he had noted on objects, particularly engraved stones, from that island. He was in a position to invest in his enterprise his sizable fortune as well as his considerable energy. He was also a scholar of broad vision who was at the same time extremely conscientious. He had a valuable assistant in the Scot Duncan Mackenzie, who unfortunately died at an early date; he was particularly helpful in deciphering the stratification and classifying the ceramic finds. At this time the Italian archaeologists Federico Halbherr, Roberto Paribeni, Luigi Pernier and Luigi Savignoni commenced excavation work at the palaces of Phaestos and Hagia Triada, in the south of Crete. The results were magnificent. At this time most of the palace of Mallia, on the north coast, was investigated by a French mission led by Fernand Chapouthier and Pierre Demargne. American, British and Greek expeditions were also mounted. In the east of Crete Richard B. Seager explored the early graves on the little island of Mochlos and the small port on nearby Pseira, while Harriet Boyd Hawes carried out work at the town of Gournia on the Gulf of Mirabello. The settlements of Palaikastro and Zakro on the east coast and the hill sanctuary of Petsofa near Palaikastro were excavated by three Englishmen: Richard C. Bosanquet, Richard M. Dawkins and David G. Hogarth. Joseph Hazzidakis, the Greek pioneer of Minoan archaeology, explored some fine private houses near Tylissos, to the west of Knossos. His successor, Stephanos Xanthoudides, was mainly concerned with the early *tholoi* in the Messara, in the south of Crete. In the other parts of the island there were no discoveries that bore a similar epoch-making character. The most important were the excavations carried out by the Greek archaeologist Christos Tsountas and the Englishman Alan J. B. Wace in Thessaly, which gave a glimpse of the Neolithic era, and Tsountas' investigations into the culture of the Cyclades. The chapters on the Aegean in the relevant volumes of the *Cambridge Ancient History*, which appeared between 1930 and 1932, incorporate the knowledge gained by the end of this second period in the history of discovery.

Third phase: from 1930 During the third phase scholars were concerned with the task of filling out a framework that had already been established. Whether this phase should now be seen as concluded is none too clear. One of its characteristic features has been the re-examination, in the light of new evidence, of old problems that seemed to have been solved already. For example, at Troy Dörpfeld left large mounds of earth standing to serve as a means of controlling his observations later. This task was undertaken in six campaigns carried out between

1932 and 1938 by an American expedition led by Carl W. Blegen. The outcome of their labours was a monumental work in several volumes containing a brilliant confirmation of Dörpfeld's results, and also expanding on them in many essential respects. Instead of the nine strata discovered by Dörpfeld we now have no less than forty, most of which are, of course, sub-divisions of Dörpfeld's classification. This has done much to clarify the history of the construction of Troy, and has also thrown a good deal of light on the chronology of nearby cultures and their relation to Troy.

Schliemann presented his finds from the shaft-graves in the citadel at Mycenae as a free gift to the National Museum in Athens, where they were made available for examination by other scholars. But the first person to study them systematically was Georg Karo, who published his conclusions in a monumental work between 1930 and 1933. The discovery of the Grave Circle B outside the citadel walls by Johannes Papadimitriou in 1952 has helped to round off our knowledge of this architectural complex.

Similar progress has been made in the study of ceramics, which is of much importance in determining questions of chronology. The work of Furtwaengler and Loeschcke has been succeeded by Arne Furumark's *Mycenaean Pottery*, which in two volumes attempts the gigantic task of ordering and systematizing the enormous amount of material that has now been collected.

There is no need to describe the countless excavations of varying magnitude that have been undertaken during the last thirty years. On the mainland the most important have been those by Carl W. Blegen at Pylos and by Alan J. B. Wace at Mycenae. In Crete the directors of the Department of Antiquities, Spyridon Marinatos and Nikolaos Platon, have enlarged our knowledge of archaeological topography and elucidated a large number of questions relating to chronology and art history at the old sites and elsewhere. The follow-up explorations by the English scholars John D. S. Pendlebury, Richard W. Hutchinson and Sinclair Hood at Knossos and its environs, and of the Italian archaeologist Doro Levi at Phaestos, have been characteristic of this stage of research.

The most important of the long-standing problems that have undergone re-examination in the light of subsequent information do not lie within the field of archaeology proper. In 1953, after many earlier efforts had ended in failure, Michael Ventris succeeded in deciphering the Mycenaean script. He established that the documents in the so-called 'Linear B' system were written in an early pre-Homeric form of Greek. The detailed examination of these documents is now mainly a task for philologists. But this discovery naturally has a direct effect upon the historical picture, particularly in so far as the assessment of finds is concerned. We are now much better informed than we were before about the relationship of this whole world to Homer and to the Greeks in general.

Finally, to appreciate the present state of research it is necessary to bear in mind the extent to which the results of excavations in the Near East have clarified the connection between the still largely prehistoric Minoan and Mycenaean cultures on one hand and neighbouring historic cultures on the other. In this connection we may consider Boğazköy, the capital of the Hatti kingdom, and Ras Shamra, the notable commercial centre on the coast of Syria. Our knowledge of these two cities throws as much light upon the links between the ancient cultures of the Orient and the Bronze Age Aegean as the deciphering of 'Linear B' has thrown upon their links with Hellas in later times.

Present state of Aegean historiography It is no accident that emphasis is laid here upon the incomplete state of our knowledge at the present time. Many details still remain to be added, many points to be clarified; many questions are still open. Among the tasks awaiting archaeologists in the future is the study of the art of Minoan Crete and pre-Hellenic Greece. The material is there, mainly in the shape of finds discovered through excavation. One of the delights of archaeology is that, to a greater extent than in any other branch of historical study, the researcher is constantly surprised by new discoveries and has to take fresh source material into account. One's picture of a given epoch is necessarily provisional — as is also the case with the results of research in other related disciplines. This glimpse of the history of discovery has led us naturally to consideration of the whole problem of the ancient civilizations, and so to the view taken of them by modern historians. The latter is based, not only on the existing source material, which is of course limited and incomplete, but also on scholarly interpretation, and thus on more general factors as well. This means that we, too, in this volume must endeavour to establish a coherent historical picture. The point made above with regard to geographical factors is equally relevant to historical factors. At present the chief task facing archaeologists seems to be to examine the evidence relating to the incipient dichotomy between East and West, in so far as this finds reflection in art. This then is the object of our survey, as far as art history is concerned. It differs from existing studies of Minoan and Mycenaean culture, including those written by the author in other circumstances twelve and six years ago.

PLATE 1 — Polished red bowl. Neolithic. Sesklo, Thessaly. Appróx. 3000 B.C. *National Museum, Athens. Height 12.5 cm. Cf. pp. 24, 32.*

PLATE 2 — Sub-Neolithic bowl, painted in a dark colour on a light slip. Dimini, Thessaly. First half of the 3rd millennium B.C. *National Museum, Athens. Diameter 22.5 cm. Cf. p. 28 and p. 32.*

I. INCUNABULA
Styles of the Neolithic

'Language of style'

The student of Minoan and Mycenaean Bronze Age art and culture who sets out in search of the links with classical Greece cannot afford to ignore the finds dating from the Stone Age. The term 'Stone Age' should of course not be applied too strictly, since metals were known already long before the dawn of the Bronze Age. But for a long time their influence upon cultural development was not appreciated. What do these early finds contribute to our understanding of the era with which we are primarily concerned? This question is obviously of importance from a historical point of view. For at the very basis of modern scholarship lies the concept that prehistoric material can serve as a historical source if the problems which its evaluation raises are approached in a proper spirit — that is to say, within a sufficiently broad framework. It can tell us something about cultural affinities and movements of population. But it can also do more than this. It is not simply a phrase to speak of a 'language of style' in relation to works of art. The decoration on a prehistoric object can be a substitute for a written document, and can convey to us the thoughts of the man who designed it, provided that it is treated in a correct manner. Naturally, the differences in means of expression should not be overlooked. Ornamental elements — or motifs, as they are usually called — possess a freedom that we only find in certain special circumstances when dealing with linguistic material. But in the relationship between an ornament and its wearer we can establish typological differences, i.e. we can classify them according to criteria of time and space. The groups that emerge correspond to the various groups of languages known to philology.

It is a basic axiom of linguistics that these groups can be understood only as criteria of different ethnic entities. Speaking metaphorically, it could be said that in the history of decoration it is not the style so much as the 'syntax' that enables us to identify the various ethnic groups involved and to ascertain the differences between them. Of course, this cannot be done with such precision by these means as is possible with the aid of linguistic material. But the concept of 'inner form' or 'form structure' is used by modern scholars who have adopted this approach. It will be obvious that this method can be of much assistance to us in identifying the prehistoric element in classical styles. We shall find it easier to see why this is so when we examine the works themselves.

The earliest Neolithic finds to be brought to light by systematic excavation were discovered at about the same time as the palaces in Crete. Since then the amount of material available has grown enormously. During the last few years in particular our picture of this period has been changing almost annually, and this state of affairs is likely to continue in the future. However, it should not be an impossibility for us to attempt to summarize the present state of our knowledge. The series of finds is most complete in Thessaly, and it is in this region, too, that objects have been discovered from the remotest periods.

Sites

In the well-watered and fertile plain between Larissa and Volo there are more than 150 *magulas* — low hills that were inhabited for centuries, and are now covered with debris that may be as much as 10 metres thick. The largest of these *magulas* has a diameter of almost 300 metres. It is more usual to find the Neolithic and sub-Neolithic strata covered by strata from the Bronze Age. The purely Neolithic strata follow a continuous line of development which can be traced through several horizons. These may be observed most clearly at the *magulas* of Argissa (Gremnos) and Otzaki, near Larissa. On virgin soil there is a stratum that is almost entirely Mesolithic. This may be found at several sites: at Argissa, for example, it is 1 metre thick. Clay vessels are as yet unknown. The implements in use are made of stone, much of the material being obtained from nearby areas. Often they are made of obsidian, a dark volcanic substance like glass. This shows that trade was carried on with distant regions, such as Anatolia or Hungary, as well as with the island of Melos. The agrarian character of this culture is indicated by carbonized remains of crops (grain and beans) and the bones of sheep and goats. So far as we can tell at present, this is the only example in Europe of a primitive culture of crop- and cattle-raisers who had no knowledge of pottery. There are several such stations in the Near East, Palestine and Syria (Jericho, Ras Shamra), and to the east in Iraq, Iran, and even India. Since we must assume that the cultivation of grain crops reached Europe from the Orient, we find the Aegean performing, already at this early date, its historic function of bridging the continents.

Sesklo culture

This is a role it continues to fulfil throughout the early Neolithic and the Neolithic era proper. In Greece Neolithic culture is referred to by a term that came into use some 60 years ago, at the time of the first discoveries: the Sesklo culture. Sesklo is the name of a *magula* near Volo. It is used in a broader sense for phenomena of the same era found in other parts of Greece, although some authorities prefer the term 'Neolithic A'. One sub-Neolithic horizon is called Dimini, after a place near Sesklo, or alternatively 'Neolithic B'. Until a few years ago it was assumed that the people responsible for the Sesklo culture came from Asia Minor. This was suggested in particular by the high technical level of even their earliest ceramic ware and its relationship to the prehistoric 'painted ware' of the Orient. But even the first excavators noted some early phenomena which must have preceded the Sesklo horizon proper. And since then it has been shown that in Thessaly there are at least three intervening phases between pre-ceramic culture and early Sesklo. It is now customary to speak of an early ceramic stratum, a proto-Sesklo stratum, and a pre-Sesklo stratum. In central Greece and the Peloponnese the sequence has not yet been elucidated so clearly. But there is no lack of parallels to the course of development in Thessaly right up to the beginning of the early ceramic period. In Thessaly, where a pre-ceramic stratum underlies those of the early ceramic period, the latter strata are thought by the excavator to represent a new era. After that the line of development is continuous throughout the whole area. Thus the origins have now been ascertained, and it is clear that they are to be sought within the country rather than outside it.

In Boeotia the most important sites are Chaeronea, Eutresis and Orchomenos, while in Locris pride of place is taken by Halae. In Attica we may mention the finds on the southern and nothern slopes of the Acropolis, the Agora, and from Nea Makri, near Marathon; in the Peloponnese those from the temple hill at Corinth, from Nemea between Corinth and the Argolis, from Lerna on the Gulf of Argolis, and two sites in Arcadia, Asea and Hagiorgitika-Tegea. Some objects have been found on Aegina, Chios, Samos, and Skyros. In Macedonia we can add Servia on the Haliacmon. Most of these discoveries are from settlements: tombs are rare. There is a preponderance of ceramic ware, and the material preserves its agrarian character throughout.

In architecture the earliest style is usually the round hut, built of a frame of *Architecture* poles with walls of intertwined reeds daubed with clay. From the proto-Sesklo stratum onwards we have rectangular houses of mud-bricks, which at first have no stone base. In one middle Sesklo horizon in Thessaly (Otzaki *magula*) the earliest known *megaron* houses in the Aegean have been excavated. They consist of a rectangular room with an entrance on one of the shorter sides, in front of which is an open porch supported by two posts. This type of dwelling, so far as we can tell at present, originated in the Near East, but acquired a characteristic Aegean quality by virtue of its open porch with columns, projecting *antae,* or both. It survived in this area throughout the Bronze Age, plays a role in early Greek architecture, and constitutes an important element in the classical temple. There is also another type of rectangular house, which likewise had an effect upon Greek architecture in later times and also has parallels in Anatolia from the Stone and Copper Age (Haçilar I/II). It has buttresses placed inside against the walls to provide a more effective support for the flat roof, which is of beaten clay. The houses in these villages were arranged close together in straight rows. No fortifications are as yet to be seen, nor do we find any arrow-heads. The sling was a more important weapon than the bow, for missiles of stone and fired clay have been found. This too, has parallels in prehistoric cultures of the Orient.

Sculpture Female statuettes appear for the first time in the proto-Sesklo horizon. They are made of stone, and more frequently of clay; the figure is shown sitting, crouching or standing. The corpulent form and pronounced naturalism are reminiscent of the Palaeolithic figures from which they are derived. In the Sesklo horizon proper, after an intervening period characterized by more abstract styles, they again become more naturalistic. A particularly fine example, unfortunately with the head missing, was found at Lerna. The position of the hands, held in front of the chest, and the serenity of the figure, which is reduced to essentials, cannot be related to the rather similar Mesopotamian figures dating from the Early Dynastic period, since the latter are much more recent. The Neolithic statuettes invariably represent the Great Mother, the dominant object of worship throughout the Aegean in pre-Hellenic times.

Pottery The study of ceramics provides a thread to guide us through the chronology of Neolithic art in the Aegean. The value of pottery is that it enables us to establish the line of development and the relationship between local styles and those in neighbouring lands — both in Europe and Asia. We can trace the evolution of pottery design from its primitive origins, through its subsequent improvement (followed by a temporary decline), until it reaches the Neolithic proper (Sesklo stage), which can be divided into three periods.

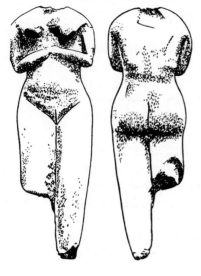

As an example we may take a popular type of vessel, the cup illustrated in the Plate on p. 19. It belongs to the pre-Sesklo stage. The conical base and curving profile are the product of an autochthonous Greek development of the simple hemispherical form. The red finish of the slip may have been deeper, and technically superior, in the preceding phase.

Fig. 1 — *Terracotta Neolithic idol. 4th millennium B.C. From Lerna, Argolis. Height 18 cm. Cf. p. 27.*

Burnished black ware, sometimes decorated with engraved or polished patterns, is the predominant type of pottery in central Greece. Already at an early date, both here and in the Peloponnese, we find the 'rainbow ware', of which parallels may be found in Thessaly and Crete. The so-called Neolithic glazed ware (Urfirnis), not known in Thessaly, is found in the Late Neolithic of central Greece, the Peloponnese and Crete. It is the prototype of the Bronze Age glaze that is typical of Minoan and Mycenaean ware and attains a peak of perfection in the vases featuring black and red figures of archaic and classical Hellas. Monochrome vessels, on which parts of the walls are decorated with impressions of finger-nails, blunt instruments or heart-shells (*isocardia*), are to be found here as well as in Cilicia, the northern Balkans, southern Italy and Sicily, and even as far afield as Spain and North Africa. In Greece, where they originate in a primitive form in the pre-Sesklo stage, they are not characteristic of the initial phase of pottery-making as they are in the northwestern Balkans and the western Mediterranean.

An examination of linear ornamentation is most helpful in clarifying the links with neighbouring Neolithic regions and subsequent cultures in the Aegean. It first appears in the proto-Sesklo stage, engraved and painted in red on a clay ground or white slip. The principal motifs are dentate bands, triangles, lozenges and arcs; they are generally placed around the rim of the vessel. This is an elementary form of the decoration which, after an interval characterized by the so-called pre-Sesklo stage, once again appears FIG. 2 as an attribute of Sesklo pottery and is then developed further on a most lavish scale. But it is also the design which we find on prehistoric painted ware from the Near East, at sites situated in a wide arc from Iran to Syria, Cyprus and Cilicia. This has long been familiar, and recently related specimens have been authenticated in Asia Minor as well. In particular, Haçilar in Pisidia has yielded pottery and ceramic idols that bear an astonishing likeness to those from Sesklo. We have indicated above the reason why this can no longer be regarded as evidence of migration from east to west. It would be more correct to speak of cultural contacts that originated in the Orient and which spread outwards from there along with the practice of tilling the soil.

But this is not all. Already in the earliest times there is a difference between *The people* the Orient on one hand and Anatolia and Greece on the other. In the former area there is a tendency to divide up the surface with horizontal stripes. In the latter area we have, from the Sesklo stage onwards, an attempt to cover the *whole* surface of the vessel with bold vertical lines. In this design there is a tendency to emphasize the meridians, in order to bring out the curvature of the vessel, and a corresponding tendency to direct the eye diagonally to

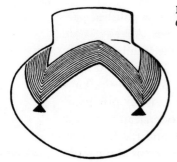

FIG. 2 — *Neolithic painted clay vessel. 4th millennium B.C. From Chaeronea, Boeotia. Cf. pp. 25 and 32.*

the axis of the vessel. Where this is done consistently, it produces the cork-screw-like spirals known as torsions. These are all 'syntactical' phenomena which, as explained above, may be interpreted in a manner similar to phil-ological criteria. In the present instance this is particularly true since we already have, in torsion, one of the principal elements in the structure of Late Minoan style. The question therefore arises whether any historical links existed between these early styles and those from the golden age of Minoan culture. If it should indeed be the case that we have here a pre-Hellenic element in classical art, this would lend special significance to our survey of the Neolithic period. These Neolithic peoples would thus include (admittedly, only in a broad sense, and at a very early stage which would still leave the future path of development open) a very early branch of the ancient Aegean people whose Bronze Age comes to such a splendid climax in Minoan culture.

THE NEOLITHIC IN CRETE
For an assessment of the Neolithic in Crete we still lack adequate stratigraphic studies, despite the work that has already been done in this field. The palace of Knossos stands upon a stratum of Neolithic deposit that may be as much as 7 metres thick. The validity of the data about its composition, obtained many years ago by means of test diggings, can only be regarded as tentative pending publication of the results gained from the systematic excavations now in progress.

Architecture
From many examples we know that in Crete caves served as dwellings and as burial-places in Neolithic times. This is a phenomenon common to the entire Mediterranean. Caves were also used by Neolithic man as dwellings in Attica and on the Peloponnese. This practice led to the subsequent development of the Cretan cave cult. That this dates back to the Neolithic period seems evident from the cave of Eileithyia near Amnisos (on the north coast, some 6 km. east of Iraklion), where the focal point of the ceremonies was a mighty stalactite.

At Knossos a rectangular house of sun-dried brick on a stone base was found in an early Neolithic horizon. From the sub-Neolithic period we have remains of dwelling-houses with rectangular rooms and inner partitions which form a honeycomb-like complex, not enclosed by external walls. This is a style of architecture not unknown in the ancient Near East. It can be traced from Early Bronze Age specimens on the Aegean islands and in Crete at least as far as the Full Bronze Age, when it was an element in Minoan palaces.

Female idols, some corpulent and others schematized, constitute a link with the Neolithic on the mainland and the extensive culture of which the latter forms a part. One male figure, made of a stone similar to marble, is remarkable both on account of its life-like modelling and the rigid stylization. (It measures some 10 cm. in height without the head and the lower part of the leg.) The posture is the same as that of the female terracotta statuette from Lerna, the Cretan figure also having the same schematized hands. It lay in an early Neolithic horizon and helps us to establish the chronology of the other work. Although its female counterparts represent a deity it must be regarded as a votive offering and the posture as that of a devotee. *Sculpture*

Fig. 1

Most of the Neolithic pottery from Crete is grey, greyish-brown, or black and burnished. In the later phases, as well as polished designs, there are some that are incised, the lines then being filled in with white or red. Many affinities can be established between them and the pottery of the mainland. But by and large Cretan Neolithic ceramic ware is a category in its own right. Painting is extant — apparently from a late date — only in red on a polished dark ground. This is a forerunner of the Early Bronze Age styles with dark grounds which reach their peak in Kamares pottery. Neolithic Urfirnis is also to be found in Crete, as on the mainland, in upper strata. Once again there is a pronounced tendency towards horizontal stripes in the design. *Pottery*

Obsidian blades and remains of obsidian-working, found in early strata, testify to the existence of connections with the outside world. Fragments of Egyptian stone vessels from the beginning of the 3rd millennium B.C., found in a sub-Neolithic horizon, indicate that the Metal Age commenced in Crete between 3000 and 2600 B.C. This is simply a chronological correlation. The really decisive connections, so far as Neolithic Crete was concerned, were those with the Orient and the Aegean. The agrarian character of the island's economy, too, was similar to that in the two last-named areas. *Contact with other areas*

In Thessaly the topmost Sesklo stratum, which belongs to the Neolithic proper, is overlaid by one that is more recent in date. The latter contains *SUB-NEOLITHIC DIMINI STRATUM)* a different cultural inventory that cannot have developed from the earlier culture. It is called the Dimini stratum, after a *magula* near Volo. Here and there copper and gold are already present. This horizon may therefore be identified as sub-Neolithic.

FIG. 3 For the first time we now come across citadels, such as Dimini itself. This citadel has several wall circuits consisting of stone slabs. The areas between them are inhabited, and are connected with one another by simple passage-ways. At the rear of the inner court, which is about 35 metres in length, opposite the gateway, there is a megaron, about 12 metres long. It has two rooms, one behind the other, with a fixed hearth in the first one. The ceiling of this room rested on internal supports.

In general this culture, too, is an agrarian one. The raising of livestock begins to be practised, in the form of pigs and cattle. A new weapon now comes into use: the club. The club-head is of stone and is perforated to take a wooden shaft. Sculptured idol figures continue to be made, but their forms are schematized.

In ceramic ware we find new and more highly differentiated varieties of styles. The development which the potter's art underwent has been eluci-dated by recent excavations. Conical bowls with upturned lips (cf. Plate PLATE 2 on p. 20), 'fruit-stands', as they are sometimes called, amphora with two vertical handles, and baggy vessels (*askoi*) have hitherto been considered the prin-cipal forms of this ware. But none of these are to be found earlier than the last of the four Dimini phases. In addition to the vessels with incised and polished decoration there are others that are painted. The colours used are duller: most of the paintings are in black on a light or rust-coloured slip. Red and white may sometimes be used as well. The spiral, meander and checkered patterns were also thought until recently to be characteristic of the Dimini horizon as a whole. But we now know that they, too, do not appear until its final phase.

Dimini strata in the proper sense of the term are only to be found in Thessaly. From the more southerly parts of the country we have imports or imitations of Dimini ware, and also local pottery influenced by it. By and large, however, the line of development is continuous until the beginning of the Early Bronze Age, which is marked by the appearance of the so-called Early Helladic Urfirnis ceramic. This brings us to the middle of the 3rd millennium B.C. (approx. 2600). From this it is clear that the population shift that caused the change of pottery style in Thessaly did not reach central Greece and the Peloponnese. Since the spiral and meander decoration must be connected with the banded ware found in the northern Balkans, southern Russia and central Europe, it was once customary to speak of the introduction of Dimini

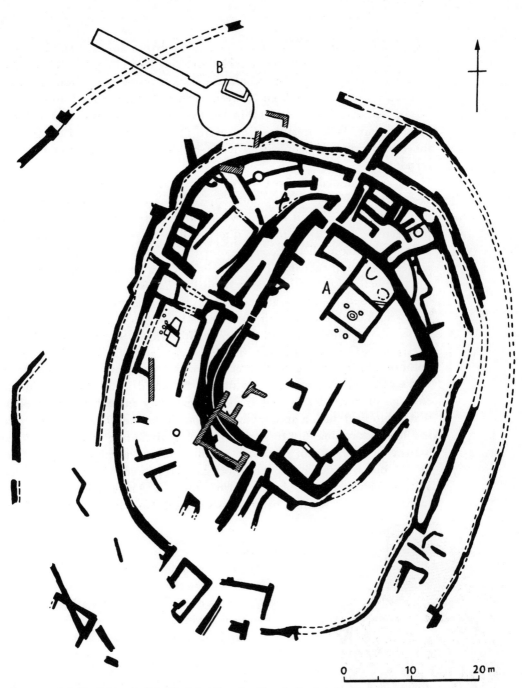

Fig. 3 — *Sub-Neolithic citadel. Dimini, Thessaly. First half of 3rd millennium B.C. A: Megaron. B: Mycenaean tholos tomb. Cf. pp. 30, 43.*

ware from these areas. But we now possess the earliest forms of Dimini ware, and from them it is clear that no such borrowing took place. For the moment it remains an open question where the Dimini people came from, or what contacts there may have been between them and other peoples. But we can accept that there is a relationship between the late Dimini styles and the banded ware. Whether these links were the result of cultural contacts or the immigration of people who made banded ware has not yet been ascertained.

Historical
significance If the works described above are considered as incunabula of Western, or even Greek, art history, they must appear so naive and primitive that one may well ask whether it is really worth while approaching them from this perspective. An answer to this query will be given in due course. But even if we look at them merely against the background of their own time we have to admit that they have a certain value in their own right. For we have here a form of European Neolithic that is not only the earliest but also the richest in variety. Its early ripening to maturity and its characteristic wealth of styles are both the result of the geographical factors mentioned above. The 'Anatolian cultural drift', which we shall meet below, exerts its effect most strongly in the Aegean lands, the area closest to its point of origin. But it extends over a much larger region: polychrome ware and associated phenomena are found as far afield as the Balkans (in the environs of Belgrade), as well as in southern Italy and Sicily. The impetus that led to its diffusion appears to have come from the spread of agriculture and livestock-raising. But it is only in the Aegean that we find a well-defined 'syntax' of styles — not of course, as the result of immigration from the Orient, but as a reaction by the autochthonous peoples of the Aegean to the cultural influences reaching them from the east. These Oriental elements, in particular the dentate band, constitute the basis for a lavish mode of

FIG. 4 — *Sub-Neolithic painted clay vessel. First half of 3rd millennium B.C. From Rachmani, Thessaly. Height approx. 25 cm. Cf. pp. 28, 32.*

expression that embraces simultaneously all three dimensions of the vessel's surface and thus leads to the emergence of genuine torsions. The patterns are clearly different from the rationally-conceived designs found in the ancient Near East, with their additive bands.

At the end of this era — already in the sub-Neolithic, which leads on into the next period — we find the first signs of influences being exerted in a reverse direction, i.e., eastwards from Europe. This trend may be observed in the banded ceramic ware of the late Dimini horizon. At first it is limited to Thessaly, and no major change takes place in the composition of the Aegean population. The tendency of this banded ware to torsion is now more clearly marked than before, and is associated with another trend alien to the ancient Near East, namely surface decoration. This may derive from the existence of a long-established relationship between the banded-ware people and the inhabitants of the borderlands between Asia and Europe. The most important point is that, despite all the Oriental influences, already at this early date we find forces at work that give the Aegean styles a European character. Seen within the framework of their connections with the rest of Europe, they acquire a special quality that later developed on a scale hitherto unparalleled.

As to the duration of this process, only guesses are possible. If one bears in *Chronology* mind that the Copper Age cannot have begun in the Aegean much before '2600 B.C., this would give the 4th and 5th millennia B.C. for the Neolithic proper. This dating is confirmed by such radio-carbon analyses as have been made, but no more precise attribution is as yet feasible.

II. THE AGE OF DEVELOPMENT
Styles of the Early Bronze Age

THE EARLY
BRONZE AGE
PLATES 1, 2
FIGS. 2, 4
PLATES 5, 6,
7, 8, 11
FIGS. 7, 8

PLATE 12
PLATES 13, 14
FIG. 11

PLATES 3, 4

A quick glance at the plates illustrating this chapter will convey better than any words the character of the new world that we are now about to enter. When compared with the Neolithic and sub-Neolithic vessels in the Plates on pp. 19 and 20, the more recent ones appear more elegant and highly differentiated. One can see at once that their form rivals those attained by craftsmen in metal. It has something vigorous, light and bold about it, whereas Neolithic pottery is heavy and clumsy. And in this new period we even have vessels of gold, silver and bronze. The difference becomes most marked when we look at the gold jewellery in the Plate on p. 61, especially if we compare them with the stone beads and mussel-shell ornaments of earlier times. The seals illustrated on pp. 62 and 63 could only have been made by a people who possessed a more sophisticated social and economic system. The fortifications shown in the Plates on pp. 37 and 38 have a monumental character that takes us beyond the limits of prehistoric architecture altogether. It goes without saying that in this period of prehistory we have to concern ourselves more than we did earlier with the final results of the evolutionary process, i.e. with later phenomena.

The discovery and working of metals, with all the opportunities that this opened up, gave an impetus to the art and culture of this phase similar to that given by the introduction of agriculture to the art and culture of the Neolithic. Many of the achievements of this period can be explained by reference to the introduction of metal-working — but not all of them. The work of this era becomes interesting to us only when we are no longer just seeking evidence of progress, but are inquiring into the reasons why various modes of expression were adopted and why there are differences between this period and the preceding one.

The existence of regional variations within this art has long since been established. At this stage Crete, the Greek mainland, the islands and the western coastlands of Asia Minor each form distinct areas from a cultural point of view. The art historian must concern himself chiefly with the study of the nature and substance of pre-Hellenic styles. For this purpose it is more important to establish the similarities than the local differences. To understand the relationship between the art of this period and that which developed later we have to remember the structure of the 'language of style'. The identification of dialects is only the first stage; what we have to attempt

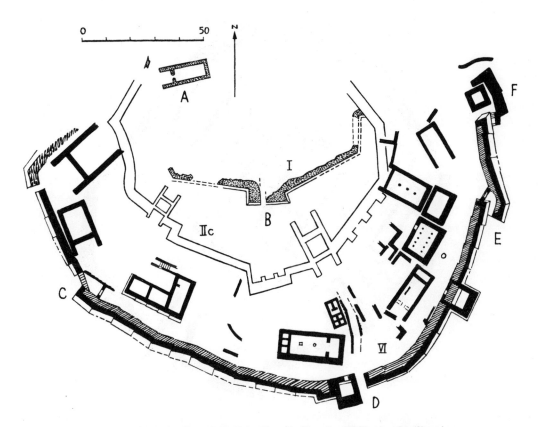

Fig. 5a — *Troy I, II and VI (detail of Troy II in Fig. 5b). Troy I: middle of 3rd millennium B.C. A: Megaron. B: South Gate. Troy VI: state in 15th cent. B.C. C: West Gate, subsequently covered over. D: South Gate. E: East Gate. F: North-eastern Bastion with cistern. Cf. p. 35.*

now is to describe the structure of the forms employed, or 'inner form', as it might be called.

Throughout the whole area places of settlement now unmistakably tend to assume an urban character. Already in Neolithic and sub-Neolithic times Knossos and some of the *magulas* in Thessaly, to judge by their size and the density of the buildings, could claim the title of cities. But they were in reality nothing more than agglomerations of houses and huts, placed together for some material reason without any architectural design. It is true that in Thessaly there were beginnings of a rectilinear and rectangular plan, but this should not lead us to minimize the primitive rural character of

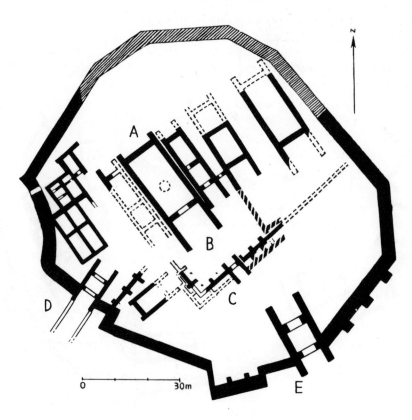

FIG. 5b — *Troy II: final state in approx. 2150 B.C. A: Large Megaron. B: Forecourt. C: Gate leading to court. D: South-west Gate with ramp. E: South-east Gate. Cf. p. 35.*

these 'cities'. On the islands some settlements have the aspect of towns by reason of their circuit walls, which are nobly proportioned and provided with gateways and turrets: e.g., Thermi on Lesbos, Poliochni on Lemnos, Chalandriani on Syros, H. Andreas on Siphnos, and Colonna Cape on Aegina. On several islands we have evidence of paved streets, squares, fountains and cisterns for water. In Poliochni the walls of the houses were covered with stone slabs right up to roof level. In many cases, particularly in eastern Crete, the fact that these towns are located on the coast suggests that the inhabitants gained their livelihood not only by agriculture but also by fishing, maritime commerce and handicrafts. Both the density of settlement and the types of dwelling built in the new phase are derived from those in the preceding period. We have several examples of megaron. Its architecture is the same as before: a stone base, walls of burnt clay reinforced with a frame of beams, and a flat earth roof; thatched gable roofs are also met with. Evidence of contact from east to west across the Aegean and impulses from the Orient during its Early Dynastic period is provided by the walls, where the stones are set in a herring-bone pattern. Such a design may be seen at Troy I, Thermi I and IV, and in Early Helladic strata on FIG. 5a the mainland (Eleusis, Eutresis, Hagios Kosmas, Lerna). In the ground plan the walls are now usually designed so that they are at right angles to one another. We also have a variant in which one of the shorter walls terminates in an apsidal form. In the latter case we may assume that the roofs were hipped on one side and gabled on the other. Both types are met with in urban dwelling-houses from the so-called Early Helladic culture in mainland Greece. In the culture of western Asia Minor the megaron is found without an apse. The oldest inhabited stratum of Troy (Troy I), Thermi on Lesbos, Poliochni on Lemnos, and Samos (Heraeum) furnish examples of this. It is no coincidence, in view of the finds registered from later periods, that we do not come across such megara in Crete. At this time the little ports in eastern Crete were still built without any plan, as was sub-Neolithic Knossos. This is also the case with Thermi, Poliochni, and H. Kosmas, near New Phaleron on the coast of Attica — the last-named site was influenced by the culture of the Cyclades.

Circular dwellings are no longer simply huts built of poles with walls of intertwined reeds daubed with clay. In Orchomenos, for example, they were dome-shaped, and were built of clay over a stone base (approx. 6 metres in diameter). In many cases such buildings doubtless have served as granaries. A vessel of green steatite found on Melos is a representation of five FIG. 20 such silos grouped around a court. Little is as yet known of the architecture of the Cyclades.

The most important innovation is that both megara and circular dwellings now appear in monumental form.

The Prince's Hall in Troy II, when complete and before its destruction, *Troy* was a massive megaron. It faced south-east. The total length was about FIG. 5b 45 m., the width almost 13 m., and the walls were about 1.50 m. thick. The walls, which rested on a stone base covered with stone slabs, consisted of flat sun-dried bricks which were reinforced by beams at regular intervals. Beaten clay served as plaster. When viewed from the front the walls terminated in blocks of dressed stone supporting six wooden planks. These served to protect the masonry and give the entrance an imposing appearance. The shape of the roof is not as yet fully clear from the evidence brought to light by excavation. The great span of approx. 10 metres in the clear and the lack of internal supports lead one to doubt Dörpfeld's repeated assertions that the roof was built of huge cypress trunks covered with beaten clay. It cannot be ruled out that it may have had a ridged roof. In view of its size, this would have been a daring mode of construction. But considerable boldness is shown in the treatment of space within the building. In plan the porch forms a rough quadrangle, open to the front, and to make the actual hall this porch is simply doubled in size. In the middle is a large circular hearth. The doorway to the porch is thought to have been 4 m. wide. More astonishing than the manner of construction and the sheer size is the simple but impressive sense of spaciousness that is evoked. The main problem of monumental architecture has here been mastered — in primitive fashion, admittedly, but yet effectively. Rooms of such size without internal supports were unknown either in the ancient East or in classical Greek architecture: they re-appear only under the Roman Empire. Later on we shall return to this point and consider how the pre-Hellenic Aegean architects treated the problem of space.

Tiryns   Beneath the Mycenaean foundations of the upper citadel at Tiryns relics have been found of a gigantic circular structure 28 m. in diameter. It belongs to the middle period of the Early Helladic phase (EH II). It has two concentric circuit-walls, built of mud brick, over a stone base; beyond the outer ring there radiate buttresses at close intervals, which in cross-section are shaped like tongues. Nothing else is known for certain about it. It was probably the seat of the prince and constructed both as a fortress and as a residence. Similar specimens have been found elsewhere in the Mediterranean dating from prehistoric times — most notably the Sardinian *nuraghe,* which originate from the Late Bronze and Early Iron Age.

Lerna   More or less contemporary with this is the mansion on the flat summit of the citadel at Lerna. Since its excavation a few years ago it has been known as the 'House of Tiles' on account of the plaques of terracotta, which in conjunction with slates covered its sloping roof. It has no equal elsewhere in the Aegean. An 'injunctive' complex of rooms with facades on all four sides (area in plan 25 x 12 m.) approximates to the design of palaces and temples in Mesopotamia. But it has no central court. From the nature of the floors and walls we may assume that there was a roof over the two large inner rooms, which are surrounded by smaller chambers and corridors. We know of a forerunner of the 'House of Tiles', shaped like a megaron and about 12 metres in width, which faced north and south instead of east and west. The towns of the Early Metal Age have circuit-walls, paved streets, squares

PLATE 3 — Troy I: wall of citadel with bastion of South Gate. Approx. 2600—2500 B.C. *Cf. pp. 32, 43.*

PLATE 4 — Troy II: ramp leading to South-west Gate and citadel wall, showing the later extensions. In the background are the Scamander valley and the Dardanelles. *Cf. pp. 32, 36.*

PLATE 5 — Amphora with crowned lid. Poliochni, Lemnos. Style: western Asia Minor. Late 3rd millennium B.C. *National Museum, Athens. Height approx. 40 cm. Cf. pp. 32, 46.*

PLATE 6 — Beak spouted cup (sauce-boat) covered with 'Urfirnis' ('primeval glaze'). Raphina, Attica. Early Helladic II, 2200— 2000 B.C. *National Museum, Athens. Cf. pp. 32, 50.*

PLATE 7 — Amphora covered with 'Urfirnis'. Orchomenos, Boeotia. Early Helladic II, 2200—2000 B.C. *National Museum, Athens. Cf. pp. 32, 50.*

PLATE 8 — Beak-spouted jug covered with glaze paint. Hagios Onouphrios, southern Crete. Early Minoan I, 2600—2300 B.C. *Iraklion. Height 28 cm. Cf. pp. 32, 53, 56.*

and closely-packed buildings; it is these characteristics, rather than their size, that mark them out. In the same period the citadel was developed as a royal residence. The stone foundations of the walls at Dimini, which date from the sub-Neolithic, are of such modest proportions that they have erroneously been interpreted simply as bulwarks against attacks by bowmen. In contrast the fortifications of Troy I, which originate from the Copper Age, could almost be called monumental (cf. the South Gate, shown in the Plate on p. 37). It may be more or less contemporaneous with Dimini. But the comparison between these two sites shows that we are dealing here with two different phases. For we know that the Metal Age began earlier in Anatolia than it did in Greece. Yet during the Early Bronze Age styles evolved in all areas precisely along the lines indicated here. On the right-hand side of our illustration one can see the escarping of the south wall. Its western face adjoins a bastion more than 15 metres wide. Through the middle of the latter there runs a narrow corridor forming the gateway. Nothing is to be seen now of the superstructure of clay itself, which must once have presented an imposing sight. Within the walls, but independently of them, the houses were arranged in rows, in a pattern similar to that noted at Otzaki *magula* in Thessaly during the Neolithic. This again shows how functional the architecture of Troy was, despite its apparent monumentality in comparison with Dimini. As a result of the American excavations it is now well established that Troy I marks the beginning of a more or less continuous line of development that is broken only by the destruction of Troy II between 2200 and 2100 B.C. During this long period the southern half of the citadel was enlarged several times, until it eventually measured more than 100 metres in diameter. The escarped foundation rose to a height of at least 8 metres and at the top was some 3–4 metres thick.

Among the innovations made are the strengthening of the walls by means of massive towers, placed in front, the substitution of a new gate for the old one located in one of the bastions, and the systematic arrangement of hall, forecourt and main gate. The new style of the gate is derived from the megaron. Two longitudinal walls, with wooden *antae* in front, enclose two covered halls and a gate-house, also covered, which has an outer and inner door. Incidentally, this type of building finds its most splendid realization in the Propylaea of Mnesicles. We shall come back later to the intermediate elements from the Bronze Age. The main gate lay in the south-east. A somewhat smaller gate, situated in the south-west, and built in a similar style, may be seen in the Plate on p. 38. It is approached from outside by means of a ramp at least 4 metres wide and paved with polygonal slabs. The wall shown in the centre of the illustration, which reaches up to the level

FIG. 5b

PLATE 4

Troy I and II

FIG. 3

PLATE 3

FIG. 5a

of the gate, was covered over when the gate was built, as was also part of an old bastion visible at the end of the wall. Of the wall built at the same time as the gate only a remnant can now be seen, in front of the older wall. Its upper part has been destroyed.

After one had passed through the main south-east gate one found oneself in front of a small gateway, built in the same style, leading into the palace court. This, together with the large megaron and the portico in front of it, which was supported on wooden poles, formed a rectangular design, the axis of which was located somewhat to the south-west of the gate leading into the courtyard. In some megara with small courts and approximately the same orientation the complex was extended both to the east and to the west.

Of all the citadels with which we are familiar Troy is the most perfect. Lerna and Tiryns differ from Dimini in the monumental character of the royal residence, and Lerna also in the stoutness of its fortifications (none of which are left at Tiryns). At Lerna they are simpler than at Troy — for one reason because the gateway, which has survived, is just an opening in the wall. The round bastions which jut out in front at Lerna have parallels on Syros and at Copper Age sites in Spain. On Cape Colonna, near what was to become the capital of the island of Aegina, we have the city gate that faced to the landward side, which dates from this period and reproduces in an accentuated form the early fortifications of Troy. The corridor through the bastion is so designed as to prevent easy passage.

Troy was not only an example of technical perfection in monumental architecture: it was also a work of art in its own right. The forbidding solemnity of the main gate is repeated on a smaller scale in the gateway to the court behind it. The latter does not form part of the fortifications, but is an expression of the power and prestige attached to the prince and his household. This is true in even greater measure of the great hall. This not only occupies the centre of the site and exceeds all other buildings at Troy in size, but, situated as it is on top of the citadel mound, dominates all the walls, towers, gates and houses within its compass. It measured some 8 metres in height, its elevation being emphasized by its setting, some 20 metres above the Scamander valley. It must have had a colossal effect upon those who approached it. We do not find compositions with such deliberate employment of emphasis anywhere in the Orient. There, in similar situations, the architecture is made up of isolated elements that are simply added on successively (as, for example, in the oval temple at Khafaje). But here, so far as we know, the elements employed are on the whole ancient Aegean in character, and not ancient Anatolian.

The Troy of the Copper and Early Bronze Age owes its unsurpassed setting to its favourable geographical location. At this time the Dardanelles did not of course have their modern importance as a route to the Black Sea. Nor was Troy of significance as an entrepôt in the metal trade between Asia and Europe, for in Europe the Bronze Age does not begin until long after Troy II had succumbed to a terrible catastrophe. But it was situated at the spot where the ancient route from Asia to Europe, along which many migrating peoples had passed, reached the Aegean. This meant that it was well placed to transmit the cultural wealth of the Orient to the Aegean lands that were now burgeoning into life. Copper appears to have played some part in Troy's rise to greatness: it was mined in Cyprus, whence it was transported overland, while tin was obtained from Asia Minor.

No graves dating from this period have been found at Troy. Those so far *Graves* discovered elsewhere in the western part of Asia Minor are simple burials in flat graves or large clay jars (*pithoi*); the dead are interred in a crouching posture. The picture is similar in Early Helladic Greece, where we also find cist graves made of stone slabs (on Leukas they are enclosed by stone circles and mounds) and mass burials in ossuaries. Stone cist graves are also known in the Cycladic culture.

There are tombs as well as graves of a more primitive type, both in Crete and on the Cyclades. Elegant round tombs (*tholoi*) were first discovered, shortly after the palaces were found, in the Messara — the large fertile plain that lies at the foot of the southern flank of Mt. Ida, which is barred off from the sea by the Kophino range and therefore opens out towards the west rather than the south. Such *tholoi* have now been discovered in the centre and east of the island as well. They are domed structures resembling bee-hives, made of stone, with a low entrance facing east. The largest known specimen (near Platanos) has an internal diameter of at least 13 metres. An excavation recently undertaken near Lebena, to the south of Mt. Kophino, has shown that the vaulting consists of roughly dressed stones held together by clay. Outside, next to the entrance, there were as a rule small rectangular chambers, used both for burials and for the cult of the dead. They were family vaults, which were in use for several centuries. When additional interments took place the earlier remains had to be pushed to one side, or else removed to one of the rectangular ossuaries. We shall come back later to the large amount of funerary gifts found there: jewellery, arms, seals, stone vessels and ceramic ware. The earliest vaults were constructed at approximately the same time as the destruction of Troy II. Some of them continued to be used until the 19th century B.C.

On the little island of Mochlos, which was then still a peninsula, there stood, on the beach, small rectangular burial houses or tombs, which had an entrance corridor and an inner chamber reached by a right-angled turn. They are built into clefts in the rock and are copies of the dwellings used in daily life. In eastern Crete we also have ossuaries, roughly rectangular in plan, with several inner chambers approached from above. They are related to the rectangular annexes of the *tholoi*.

Smaller versions of the *tholoi* are found on the Cyclades, near the Cycladic settlement of Hagios Kosmas near New Phaleron on the coast of Attica, and on Euboea. They are built below ground level. The small chambers have walls of stone slabs which slope inwards, an entrance with small *dromoi*, and a covering slab on top.

The *tholoi*, or round graves, are reproductions in architectural form of caves used for burials. Like the small burial houses on Mochlos, many of them are built against a cliff face. Their style is a specifically Aegean one, but is linked to styles found as far afield as Syria, the Iberian peninsula and the British Isles. Dolmens and rock-cut tombs are also in essence architectural reproductions of natural burial sites, but they may perhaps also bear some relation to the cults performed in them. Megalithic architecture provides us with a link here. Recent research has established that at various sites the original primitive form is echoed in important buildings erected during historic times. In the Aegean such structures attained veritable monumental proportions already during the Bronze Age.

POTTERY

Pottery is of more value than architecture in clarifying local differences, which are of considerable importance for art history as well as for history in general. In due course, after dealing with the various ceramic groups, we shall discuss the question whether there existed, over and above the local styles, anything that could be called an artistic achievement common to them all — an 'expression of the age', as it were.

Western Asia Minor (Troy)

The vessel shown in the Plate on p. 39 illustrates the ceramic ware of western Anatolia. It was found at Poliochni and corresponds to a group of

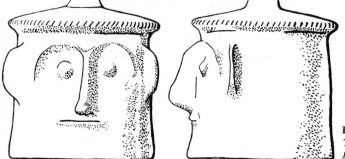

FIG. 6 — *Lid of a clay vessel from Troy II-III. Late 3rd millennium B.C. Diameter 12 cm. Cf. p. 47.*

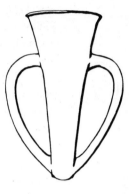

FIG. 7 — *Clay vase, so-called depas, from Troy II-III. Late 3rd millennium B.C. Height 9 cm. Cf. pp. 32, 47.*

jars found in Troy II, i.e. dating already from the time of the city's destruction. It has a brownish slip, not very carefully executed, and was made without the aid of a potter's wheel — although this tool was of course known in the later phases of Troy II. The large handle-like projections, which are joined to the main body of the vessel by means of plastic volutes and curve inwards like hooks over the shoulder of the jar, have parallels in a copper vessel discovered in one of the treasures buried at the destruction of Troy II, as well as in some other pieces from the interior of Asia Minor. The lid with the handle like a crown is quite characteristic of the later FIG. 6 phase of ceramic ware from the west of Asia Minor. Human features were often modelled on afterwards.

The form of the lid and handle illustrate very clearly the parallels that exist with similar styles in metal work. In this connection we may note the so-called Trojan *depas,* which has still retained the Homeric name given it by FIG. 7 Schliemann although it has nothing to do either with Homer or the Greeks. This is a slender funnel-shaped beaker, without a base support, and has two staff-like handles which curve outwards and connect the upper part of the vessel with the base. Finds of such beakers in central Anatolia in strata that can be dated are useful in establishing Trojan chronology.

The beak-spouted vase, the principal form throughout the Aegean in the Early Metal Age, is also present at Troy and nearby sites in the western part of Asia Minor. But of the equally characteristc sauce-boats we have but a single example. It is in gold, with two spouts, and was found in one of the treasure-stores. Engraved designs are infrequent, and painting on the vessels FIG. 8 very rare indeed. Excavations carried out in the 1930s yielded a considerable amount of imported ceramic ware of the so-called Early Helladic group, together with copies made at Troy itself. These have proved useful in establishing the chronology of Troy's contacts with the Greek mainland.

On the Cyclades ceramic production was more varied in character. By the Cyclades we mean the islands in the south of the Aegean, situated in a circle around the rocky island of Delos. The Pelos group, named *Pelos group* after a site on Melos, is followed by the Syros group. The small Kampos group, so called after a site on Naxos, occupies an intermediate position.

47

The Pelos group is confined to simple compact vessels which, however, again bear a resemblance in style to those in metal. They often have in addition a slip of Urfirnis. Jugs and flasks with conical necks, spherical jars on a tall base, and pyxides with lids in the shape of a cylinder or flattened sphere, are among the forms favoured. Where there is decoration, it is engraved. The elements employed are herring-bone patterns, hatched triangles and dentate bands. Although these styles are not unusual and are widely diffused, the similarities between them and the more ancient Neolithic styles suggest a connection. The articulation of the surface by meridian lines and torsions is more clearly marked than in Neolithic pottery, and in the case of the horizontal striped patterns the spaces between the lines are so slight that we have what is virtually surface decoration.

Syros group

Pelos pottery must have ceased already before the destruction of Troy II, for the following group, that from Syros, has parallels with ceramic ware found in Troy II. Links with western Anatolia can be seen in such Syros group products as beaked jugs and sauce-boats, pyxides, 'pedestalled' goblets and bell-shaped vessels corresponding in form to some made of silver that were found in oné of the Trojan treasure-stores. Side by side with this ware we have old Cycladic styles, for these continued to be used in this period. Among the new styles were the so-called Cycladic pans, some of which have anthropomorphic features suggestive of female idols. They were probably used to hold the offerings of fruit that were interred with the dead. Engraved decoration is combined with notching. There are also some stamped designs. In pottery where these patterns occur the dark clay is covered with Urfirnis, which gives it a highly-polished black surface. The impressed designs are mainly composed of concentric circles and spirals. The lines may be combined to give the effect of a network of spirals — in other words, we have here genuine surface decoration, covering large areas of the vessel. The fact that spirals, although in a different style, appear simultaneously on Crete (cf. p. 140), and the black colour of this ware have led to the supposition that it may have been influenced by the banded pottery from the Danube region. But this cannot be so, since there are no bands in these patterns, and there was dark-coloured ware on the mainland already in the Late Neolithic era. We have drawn attention above to the links between the decoration of the Late Neolithic and the Pelos pottery that preceded that from Syros. It is also worth mentioning that these contacts are still more plainly visible in one type of Cycladic pottery dating from this period which has dark painting in Urfirnis upon a light ground of clay. Here the designs consist mainly of dentate bands and lace-work patterns. From a syntactical point of view the preference for horizontal bands is greater now than it was during the early Cycladic phase. This can be explained as due to the normal course of stylistic development, indicative of a tendency towards rigidity. In the circumstances it would be nearer the truth to derive the Cycladic spirals from influences associated with the newly acquired techniques employed in metalworking, in particular the use of coiled gold and silver wire. We have pieces of jewellery from the Aegean area dating from this period in which this wire is used, and it is to be found in Oriental designs as well. In the Cyclades we have, for example, silver pins with coiled heads. *Metal work, stone vessels*

Another group of Cycladic products consists of vessels of green steatite (soap-stone) with *en rapport* designs in which S-shaped and C-shaped spirals predominate. Among Cycladic marble vessels made of unveined material, the cylindrical pots and goblets without handles coincide with traditional ceramic styles. We have silver vessels from Amorgos that possess forms found in ceramic ware. Some gold and silver bowls from Euboea, which may have been imported from Asia Minor, bear designs of hatched triangles that are related to the familiar ornamentation on clay vessels. FIG. 20

These data render untenable the former view that Cycladic culture in general and Cycladic ceramic ware in particular derive from Anatolian models. Our final verdict cannot be wholly conclusive owing to the almost total lack of Neolithic remains on the islands. But this is due to insufficient investigation: there is little doubt that the Cyclades were inhabited in Neolithic times, and one day we shall have evidence to this effect. For the moment we must content ourselves with saying that the islands did not lag behind the mainland. The connection between the two areas, which can be observed in Cycladic pottery, leads to the hypothesis that the latter was derived from Neolithic forerunners under the sudden impact of the introduction of metals from the east. Much the same was probably true of mainland Greece at this time and also of Crete. *Historical significance*

On the mainland the culture of the Early Metal Age is known as Early Helladic. Not without good reason its pottery is loosely termed 'Urfirnis ceramic', although this type of glazed painting was also executed in the Cyclades and Early Minoan Crete. The technique was developed to a high pitch of perfection in the second of the three stages through which Early *Mainland Greece (Early Helladic)*

49

Helladic Urfirnis ceramic passed. As in the preceding stage, it dispensed almost entirely with ornamentation. Even when judged purely from the standpoint of technique it is of an astonishingly high standard of excellence. The thin walls, made of clay well tempered with water and fired rock-hard, are almost like porcelain. For the slip preference was given to light colours, which in particularly fine specimens can be of a silvery white hue. The elegance and expressiveness of these vessels are all the more remarkable when one takes into consideration the fact that they were hand-turned, without the aid of a potter's wheel. Two typical specimens are illustrated here:

PLATE 6
PLATE 7 the beak-spouted cup from Attica in the Plate on p. 40 and the amphora from Orchomenos in the Plate on p. 41. The beauty of the former vessel lies in the gradation of its bold sweeping contours and the tightly stretched curvature, giving it a form that is both functional and expressive. The oval vessel itself, which rests upon a flat conical base, projects in a spout that rises up as high as possible, so that the liquid in the vessel may be poured exactly in any desired direction simply by pressing upon the handle with one's thumb. This bold feature lends the vessel a special charm, as does its general shape, clearly taken from that of a metal vessel, which is emphasized by the glazed slip. Articulation is found only at the edges — i.e. on the base, handle and spout. Its simplicity undeniably enhances its artistic effect. As well as being a beautiful work of art, it is excellently suited to fulfil its functional purpose. For this reason it bears little ornamentation, and the lower part, resembling a dado, is painted brown.

The amphora from Orchomenos illustrated on p. 41 is covered with Urfirnis in a darker hue, so that — again copying metal models — the reflected colour helps to make the surface more expressive. The neck, shaped like a trumpet, with thin walls, looks as though it were made of metal. The four little ribbon handles, placed crosswise at the points where the vessel attains its maximum projection, serve only as a means of accentuation. So also do the vertical incisions linking them to the base of the neck. In general it may be said that this is a simple and elegant expression of a functionally limited form, conceived as a unity and realized on a handsome scale.

This pottery is related to that found elsewhere in the Aegean not only through its beak-spouted cups (sauce-boats) but also its numerous beak-spouted jugs. In addition to these asymmetrical vessels we have tubular flasks known as *askoi* — these being typical products of potters obliged to work without the aid of a wheel. All the elegant works of art mentioned here are designed for use at table, but most finds are of course simple objects made for daily use. As a result of the excavations that have been carried out we have an enormous amount of potsherds, which in the course of time will be of considerable assistance in elucidating a development that extended over some six to seven centuries (from approx. 2600 to 1900 B.C.). Already in the later strata of Troy I we find imported Urfirnis ware. Chronological classification is facilitated by vessels from Troy II, such as the *depas* or the two-handled beaker found at sites on the mainland. Coarser stamped pottery with spirals or bands discovered on the mainland has generally been interpreted hitherto as an import from the Cyclades. But it may perhaps have been imitated in local workshops.

In the last phase of Early Helladic (EH III) we find various types of pottery bearing painted designs. One of them has dark decoration on a light clay ground and thus corresponds to the ware produced at this time in the Cyclades, although the patterns there are different. It was made for the houses of noblemen living in the north-eastern Peloponnese. In central Greece the local style is known as the Hagia Marina ware, after a site in Phocis. It has white designs on a dark ground covered with Urfirnis. In these groups we again find the styles we met in painted Neolithic pottery: bands of large and small dentates, interlocking dentates, triangles and lace-work patterns. We also come across such designs in the Cyclades during this period, and later, as we shall see, they are to be found in Early Minoan pottery as well. In addition there are a number of parallels in the west of Asia Minor, where they date back to the horizon of Troy I, centuries removed in time from the later Early Helladic groups. We cannot say whether there was a direct connection between these two types, which are surprisingly alike. In Thessaly they are separated by the intervening Dimini strata, which were more important and of longer duration than has previously been supposed. But on the Peloponnese and in central Greece the stratigraphic relationship between the Neolithic and the ensuing Early Helladic has as yet been far from adequately explored.

Historical significance

It will be the task of future scholars to explain whether these similarities between Neolithic and Early Metal Age styles are the product of continuous development or whether the chronological and geographical distance between them was so great that we are dealing here simply with a coincidence, due to the prevalence of similar circumstances in both these areas. Whichever of these hypotheses turns out to be correct, one thing is certain: taking into consideration the correspondence between the 'stylistic syntax' and the ethnic origin of the people concerned, the similarities we are discussing must be seen as an indication that a large ethnic group was in process of formation — a group that was distinct from neighbouring peoples both in Asia and in Europe, even though the differences were not so clearly marked at the beginning as they became later. In any case, it is now clear that the Neolithic tradition was at least as important as the changes that were now introduced. Moreover, information recently obtained indicates that the Neolithic strata in Greece and Anatolia were in essentials akin to one another. Therefore, despite the fact that many minor shifts of population took place in the area at this time, we must discard, not only the hypothesis that there was a considerable superimposition of new elements as a result of immigration from the northern Balkans, but also the theory of 'Cycladic migration', which did duty for a long time as an explanation of the changes wrought in the Aegean in the Early Metal Age. According to this theory the innovations were the work of a people that arrived in Hellas from Anatolia. Since the Neolithic substratum on either side of the Aegean is now known to be related, the real explanation for the similarities that exist must lie elsewhere.

It is only to be expected that the introduction of metals should have had a revolutionizing effect upon all spheres of life, including art. In this connection we sometimes speak of 'the shock of metal', to emphasize the drastic nature of the changes it brought about. Its effects were first felt in the Orient at a relatively early date, and later in areas situated progressively further to the west, until the southern Balkans were reached, when the movement temporarily came to a halt. One consequence which this had upon future developments may be singled out for attention here. When the Achaean Greeks, the forerunners of the men who created the Mycenaean culture, reached the Aegean lands in the early part of the second millennium B.C., they found there — not a population divided into two groups — but the autochthonous ancient Aegean inhabitants, who had been only slightly affected by external influences. The pre-Greek language can be traced in the topography of Asia Minor, the Aegean islands (including Crete) and Greece itself, where we find names of mountains, rivers and towns that contain the consonants -ss-, -tt-, -nth- or -nd-. Here, up to the end of the Early Bronze Age at least, philology can supplement the evidence of Neolithic architectural remains: e.g., Hymettos, Larissa, Knossos, Lyttos, Tylissos, Assos, Tarnessos, Mykalessos, Pednelissos, Korinthos (Corinth), Erymanthos, Kynthos, Olynthos, Tiryns, (gen. Tirynthos), Xanthos, Labranda, Alabanda, Alinda and Isinda (cf. Labyrinthos; asaminthos means 'bath-tub'). The people of whom we are speaking are identical with the Carians, Leleges and Pelasgians referred to in the Greek literary tradition. We shall have something more to say in due course about their history during the Full and Late Bronze Age.

'Individuation' To understand the evolution described above we have to bear in mind the differences, as well as the similarities, between conditions in the earlier and later epochs. These differences are evident in a refinement of artistic quality,

in increased compactness, and in greater clarity. That this constitutes progress is undeniable. The atmosphere becomes brighter — and this presupposes the existence of men who were awakening for the first time to new sensations and reacting to their environment with a mental awareness hitherto unknown. It was they who were responsible for the new styles. But this progress went hand in hand with greater differentiation. We have already noted the existence of various regions within the Aegean world, as well as their characteristic common modes of expression which linked these regions together. It should also be pointed out that the differences between these various groupings were now becoming more clearly marked and precisely formulated. Thus it may be said that the really characteristic feature of this entire phase is the tendency towards a greater accentuation of individuality. Although we cannot of course yet speak of the achievements of individuals, it nevertheless seems certain that, corresponding to the greater degree of differentiation between local (and thus probably also tribal) groups, we have a breakdown and 'individuation' of the single universal character of this age in comparison with the preceding one.

We have already considered the differences between the west Anatolian, Cycladic and Early Helladic cultures, in so far as these are reflected in their pottery. We have now to examine the Cretan group. This is treated last here because it throws fresh light upon this whole question, and also because it occupies something of a special position in Aegean art as a whole.

In attempting to elucidate the chronology and stratigraphy of Knossos archaeologists have resorted to a threefold system of classification. Of the three levels in this triad we are here concerned solely with the first, known as Early Minoan. It already replaces the sub-Neolithic prior to the middle of the 3rd millennium B.C. and comes to an end in the 20th century B.C., just before the palaces were built. These are the terminal dates of the Early Bronze Age in Crete, which is thus already over before the Full Bronze Age has begun elsewhere in the Aegean. Of the three Early Minoan sub-periods the first (EM I) seems to have been relatively long (from approx. 2600 to 2250 B.C.) and uneventful. The next one (EM II) apparently overlaps the last (EM III) to a considerable extent.

Early Minoan pottery

The beak-spouted jug illustrated on p. 42 belongs to the end of the first sub-period. It comes from the *tholos* at Hagios Onouphrios near Phaestos. It has a slip of clay well tempered with water that is a yellowish white in colour. For the decoration a reddish glaze has been used. The design consists of three identical groups of interlocking angles, with their vertices pointing upwards. Below them there is a lace-work lozenge, formed by prolonging the sides of the inner angle to touch the outer ones. Of these groups the

PLATE 8

one in the middle has its vertex diametrically opposite the handle, so that each of the three occupies one third of the total curved surface of the vessel.

Of the three empty spaces between the angles the two in front are filled in with meridian-like lines, while the third contains the socket of the handle, and below this some crossed lines. This is obviously nothing else but a disintegrated dentate band. Confirmation of this is provided by the fact that in the entwining lace-work ornaments we may recognize affinities with similar designs from the Neolithic and Early Metal Age, the significance of which has already been discussed. Nowhere outside Crete do we find such a vigorous and consistent effort to achieve a torsion effect, and to direct the eye of the beholder diagonally to the axes of the vessel, thereby enabling him to perceive it three-dimensionally.

'Mottled ware
PLATE 11
From the little town of Vasiliki, near the Gulf of Mirabello in eastern Crete, come the teapot vessel and the small beaker shown in the Plate on p. 61. Both illustrate a style of pottery known as 'mottled ware', which found favour in the east of the island during the middle of the Early Minoan phase (EM II). The vessel was covered unevenly with glaze, and while being fired was exposed repeatedly to the flames, or touched here and there with red-hot charcoal, so that the surface acquired a mottled effect. In this way nuances of colour could be obtained and the dots made to melt into one another, forming a single shade ranging from a dark brownish black, by way of a yellowish gold similar to amber, to bright yellow. The teapot vessel illustrates the high degree of perfection that could be attained by this method. The mottling was carried out in such a way as to produce a design. Two bean-shaped band ornaments were arranged symmetrically, and this design is continued in a different fashion on the spout. By means of painted lines the latter is made to represent a bird's head, a knob being affixed to suggest the eye. This specimen also makes it clear why we can no longer speak of Urfirnis in Early Minoan Crete, as we can in regard to the pottery produced at this time on the mainland and in the Cyclades. The artistry with which the glaze was produced and applied could hardly be surpassed.

Mottling was one way of producing surface decoration, which is met with frequently in Aegean ornamentation already at an early date. These patterns foreshadowed the truly classical ornamentation that came in later, during the age of efflorescence. They deserve our special attention since this style was unknown in the decorative 'syntax' of the Orient and Egypt.

When one considers how attractively the contrast is brought out between the bizarre mottling and the deliberately simple form of the vessel, one can appreciate that this work is a composite entity, its sense of wholeness being brought about by means of the surface decoration. In glyptic art we also have ornamental bands from this period which are still produced at the height of the Minoan era. The Minoans' feeling for movement, expressed in swirling curves, must have been inspired by these flowing wavy bands. The transition to a naturalistic form, in the spout of the jug, has parallels in Trojan crown-like lids and elsewhere. It is executed with absolute accuracy. That such a work should have been produced in Crete is doubly significant because here this phase developed along lines radically different from those followed elsewhere, in that the design was prepared. We can follow this process as it develops both on seals and painted vessels: the basis is a combination of Oriental models and Aegean ornaments. A somewhat similar process occurs in the blending of functional and natural elements on the 'teapot' from Vasiliki. The little jug of red and white stratified stone, probably stalactite, depicted on p. 60 was found in one of the family tombs on Mochlos. It, too, belongs to the second Early Minoan period. The decoration is related to that on the mottled ware. The contrast between the marbling effect and the shape of the vessel is even more marked than in the latter instance, because here the material is more difficult to work, since it has a greater abundance of natural colours. The wavy lines lend this manifestation of wealth and splendour a more spirited and cheering note, which is as far removed from the staid prehistoric ware found elsewhere in the Aegean as it is from the heavy monumental style of Egypt and the Near East.

Stone vessels
PLATE 10

Early Minoan stone vessels belong to a tradition that reaches back to Neolithic times. Adaptation of the graining in the stone for decorative purposes is also no innovation, and the same is true of the polychrome mottling produced by the use of conglomeratic stones. In their variety of colours and the degree of technological refinement attained they surpass all the works produced up to this time and all those produced outside Crete. They also excel in the consistency and vigour of the decoration. This passion for utilizing brightly-coloured precious stone to obtain an ornamental effect found expression later in the Minoan palaces.

Turning to the other kinds of pottery produced at this time, before the Palace period, we may note that the engraved grey ware found earlier soon died out. It was the Cretan equivalent of the Pelos group from the Cyclades, many of the vessels being similar in shape. Characteristic is the substitution of concentric semicircles for the pattern of bands of disintegrated interlocking dentates.

Other groups of pottery

Also of early date, but probably more enduring, is the Pyrgos group, as it is called, which is dark in colour with a design consisting of burnished straight lines. The technique used in producing these vessels was already known on

PLATE 8

the mainland in Neolithic times. The principal form is the goblet on a tall pedestal. It is often associated with the light-coloured group represented here by the beak-spouted jug from Hagios Onouphrios. Both these styles are related to those of the Cyclades, the links between them being evident already in the case of the Pelos group.

To appreciate the special position held by Crete in the Early Bronze Age, we can do no better than to compare the elegant pottery that has white painting upon a dark glaze with the Hagia Marina ware produced at the same time on the mainland. The Minoan pottery that now developed in eastern Crete was to become predominant throughout the island at the beginning of the Palace era. It commences as early as the middle of the period we are now discussing (EM II), when it supersedes the mottled ware that was also made in eastern Crete. Beak-spouted vases, teapot jugs and beakers, which may be either conical or spherical in shape and either have handles or lack them — these are the most frequent forms. The addiction to spirals, meanders and torsions prepares the ground for the brilliant achievements of the following period.

Abundant information concerning gold jewellery in the Early Metal Age has been yielded by the treasure-stores buried by their owners when Troy II was destroyed. As they were housed in the Museum für Vor- und Frühgeschichte in Berlin, where they perished during the Second World War, a contemporaneous find from Poliochni which bears a resemblance to them must do duty instead. This find comprises half an ear ornament having a clasp to which is affixed a basket with three horizontal rows of tiny gold beads on either side. The latter are soldered on to the gold leaf by means of the so-called granulation technique. The pendant itself consists of five fine chains decorated with scales, to the bottom ends of which are fixed tassel-like ornaments of beaten gold leaf. These are images of idols whose function is to give protection and good fortune to the wearer.

Similar to this is a lavish Trojan ornament worn on the forehead, which has countless pendants of this kind. We also know of tubular ear-rings of an Oriental type, hair spirals, bracelets in the form of spirals, and of broad bands with small spirals and rosettes soldered on, and furthermore pins with magnificently worked heads, decorated with coiled wire, either soldered

FIG. 9 — *Cycladic marble idol. From Syros. Last third of 3rd millennium B.C. National Museums, Berlin. Height approx. 25 cm. Cf. p. 57.*

on or freely rolled, and small plastic vases of embossed gold leaf. The piece PLATE 12 from Poliochni (Plate on p. 61) which has two plastic quadrupeds in embossed gold leaf, is of a rather similar type. The technique, and partly the styles as well, are derived from the Orient. This is particularly true of the granulation.

The same processes were employed in making jewellery on the Greek mainland. The museum in Berlin used to possess a treasure-store from Thyreatis (Peloponnese), now unhappily lost, which would have served to illustrate this point. Other examples are found in the Cyclades and Crete. The existence of movable parts and the delicate workmanship which this involves mark these objects out as of Aegean manufacture. Pins crowned with figures of wild goats or the heads of such animals, or alternatively with wire spirals, are found both in the Cyclades and the Peloponnese. We have silver diadems worn by the dead, some of which have a beaten decoration, from both these last-named areas, and similar articles in gold from Crete (Mochlos, Lebena). The *tholoi* of the Messara have yielded a small gold cylinder with wire spirals soldered on and a little lion with a mane of granulated work. Lavish funerary jewellery has been found at Mochlos (EM II): delicate pendants in the form of chains, which from a technical standpoint are akin to the jewellery from Troy and the Peloponnese. The early representations of flowers have been improved upon: we know of pins being modelled in this form, and of olive leaves in gold combined with small chains. In this way Minoan production is distinguished from that of other areas, so far as this branch of art is concerned, less by superior quality than by its more complete, compact and specific mode of expression. From this alone it is clear that in decoration the objective is to fuse the ornament with the natural form.

In place of the Neolithic idols — among which were some splendid specimens *Statuettes* FIG. 9 made of clay, such as that from Lerna — we have the marble idols of the Cyclades. The marble quarried on these islands, which was to be used to such effect in historic times, made it possible for these workshops to flourish as they did. Their products reached Crete as well as the mainland.

Most of these statuettes are naked female figures, depicted with the arms crossed over the abdomen. They are generally not designed to stand erect. Groups of up to twelve of them have been found in graves in the Cyclades. The head from Amorgos (height 29 cm.) illustrated in the Plate on p. 59 PLATE 12 is characteristic of this style, although its size, and the fact that the head is separated from the body, make it unique. The eyes were represented by painting, and tattooing was suggested by red and black lines painted on the left cheek. These tombs have also yielded rectangular marble palettes and lumps of red colouring-matter, in addition to engraved hollowed-out bones containing blue paint. These were used to colour the body. From an anatomical point of view these idols are remarkable for their distended form, as in the elongated neck, oval face and nasal ridge. These features, together with the receding forehead, are typical of the human figure as we find it depicted in Late Minoan works. They seem to be characteristic of the ancient Aegean people as a whole. After the spontaneous naturalism of the Neolithic works one is struck by the degree of schematization and the way in which isolated parts are co-ordinated so as to form a unity. Their combination in a plank-like fashion, such as we find in the torso, for example, leads to a loss of the former unrestrained plasticity. If works such as these have an appeal for modern artists, this appears to be due to the abstract nature of this style. In comparison with earlier figures, these' statuettes reveal a new awareness on the artist's part. The secret of their effectiveness is to be found in the fact that they express with such immediacy the outlook of man at this early stage in his evolution. These works exemplify the clearer definition that characterizes this whole phase of stylistic development.

These Cycladic idols are related to those of the Neolithic era by their corpulence and the squatting posture. They are illustrative of a large group of highly schematized clay and marble idols found throughout the area. These symbolic styles are derived from the squatting motif. In the Cyclades a shape resembling a violin is favoured. Schematization took place in

FIG. 10 the Neolithic: one can detect it in the figures from Asia Minor which served as a model for those of the Aegean. Idols such as these are also to be found in Aegean settlements, which provides evidence of both the limited nature of, and the common elements in, religious beliefs. The Great Goddess, the giver of fertility in the broadest sense of the term, was represented by a powerful symbol which could be treasured by the living and the dead: its multiple portrayal, which we have already noted in western Anatolian metal work, served to guarantee its effect. It would therefore be wrong to envisage them as cult images, although there must have been a strong element of magic in this idol cult.

This helps to explain why already at an early date we find representations

FIG. 10 — *Cycladic marble idol in the shape of a violin. From Paros. Last third of 3rd millennium B.C. National Museum, Athens. Height 11 cm. Cf. above*.

PLATE 9 — Cycladic marble head with traces of painting. Amorgos. Latter half of 3rd millennium B.C. *National Museum, Athens. Height 2.9 cm. Cf. p. 56.*

PLATE 10 — Small stone jug, probably of stalactite. Mochlos, eastern Crete. Early Minoan II, 2300—2000 B.C. *Iraklion. Height 12 cm. Cf. p. 55.*

Opposite Top:

PLATE 11 — Cup and vessel with spout covered with glaze paint. Mottled ware. Vasiliki, eastern Crete. Early Minoan II, 2300—2000 B.C. *Iraklion. Height of cup 6 cm.; height of vessel 14 cm. Cf. pp. 32, 54.*

Opposite Bottom:

PLATE 12 — Gold ear pendants and fibula. Poliochni, Lemnos. Style: western Asia Minor. Late 3rd millennium B.C. *Length of ear pendants 7.8 cm.; length of fibula 9.8 cm. Cf. pp. 32, 56.*

PLATE 13 — Ivory seal bearing an ox and two lions bordered by spiral ornamentation. From a *tholos* tomb near Platanos, southern Crete. Early Minoan II, 2300–2000 B.C. *Iraklion. Length 3 cm. Cf. pp. 32, 67.*

PLATE 14 — Ivory seal in the form of an ape. Trapeza, eastern Crete. Middle Minoan I, 2000—1800 B.C. *Iraklion. Height 55 cm. Cf. pp. 32, 67, 72.*

PLATE 15 — Palace of Knossos: North Propylon, seen from the north-east. Foreground: Pillar Hall. Centre: reconstruction of buildings on western side of inclined path leading to central court. Background, left: reconstructed rooms on the western side of the central court. 16th cent. B.C. *Cf. pp. 79, 91.*

Opposite Top:
PLATE 16 — Palace of Knossos: Hall of Colonnades in Royal Apartments, seen from the western vestibule. The columns in the rear belong to the eastern vestibule. 16th cent. B.C. *Cf. pp. 79, 91.*

Opposite Bottom:
PLATE 17 — Palace of Phaestos: Ante-room with vestibule and light-area (in front, on the left), in the north wing of the Second Palace (1700—1400 B.C.). *Cf. pp. 99, 102, 105.*

PLATE 18 — Palace of Knossos: ground level of stair-well adjoining Royal Apartments ('A' on plan in Fig. 16), looking south-east. 16th cent. B.C. *Cf. pp. 79, 91.*

of men as well as of the Goddess. The former can be identified as votive offerings. Among these figures are seated harpists and a standing flutist. Music was an element in the funerary ritual, and even the dead were not deprived of it. The idea probably was that it would propitiate the gods and give vigour to departed souls.

An abundance of sculpture is found only in Crete. The best works, it is interesting to note, are miniatures: ivory seals carved in the shape of figures, which have been discovered in graves. Examples of these are the ox from a *tholos* near Platanos illustrated in the Plate on p.,62 and the ape from interments in the Trapeza cave, at the edge of the plateau of Lasithi. We also have a dove with two if its young, a boar's head, a lion killing a man, and heads of quadrupeds and birds. These were modelled directly upon Egyptian seals from the so-called First Intermediate period, i.e. the era between the Old and Middle Kingdoms (2360–2000 B.C.). They originate in the ancient Orient. The crouching ape motif is likewise Egyptian. On the other hand, the voluminous three-dimensional carvings, arranged in a decorative scheme and executed in an unconstrained naturalistic style, possess Cretan features clearly distinguishable from those of the carved idols from the Cyclades. The motifs show whence the impulses came for such non-representational works. It is all the more remarkable that it is precisely their naturalistic features that distinguish them from their models.

PLATE 13
PLATE 14

Finally, one may note some vessels featuring figures from Cretan graves. Bulls with diminutive men hanging on to their horns, birds, and a beaked jug with men clambering up to the rim — these are still more vigorous in their naturalism and plasticity.

Only Early Minoan glyptic art can compete with the pottery of this period in artistic expressiveness and in its interest for the student of art history. The medium used is either bone or steatite. The scenes or patterns on the surface of the seals are engraved, the drill being as yet unknown. In addition to signets, on which the design may be either representational or ornamental, there are many button seals, discs, prisms, and — last but not least — ivory cylinders. In the latter case it is the ends that are decorated, and not the convex surface, as is the rule in the Orient. This whole group of objects, except for the seals in Fig. 11, is illustrated here only by the Plate on p. 62, which shows the lower side of a small ivory ox. Two striding lions are enclosed within a framework of S-shaped spirals. Such combination of Aegean spiral ornamenation with figures of Egyptian or Anatolian origin is typical of Cretan art in this period. The ornamental elements of these seals include bands, S- and C-shaped spirals, meanders, swastikas, crosses and stars. Among the figures that occur we may mention the lion, ox, wild goat, wild boar,

Seals
FIG. 11

PLATE 13

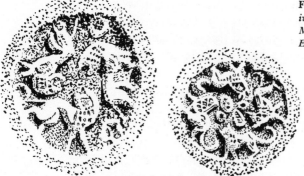

FIG. 11 — *Impressions of Early Minoan ivory seals featuring lions. From Platanos, Messara. End of 3rd millennium B.C. Enlarged. Iraklion. Cf. pp. 32, 68, 71.*

ape, animal's head, scorpion, spider and bee. Human figures are also found, while flora is represented by foliate designs and rosettes. This whole repertoire of figures, like pictorial representation in general, is alien to the rest of the Aegean during this period. There can be no doubt that it originated in the Orient.

The other group of motifs, consisting of ornamental designs, developed in the art of the Early Metal Age all over the Aegean lands. We can follow the impulses that led to its emergence both in Europe, where banded ceramic ware was produced in primitive times, and in Anatolia, where metal was already worked. It was the achievement of the Minoans of this period that they succeeded in fusing these elements to form a new unity, as is evident from the stylistic 'syntax'. The new elements are the S-shaped and whorl motifs, and surface decoration that follows the *en rapport* pattern. Also present are the 'syntactic' styles found in curvilinear compositions of ancient Egypt and the Near East: in the former area cruciform arrangements and segments, and in the latter concentric circles. But with the passage of time these styles become less frequent in Minoan glyptic, and the motifs, which are now pictorial in character, follow the new syntax. As an example of this process we may note the changes undergone by the lion, which was a popular figure. The animal develops a pronounced twist, until its forelegs curve around parallel with the lower part of the circumference of the seal, and the hind legs are parallel with the upper part. The influence of spiral and whorl motifs is obvious. In this way spirals and wavy lines now determine the design of the pictorial elements as well.

FIG. 11

A find of clay seal impressions from the 'House of Tiles' at Lerna throws some light upon the historical background of these early Minoan seals. These lumps of clay often bear traces of the cord used to fasten the boxes and vessels that they secured. Seventy different seals can be identified. The impressions were buried when the building was destroyed at the end of the second Early Helladic phase, and are thus roughly contemporary with the earliest Minoan seals. The seals themselves were probably carved from wood. The only pictorial designs here are of a bee and jugs; in the main the decoration is ornamental. Most frequent are patterns of bands. Meanders and swastikas are rare, and S- and C-shaped spirals rarer still. Motifs from the plant world make an inconspicuous appearance in a few cases, where the pattern reproduces that of leaves. The most striking feature is the difference in syntax. There are no more than attempts at *en rapport* patterns and whorls, while division into several segments and cruciform arrangements are popular. The patterns of three or four circles formed by bands serve rather as a means of articulation — unlike kindred forms in Minoan art, which tend either to become surface decoration or to close the circle. Some impressions found at Lerna that are divided into two segments are nearer than any of the Cretan seals to Egyptian button seals or to their prototypes from the ancient Near East, with their loops. The entire group is not only earlier in date, but also more restrained, despite its character and high artistic quality. On the mainland it left no trace upon later works.

This shows that the influence of patterns from the ancient civilizations of the East was more intensive and productive in Crete, which in turn indicates the special position occupied by this island in relation to the other Aegean lands. This was evident already in the case of its pottery, sculpture and gold jewellery. The effect of its favourable geographical location is immediately obvious. The influences that radiated outwards from the east and south-east came together in Crete, which so to speak acted as a lens, focussing them and then transmitting them to other parts of the Aegean. This possibility of exporting its wares, as we shall see below, gave Cretan production an impetus unparalleled elsewhere. Equally important, from the standpoint of art history, is the relationship of Cretan art in this period to later Minoan developments during the Palace era. At this point we should note that its organic inner consistency of style, to which attention has already been drawn, continues without interruption. Our glimpse of the way in which pictorial elements were transmuted by the syntax that had hitherto developed only in decoration throws light upon a new and specifically Minoan reciprocal relationship that now came into being between pictorial motifs and decoration. This was based upon principles common throughout the Aegean world, but now became separate and distinct from them. Thus we now have a tangible Minoan stylistic structure — an 'inner form' that is specifically Minoan. We shall see in due course how the whole of Minoan art rested on this basis during the Palace era.

When the palaces were discovered the affinities between their motifs and those found in the ancient civilizations obscured the true picture. These affinities were explained by reference to waves of immigrants from Anatolia and Egypt in primitive times. This view, characteristic of the 'heroic age' of early scholarship, is still met with occasionally today. Systematic comparison of styles only became possible once we had the seals, and these were discovered at a later date. When they were studied it was found that precisely the reverse was true: Minoan style was not a fortunate blend of heterogeneous elements but a very definite, and highly characteristic, expression of the ancient Aegean substratum.

The history of art is more than a mere record of styles: it is also the history of the way in which certain ideas have been expressed. It is therefore closely related to history in general — whether social, economic, political or religious. In the prehistoric period with which we are concerned we have no written sources. The same documents have to provide us with information about art and much else besides. For this reason the historical background, although it is only possible to sketch it in broad outline, is nevertheless important to our theme.

SOCIOLOGY Here, too, the changes that took place during this period may be explained in the last resort by the introduction of metals. This led to the emergence of groups of craftsmen, traders and mariners. Where the bulk of the population was still engaged in agriculture these classes of persons naturally acted as a ferment. The primitive equality that had generally prevailed hitherto was subject to stronger disruptive pressures. It now had to contend with forces more powerful than the differences between those owning various amounts of land. The existence of princes who enjoyed considerable wealth and power, such as we find at Troy, Lerna and Tiryns, presupposes a degree of social, economic and military organization which, for all its undoubtedly primitive character, must have surpassed by far the conditions that had existed under the old tribal chiefs. For evidence of this we may once again look at Dimini. The ancient civilizations of Egypt and Anatolia provided, as well as metals and the values attaching to them, many other things that helped to raise the level of human existence and to improve its quality. Greater effort now had to be expended in order to ensure its protection, as we can see from the fact that fortified towns now came into being alongside the princes' residences, and that metal weapons were made, first of copper and then of bronze. We have daggers in the shape of laurel-leaves or triangles, with short tangs to hold the hilt, which is of wood or bone. Lance-heads, too, are shaped like laurel-leaves and are affixed to the shaft with cords. No swords are as yet to be found. Still in use are stone weapons, such as the battle-axe and club-head, and long-range weapons such as the bow and sling.

The graves in Crete are family sepulchres. They are often situated close together, which suggests the existence of an enclosed settlement in the area. One may also probably conclude from them that property in land was inherited within the family. The large number of seals found in the graves indicates that the heads of the various clans were concerned to establish their title to their property. The use of seals was probably connected with belief in magic, namely that an individual's force could be transmitted to an inanimate object. Prisms, for example, may be identified as amulets, and the appearance, at the beginning of the Palace period, of one group of these which served as talismans may be based upon such ideas. We can also see further traces of the tendency towards 'individuation'. The seal impressions found in the prince's house at Lerna show that already at this time the prince's officials made use of seals for their own purposes. In view of the function later performed by seals in the Aegean during the Bronze Age, we must presume that in this case, too, there was some interrelationship between the object secured and the possessor of the seal. The use of seals in commerce is also evidenced by stamped clay vessels from Troy, the Argolis, the Cyclades, and Crete.

The cult objects are in general similar to those we came across during the Neolithic. Most frequent are likenesses of the Great Goddess — an important point to bear in mind when considering the links between this phase and the preceding one, and the elements during this phase that are common to the whole area. One can also see from this that Aegean culture during the Early Metal Age still has a prehistoric character. The affinities between the cult of the dead in Crete and in the Cyclades lead one to assume that similar practices were carried on in western Anatolia and on the Greek mainland.

RELIGION, RITUAL

The presence of idols in the graves at least suggests a chthonic note in the concept of the Goddess. Only in Crete do we have evidence that she was associated with the bull. Votive vessels in the shape of bulls from the *tholoi* of the Messara show that the so-called 'bull sport' was already familiar at this early date. This is a ritualistic imitation of the action of catching the bull for sacrifice, which shows that this animal was of importance in the cults of the Early Minoan era. At this stage we also find the first Minoan double axes, which are likewise symbols of bull sacrifice. Thus the Early Minoans succeeded in turning the bull god of their Mediterranean and Anatolian neighbours into the means of expressing fresh and original ideas of their own. The antithetical relationship between the Goddess and the bull is an incomparable, and truly Cretan, way of manifesting the Goddess' power.

One of the clearest and most characteristic new features on the historical scene was the increase in communications, and thus also the exchange of goods and ideas. This traffic was carried on between the Aegean and the ancient civilizations as well as within the Aegean itself. Most of it, naturally, was by sea. The vessels used were almost exclusively flat-bottomed craft manned by a number of oarsmen. We are familiar with them from engravings on Cycladic clay vessels or Minoan seals, and from reproductions in clay and silver found in graves in Crete and the Cyclades. It was at this time that the art of navigation appears to have become known. Sailing-ships had long been a familiar sight in Egypt, but we have definite evidence of journeys by Egyptian seamen only as far as the coast of Syria.

We have already referred above to one of the routes by which metals were introduced. It is known for certain that tin was obtained from eastern Anatolia, and the demand for copper could be satisfied with ease from the mines of Cyprus. Copper from the Iberian peninsula and tin from Britain do not seem to have played any part in Aegean commerce at this stage. All that can be established with certainty from excavations is that Aegean merchants traded westwards as far as Sicily and Dalmatia. There seems little doubt that the copper and tin came overland to Troy and from there reached the Aegean. Absolutely reliable evidence, at least so far as copper is concerned, is available as regards the southern route: i.e. the maritime route to Crete along the south coast of Asia Minor. It was this route that served to link the Aegean with Egypt. There is no evidence of direct trade across the eastern Mediterranean to the Nile, and this seems unlikely.

In addition to the raw material for bronze-casting, gold, silver, and many other craft products must have reached Crete in this way from the east and south-east. Other articles became known through the merchants themselves. It is difficult to gain any idea of the commodities that the Aegean lands sent in exchange. Perhaps they were the same products that were exported during the Palace period: olives, shells, wine, oil, wax and wool. Much becomes clear when we bear in mind that this trade was not carried on directly but through a number of local entrepôts. Most of the articles that possessed a cultural significance will thus have reached the Aegean by stages.

Fig. 11 As examples of imported Oriental motifs we may mention the Aegean lion, wire spirals, and the plan of the residence at Lerna. The herring-bone method of building walls already mentioned also comes into this category. The links between Crete and Egypt are exemplified by Minoan reproductions of EgyptPlate 14ian stone vessels, the influence exerted in Crete by Egyptian button seals
CHRO-
NOLOGY and the carvings of crouching apes found on the island.

In Mesopotamia and the Nile valley, where civilizations existed that possessed written scripts, we can reconstruct with their aid a fairly reliable chronology going back some distance into the 3rd millennium B.C. Cross-references can help us to establish some firm dates for the history of the Aegean lands as well. Remains of Egyptian stone vessels from the first half of the 3rd millennium B.C., found at Knossos, give us a *terminus post quem* for the beginning of the Copper Age (EM I). But as imperishable objects they may have been produced long before they were buried. The earliest synchronisms that are of any use are provided by the seals. Their Egyptian prototypes are typical products of the so-called First Intermediate period (6th-11th dynasties, i.e. 2345-1991 B.C.). In Crete they are found during the second Early Minoan period (EM II). They continue in the *tholoi* of the Messara and some way into the early Palace era. In one *tholos* near Lebena subsequent interments have been found which could be dated by a scarab to the 20th or early 19th century B.C. The oldest interments in this grave contained early seals and pottery from EM II. On account of its inartistic and impermanent construction such a grave can scarcely have survived for more than 300 years, even allowing for renovations. On the other hand it has become steadily clearer that objects assigned to the third Early Minoan phase belong chronologically with those of the second. For reasons given above, the latter must have begun during the First Intermediate period in Egypt. The earliest date that can be set for the beginning of the second Early Minoan phase is between 2300 and 2200 B.C., since its origins overlap with the later phase of Troy II, and from the links with Near Eastern chronology it is clear that the end of Troy II cannot be put earlier than 2200-2150 B.C.

For the earlier period we have to confine ourselves to conjectures. It would be useful to know the approximate date of the beginning of Troy I and the Copper Age in western Anatolia. This must depend on the duration of Troy II. In this connection it is firmly established, as we have just pointed out, that the end of Troy II overlaps with the beginning of EM II. An approximate upper limit, at least, is set by the appearance of EH I ceramics in Troy I from the middle strata onwards. The Urfirnis ceramic horizon, and with it the Early Helladic culture, come to an end between 1900 and 1800 B.C. Its beginning falls some time during EM I and the Early Cycladic period (Pelos phase). But it cannot be dated back indefinitely into the past— otherwise we should have to allow a vast space of time for the whole Copper and Early Bronze Age, which would not accord with the relative scarcity of finds or what we know about their development. If the Copper Age does indeed begin earlier in Crete and western Anatolia than it does on the Greek mainland, we cannot put it much earlier than 2600 B.C.

We can therefore date the beginning of Troy II, which developed directly out of Troy I, to 2400 B.C. and its destruction to 2150 B.C. Seven stages can be identified in the extensive restoration work carried on within this horizon, the terminal dates of which must accordingly be placed as far apart as the evidence permits. On the other hand synchronisms with discoveries on the Anatolian plateau that can be dated by Near Eastern chronology allow us to put the catastrophe that befell Troy II about two hundred years before the end of the 3rd millennium B.C. This would accord with the affinities with EM II. Troy V was replaced by the Full Bronze Age citadel of Troy in, or shortly before, 1800 B.C., and in early Troy V we still come across late Urfirnis pottery (EH III). We thus still have six to seven centuries left (2500–1900 B.C.) in which to place the Early Helladic phase. The second Early Helladic phase, when this culture reached efflorescence, would then coincide roughly with EM II, likewise a highly productive era, and in its early part also with Troy II. The border-line between the earlier and later periods in the Cyclades (Pelos and Syros phases) thus corresponds to that between EM I and II and EH I and II. It, too, occupies a place approximately in the middle of Troy II.

Thus in general the beginning of the Metal Age in the Aegean can be put at 2600 B.C., or shortly before. It cannot be excluded that on the Greek mainland it may date only from the following century.

As we can see, in the chronology of the Aegean during the 3rd millennium B.C. we have two principal aids to guide us. One consists of the synchronisms with Egypt and the Near East, the other of stratigraphic findings. The various interpretations still current today are due to differences in evaluating these factors. The most important stratigraphic material has been obtained by American excavators at Troy. It is not surprising that they should tend to accept an extended chronology and to set the origins as far back in time as possible, in view of the astonishingly large number of construction periods and strata they have succeeded in identifying and their measurements of relative thicknesses of debris deposits. Their findings are incontestable and their deductions arrived at with exemplary circumspection. But it is in the nature of things that the chronological conclusions drawn from these facts have to remain simply estimates, since where so many unknown quantities are involved they alone cannot support the entire edifice.

On the other hand, since the 'landslide' of dates for the reign of Hammurabi which occurred about 15 years ago, Near Eastern chronology must make us inclined to set the origins at as recent a date as possible. A short chronology is also suggested by an analysis of the information relevant to Aegean history contained in Egyptian button seals. Their importance deserves to be stressed since their range of distribution continues to be generally underestimated.

This means that we have to attach the shortest possible values to estimates attained from stratigraphic evidence. It is with these considerations in mind that we have made our suggestions here. It may be added, merely for the sake of completeness, that recently a proposal has been put forward that the Neolithic in Crete should be dated some way into the latter half of the 3rd millennium B.C. This is a generalization from stratigraphic observations at Phaestos. It is in hopelessly irreconcilable conflict with the accurate data relating to kindred neighbouring cultures, and shows the dangers involved in overrating the importance of stratigraphy in establishing an *absolute* chronology.

We are now in a position to sum up the historical significance of the art discussed in this chapter. It bears a prehistoric character, as does the art of the preceding era. But the forces that were then only beginning to stir now make themselves felt more clearly. There is a greater number of styles, and they are more varied. It is this that makes the process of development interesting for us. Only by looking back in time can we appreciate the extent to which this art derived its character from links with Egypt and the Near East. These connections mark early Aegean civilization off from the other cultures elsewhere in prehistoric Europe, with which it may be compared. The clearest indication of the difference between them is to be found in the emergence of the fortified town, and the way of life which this implies. There can be no doubt that we are now close to the border-line of what can properly be called prehistoric.

In other respects Aegean art in the Early Metal Age is as obviously European as it is prehistoric. It is the combination of these two features (the prehistoric — ancient European basis and the creative adaptation of contacts with the great civilizations of the Orient) that constitutes the 'individuation' which, as we have already mentioned, is the real achievement of this era. The differentiation between the various sub-regions, we can now see, is simply the reverse side of this phenomenon.

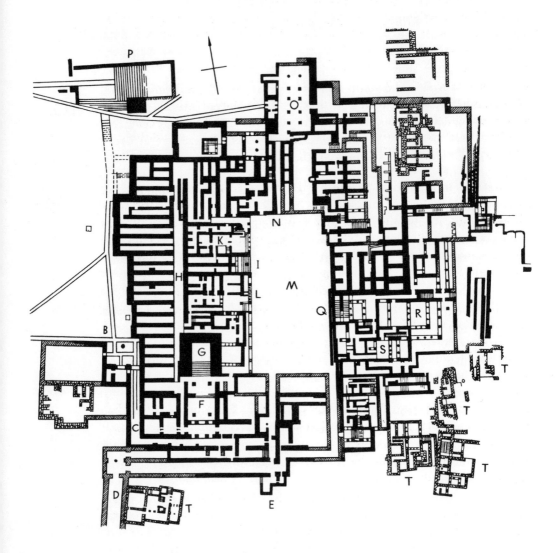

FIG. 12 — *Knossos: ground plan of the Palace before its destruction in approx. 1400 B.C., based on the plan drawn by Evans but simplified. A: West Court. B: West Propylon. C: Corridor of the Procession (in the eastern part the basement is not distinguished from the main storey). D: 'Stepped Portico'. E: South Propylon. F: Vestibule. G: Stairway to State Apartments. H: Corridor leading to magazines. I: Stairway from State Apartments to Central Court. K: Little Throne Room. L: Ritual Facade. M: Central Court. N: Path along ramp. O: North Propylon. P: False stairway and path leading to Little Palace. Q: Eastern stair-well. R: Hall of Colonnades. S: Queen's Megaron. T: Private houses. Cf. p. 77.*

III. THE AGE OF MATURITY
Minoan Style in the Palace Period

THE
PALACE
PERIOD

The palace of Knossos was built soon after the turn of the millennium, and Mallia and Phaestos followed a little later. The palaces remained standing until they were destroyed in or about the year 1400 B.C. These six centuries, which we call the Palace period, constitute the Full Bronze Age in Crete. One may distinguish two sub-periods, the dividing-line between which falls in approximately 1700 B.C.

The residences of earlier times (Troy, Lerna, Tiryns) were splendid enough for the prehistoric world. A palace presupposes the existence of an advanced culture. This is the difference between the buildings we are about to consider and those constructed hitherto. Even in this period we lack the written sources so essential for a full understanding of the past. This statement still holds good, as we shall see, despite the deciphering of the Linear B script, which in any case is relevant only to the last hundred years of our period. To appreciate the significance of this period for the history of art, we have to bear in mind the following point: the stage now reached on the road from prehistory to history must have played just as important a role in determining the artistic features of this phase as did its geographical location on the border between East and West.

We shall not deal separately with the monuments of the Early and Late Palace periods, although it is not our purpose to pass over the differences between them in silence. These differences ought to be of assistance to us in elucidating what is common ground in the structure of the new style. Let us take architecture first, and begin with the palace of Knossos, the greatest achievement of the period.

FIGS. 12, 13

Its builders were not free in their choice of site. It may be assumed that there was a royal residence in the ancient settlement, the extensive debris of which lies beneath the palace. Its location nearly 6 km. inland from the coast was dictated by elementary considerations of security. The choice of a site halfway along the north coast was not due simply to a desire to be equidistant from the eastern and western extremities of the island. Right up to the very end of this period everything to the west of Mt. Ida remained overshadowed by Minoan culture. Despite this, Knossos occupied a special place in the trade carried on between one part of Crete and another, because here the route leading from the densely populated Messara to the north coast, via the depression between Mts. Ida and Lasithi (Dikte), met the coastal road

ARCHI-
TECTURE
Knossos

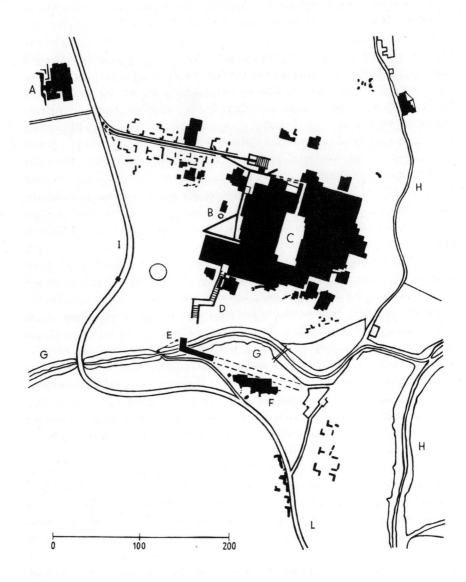

FIG. 13 — *Knossos: the Palace and its environs; state in 16th and 15th centuries B.C. A: Little Palace. B: West Court. C: Central Court. D: 'Stepped Portico'. E: Viaduct. F: Caravanserai. G: Vlychia (stream). H: Kairatos (stream). I: Modern road. Cf. pp. 77, 95, 105.*

leading from the equally densely populated eastern part of the island. This was therefore the most favourable site from which Cretan influence could spread northwards throughout the Aegean, and in particular to the Greek mainland. It was not exactly well suited to fortification. True, its position, at the junction of the valley of the little river Kairatos and the gorge of the Vlychia — one flowing north and the other east — is not readily accessible either from the east or south. But to the north and west the plateau, situated some 200 feet above sea-level, had no natural barriers. Yet for six centuries life flourished in this palace, and despite the fact that it was frequently destroyed by fire and earthquake it was repeatedly rebuilt without the protection that fortifications could afford. This is one of the strongest pieces of evidence of the Minoans' command of the sea, which dates from the beginning of the Palace era, and of the secure internal conditions prevailing on the island, which presuppose the existence of a strong centralized authority. Apart from the east wing of the palace, which is built into the knoll, so *Present* that its two lower storeys lie below the level of the central court, the excava- *condition* tions have yielded little other than the walls and foundations of the basements. But we do have evidence of the shape of the multi-storeyed superstructure that rose above these foundations. This is to be found in sketched reconstructions, which should not, however, be taken as entirely reliable. Attempts have also been made to restore the ruins after excavation, using cement instead of wood and different kinds of paint to suggest the various materials used for different parts of the building. The resultant effect is one that arouses mixed feelings in the viewer. But it would not be doing justice to those who have charge of the site if we did not bear in mind that excavated remains are necessarily subject to slow decay. Everything that serves to delay this process therefore deserves to be welcomed. Nor need we minimize the value of this restoration work in giving the visitor an idea of the inner rooms. In many places corrugated plexiglas roofing has recently been put up, resting on steel supports. But this, too, can only be an emergency measure. The Plates on pp. 65 and 66 give some idea of the recon- PLATES 16, 18 struction of certain rooms in the east wing. The view of the northern entrance-rooms in the Plate on p. 64 shows how the projections above ground PLATE 15 level help to make parts of the building visible in their original size and condition.

Finally, to assist in understanding the following description, we may add that the palace covers an area of about 10,000 square metres, and that the central court forms a rectangle in plan, facing north and south, and measuring some 50 by 28 metres in area.

The continual rebuilding carried on, beginning already in Minoan times, has obscured or destroyed all too many of the earliest features. To understand the remains that are still extant, and the history of the building in general, we need to have a clear picture in our minds of the appearance of the palace immediately prior to its destruction. This is the state in which the present ruins are being conserved. We may begin with these and then work our way back to the original building.

One cannot really speak of a building as such — so *open* is the palace in every sense of the word. In lieu of a continuous line of wall we have on the exterior a mass of projections and recesses, apparently arranged in a quite arbitrary manner. There are entrances and other openings on all four sides, as well as windows, loggias and verandahs. The differences in the thickness of the walls allow us to draw conclusions as to the height of the various storeys, which again seem to lack any kind of order or symmetry. Thus there *West Wing* is no facade, but only parts resembling facades; nevertheless the west side seems to have a more imposing character than any other. The combination of the paved forecourt (without buildings in the north or west) with its paths covered by slabs; the base of the palace wall, lined with alabaster orthostats about 1 metre high, standing on a plinth; and the monumental gateway leading into the whole complex — all these features, taken together, give the effect of a facade. The base is in two rows, with a filling of rubble. The wall above must be imagined as a solid ground-floor wall, with at the most a few slits to allow some light to reach the magazine. Like the other external and internal walls, it consisted of rubble packed with clay and strengthened by beams, or alternatively of mud-bricks with a timber framework — or of both together. We may assume that it was plastered in rudimentary fashion. The main floor and the second floor (which seems fairly certain to have existed at some points) had windows that were approximately square and were framed by beams, and possibly also loggias with pillars. Both these details are known from pictorial representations of other buildings.

The gateway on the southern side of the court has a right-angled opening leading northwards to the outer wall. This opening was about 12 metres wide in the clear. In the middle of it there stood a tall wooden column, tapering towards the base and resting upon a stone plinth. The paved vestibule was about 8 metres deep. At the rear were two rooms that may have been used by the guard. The east wall was decorated with the life-sized representation of a scene from the bull-sport, in painted stucco. Next to it, in the south wall, a passageway led off to the south. On its walls were life-sized frescoes depicting votaries, and for this reason it is known as the 'Corridor of the Procession'. It first runs to the south, but after about 27 metres makes a right-angled turn to the east. If one follows it along its full length

FIG. 14 — *Knossos: section of western façade of Central Court. Reconstruction based upon data given by Evans. 16th—15th centuries B.C. Left: ritual façade; centre: stairway leading to State Apartments; right: entrance to 'Little Throne Room'. Cf. pp. 146 and below.*

of about 45 metres and then makes another right-angled turn to the north, one emerges on the southern side of the central court. More important is another passageway which leads off from the middle of the tract that runs east and west. It leads through a magnificent columned vestibule, decorated with frescoes, to a broad staircase that probably also served as a light-well. As to the disposition of the rooms in the 'Piano Nobile', only guesses are possible. Some information can be gleaned from the walls of the foundations, which have been preserved. These, together with the monumental staircase, suggest that there were a number of formal reception rooms. After passing through the room next to the staircase one turned right (i.e. to the east) and so, by way of another broad gentle flight of stairs, gained the central court.

At the foot of this stairway, in the middle of the exit, was another tall column. FIG. 14 From an architectural point of view the basement served simply to carry the weight of the lavishly constructed rooms above. Its chief practical use was as a provision store. More than twenty magazines are arrayed along the west side of a long corridor running from north to south. They still

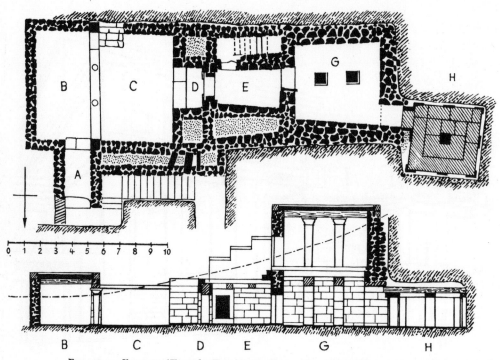

FIG. 15 — *Knossos: 'Temple Tomb', to the south of the Palace. Approx. 1500 B.C. A: Entrance. B: Hall. C: Court. D: Doorway. E: Corridor. F: Staircase. G: Ante-room. H: Sepulchral chamber. Cf. p. 115.*

FIG. 19
APPX. PL 11

contain huge clay vessels as tall as a man. Further provisions could be kept under the floor, which was covered with stone slabs, in box-shaped cavities also lined with stone slabs. Between the passageway and the central court there were more magazines, and in particular little square rooms used for religious purposes. They were rather like crypts. The ceiling was supported by pillars of blocks. No daylight penetrated into these rooms, and lamps therefore had to be used.

Central court The court, which formed a regular rectangle, must have lent a touch of calm and repose to this architectural design, with its constant dynamism and variety — even though the walls that surrounded it had many openings and were of different heights. But these were the only continuous stretches of wall in the whole building. Opposite the entrance to the court on the south (i.e. the shorter) side, which we have already noted, there was another on the north side. This gave direct access from the court to the outside world. Through it beasts of burden and sedan-chairs could also pass. At this point an open plastered ramp rises up to the north. On both sides it had colonnades resting on massive bastions. Some of these have been restored, as

PLATE 19 — Palace of Hagia Triada (1600—1400 B.C.): general view from the east. In the foreground, on the right: sloping path leading from the coast. To the rear is the basement and on the left the court. The Bay of Hagia Galene may be seen in the background. *Cf. p. 103.*

PLATE 20 — Palace of Phaestos: Central Court, looking north, with remains of the Second Palace (1700–1400 B.C.). In the background: Ida Mts. (2500 m.). *Cf. p.102*.

PLATE 21 — Palace of Phaestos: Central Court, looking north, with remains of the Second Palace (1700—1400 B.C.). In the background: Ida Mts. (2500 m.). *Cf. p. 102.*

PLATE 22 — Fragment of fresco from the Palace of Knossos: a dancer. 16th cent. B.C. *Iraklion. Height of part preserved 37 cm. Cf. pp. 119, 203.*

Opposite:
PLATE 23 — Stepped street in Gournia, eastern Crete, viewed from the east. 16th cent. B.C. *Cf. p.113.*

PLATE 24 — Ruins of the small town of Gournia, eastern Crete. 16th cent. B.C. In the background: Gulf of Mirabello.

we can see from the Plate on p. 64, which depicts the north end of the one PLATE 15
on the west side. In front of it are visible the remains of a tripartite pillar
hall, the westernmost third of which probably was open to the sky. The
actual entrance, which was very narrow, was situated in the middle of the
west wall.

Let us return to the central court and from there direct our steps towards
the east wing. Its northern, and larger, portion contains workshops and
magazines. From its terrace wall, built of ashlar masonry, which carries the
external wall, a twisting flight of steps leads down to the Kairatos valley.
In the smaller southern portion of the east wing were the royal quarters. FIG. 16
The two lower floors were built against the hillside by removing the old
debris; they have now been restored to their former appearance. They both
have the same plan and height (approx. 3.5 m.). The roof of the upper
storey was at the same level as the floor of the central court. We know that
there were two other storeys above these.

From the court one approached the stairway which acted as a light-well *Domestic*
and gave access to all storeys of the building by means of columnar galleries. *quarters,*
East Wing
On each storey the stairway had two flights running in opposite directions
parallel to the side of the court, with a landing between them. In the Plate
on p. 66 we have a view looking south-east across the light-well from the PLATE 18
point where the stairway commences at the ground-floor level. To the right
rises a row of three columns, supported by the balustrade of the stairway,
which in turn supports the flight of stairs above. The four pillars at ground
level show that there was a hall along the north and east sides of the court.
At the top of our illustration, in the centre, one can just make out the
balustrade of the eastern one on the first floor. The windows in the south
wall of the court shed light upon an ancillary staircase, to which access was
gained by means of the door in the east hall that can be seen in the shadow.
The lavishness of this arrangement may be appreciated when one considers
that the features reproduced in our illustration were repeated at least three
times on the storeys above.

In the extension of the northern part of the hall a corridor leads off to the
east. After a few steps along it we come to a door in its south wall. Through
this one reaches the complex of residential quarters, divided into two sections.
The larger section, in the north, centres upon a room measuring approximately 6 by 9 m. in area. It has a solid wall on the north side, but rows of
pillars on the other three sides. The western row can be seen in the foreground in the Plate on p. 65. This illustration also shows that there is a PLATE 16
colonnade in front of the row of pillars opposite, i.e. on the east side of
the room. The same arrangement is repeated on the south side and also —

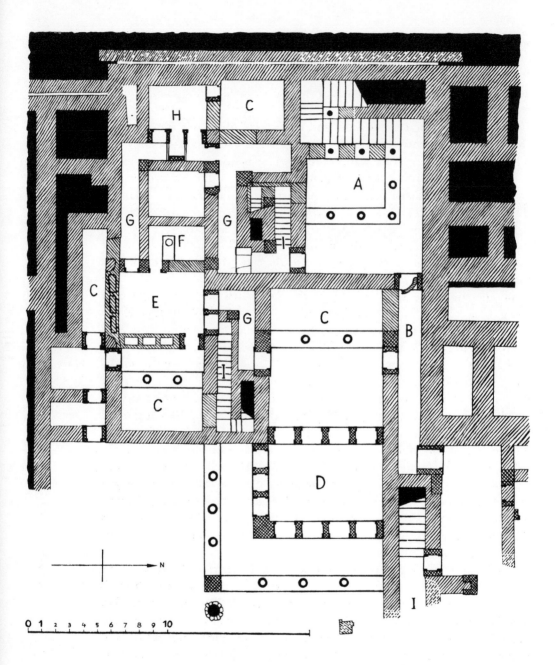

FIG. 16 — *Knossos: Royal Apartments, eastern wing of the Palace. 16th cent. B.C. A: Entrance-hall. B: Corridor running from east to west. C: Light-areas. D: Pillar Hall. E: Queen's Megaron. F: Bedroom. G: Corridor. H: Closet. I: Service staircase. Cf. p. 91.*

on a different scale — on the west side. The view shown in the Plate on p. 65 is taken from the western colonnade. This is deeper and has only two columns, as against the three we find on the east and south sides. These two columns separate the covered-in rooms from a small court that serves as a light-well. The wooden throne on the left-hand side of the picture is an imaginative modern reconstruction. Over it is a frieze of spirals, likewise a reconstruction, which gives some idea of the original decorative frescoes.

From the west antechamber of the pillar hall, opposite the door leading into it from the corridor running east and west, there is another door. This opens upon a short passageway with two turnings in it, which leads from the smaller, southern part of the residential quarters to the northern part and at the same time gives access to a servants' stairway situated between the two sections. The smaller part, too, has a pillar hall in the middle. It is less grandiose and has only two open sides, in the east and south, each with light-wells beyond them. Only on the east side do we find columns in between. Excavators have called this room the 'Queen's Megaron'. A door near the corridor in the north wall gives access to an ancillary staircase leading directly to the first floor. The 'Queen's Megaron' has an alcove on the west side, which at the time when the palace was destroyed was used as a bathroom, and had a terracotta bath-tub. It was designed to be used as a bedroom. Next to it a corridor leads westwards directly into a room in which was discovered the celebrated water-closet with its system of water flushing. Next to a light-well a corridor with two turns leads to the main stair-well. Here again, as to the east, we find another servants' staircase running from the northern to the southern part of the entire complex.

The 'Queen's Megaron' is closed off from the outside world. Although it is situated on one side of the palace it has no direct connection with it either by doors or windows. The view is also blocked by the eastern light-well, which had a high wall of ashlar masonry that probably extended at least one storey higher. The great pillar hall, however, with its portico on the east and south sides, opened upon a terrace, from which one had a clear view over the gardens that must have covered the slope to the hills across the Kairatos.

We have thus followed a devious route through the palace, starting and ending with its exterior. There were plenty of places where we had occasion to pause. One was in the ceremonial room on the first floor of the west wing. Others were in the central court and the two pillar halls in the eastern residential block. On the other hand there is a sense of dynamism in the propyla, corridors, stairways and doors. It is characteristic that, even when one is in rooms where one is tempted to linger, one feels impelled to leave by a different door from that through which one entered. One also soon notices that the places that induce a feeling of repose are not of equal value. In this sense the inner chambers are inferior to the central court.

This factor alone indicates the architectural function of the great court in the design. It moderates and gives a measured rhythmical quality to the feeling of unimpeded flowing movement. We may appreciate its central uniting function better if we do not regard it simply as a means of getting from one part of the building to another, as on our quick introductory tour of the palace, but note the fact that on all sides it has openings leading to the outside world. We have already drawn attention to the exit to the North Propylon (as well as the western forecourt, which was on the route we followed). We have also mentioned the corresponding opening on the south side, which gives access, by way of the Corridor of the Procession, to the West Propylon. There is a replica of this monumental gateway, on a smaller scale, with the entrance facing westwards, a few yards below the south wall of the palace. On the east side a propylon would have been inappropriate on account of the intimate character of the royal quarters. But we have already seen that despite this there was access here both to the outside world and to the central court.

Evans believed that at the north-west corner of the palace there was an outside flight of steps leading to the 'Piano Nobile'. This, however, is more than doubtful. We have therefore only to mention the important entrance that later replaced the little South Propylon we have just described. It is situated at the south-western corner, one storey below the Corridor of the Procession. It leads to a passageway, running from east to west at the lower level, which terminates on the south side of the palace. At this spot began the so-called 'Stepped Portico', a covered flight of steps about 80 metres long, in the form of a columnar hall, which extended down the hillside, with two turnings, until it reached a stone viaduct with nine arches. This spanned the gorge almost at right angles; on the other side was a road which led first east and then south, up the Kairatos valley and so to the south coast. The arches of the viaduct were built of well-dressed stone blocks, on the principle of the false vault, and were at least 8 metres high and 3 metres wide in the clear. The road across the viaduct was about 5 metres wide.

FIG. 18

Caravanserai
FIG. 13

FIG. 17

On the south side of the road, opposite the south side of the palace, was a small building used for the reception of visitors. Its central feature was a room open at the front and approached from the roadway by a few broad steps. A single column supported the architrave. At the rear, on the side facing the hill, was a door giving access to the servants' quarters. Its frescoes imitated the architecture of a pillar hall, the pillars themselves being suggested by vertical yellow bands on a white ground. It is worth noting

94

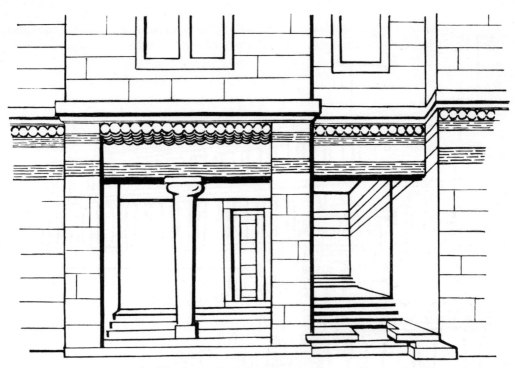

Fig. 17 — *Knossos: Caravanserai, to the south of the Palace. Based upon the reconstruction drawn for Evans. 16th—15th centuries. B.C. Cf. pp. 94, 97.*

that, unlike Egyptian interior decoration with its marked-out corners, none of the painted pillars here coincides with a corner. The lower border of the continuous frieze round the room, suggesting a wooden beam, consisted of a yellow horizontal band. The frieze above it depicted partridges and other birds nesting amidst a rocky landscape. On the west side was a spring-chamber, open at the front and rear. This contained a basin in which travellers could wash their feet. It had benches around the sides and was approached from the roadside by descending a few steps. Water flowed in, and was drained off, through subterranean pipes.

Further to the west were rooms in which one could take a hot bath, and finally, at an angle to the other rooms, a little chamber with a fountain cut out of the rock. Its walls were dressed with alabaster plaques, and it had a joist ceiling 2.40 metres above the level of the floor. Along its rear wall, on plinths and in a niche, were votive offerings and stone lamps. The water bubbled forth from the gravelly soil and was drained off by a concealed pipe.

This caravanserai, as Evans called it, catered to a demand for luxury and represented a notable level of technological achievement. Its architectural

FIG. 18 — *Knossos: south-western corner of Palace with 'Stepped Portico' and part of the viaduct. Reconstruction based on data provided by Evans. 16th cent. B.C. Cf. pp. 94, 97.*

function was no less remarkable. We can do no more than guess at its general FIG. 17 appearance, since we have actual knowledge only of the ground plan. But from the principal room, open to the north, one had an impressive view of the great palace towering up across the river. One might think this had been deliberately contrived — but let us be careful, and ask ourselves whether such an assumption does not betray a modernistic outlook. The idea of scenic beauty which it implies comes only in the post-classical period of ancient art, and occurs once again in the Renaissance. Would it not contradict the many primitive features we have noted? This question leads us back to the architectural significance of the palace as such, a question we have already broached to some extent during our tour.

Textbooks unfailingly stress the primitive characteristics of the architecture at Knossos. This view expresses the self-satisfied outlook of the late 19th century, when the apparent trial-and-error approach of the early builders contrasted so sharply with the artistic achievements of the observers' own time. We have seen how this attitude found reflection in scholarship during the years of the early discoveries. But today the tendency is rather to go to the other extreme, and to depict the impulsive and irrational element in primitive art as a positive value. Both points of view are equally far removed from a proper historical approach that seeks to explain things by relating them to the circumstances of their time. More interesting than questions of style are those concerning structure. Can the architecture of Knossos be put on the same level with the rest of Cretan art in this period? And can we see consistent or logical contrasts between this art and that of its prehistoric, Near Eastern and Egyptian predecessors?

It is still too early to give more than a general answer to the first question. But for the second we already have sufficient material at hand.

The palace of Knossos was built around a central court. The central court-yard is a constituent element of the palaces and temples of Mesopotamia and the Nile valley as well. But the relationship between the buildings and the court there is different. In the ancient civilizations it is 'injunctive': that is to say, the court is left free from encroaching buildings. Of vital importance is the cube-shaped building, which is complete in itself and can thus express a sense of timeless monumentality. At Knossos, on the other hand, the system of courts is 'conjunctive': the rooms are arranged around a court that is primarily rectangular in plan and is marked out in advance. The openings leading to the outside world correspond to those leading to the interior of the palace. This makes for a sense of dynamism that is alien to the injunctive type of palace architecture. However, this dynamism does not lose itself in impulsiveness and abnegation of form, but on the contrary obtains purpose

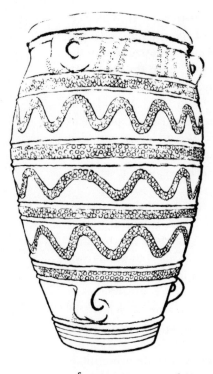

Fig. 19 — *Knossos: clay vessel used for storage (pithos), almost as tall as a man. 16th cent. B.C. From the western magazines. Cf. p. 82.*

and unity by virtue of its centralizing combining function. Elements of this 'conjunction' were to be seen already in an earlier stage of development. Despite the differences between them, the model granary from Melos and the residence from Late Troy II, with its columnar court and propylon had systems of courts basically similar to the one we find at Knossos.

The other element in Minoan palace architecture, as we have seen, existed in embryo in the agglutinative structure of sub-Neolithic Knossos and Early Minoan Vasiliki. We are now in a position to understand why we have no further examples in the Aegean of the cubistic and injunctive 'House of Tiles' at Lerna. This was a foreign body — a reproduction of an Oriental type of building. Hence we see that already in the forerunners of the Minoan palace there is a feeling for the use of space as a central, organic constituent element. Let us recall what was said above about the pillar hall and its incorporation into the rest of the architecture. This is the typical Minoan way of utilizing space. As a principle of systematic arrangement, organization around a central point is artistically equivalent to the crystalline mathematical principle of the Orient and Egypt, although the mode of expression is radically different — as is the type of human being who created it. In addition to this there are the structural affinities with Cretan decorative art of the pre-Palatial era, evident in the connection between the interior and exterior. Where before we found spirals and whorls, we now have winding passageways such as those we followed on our tour of Knossos. In the Stepped Portico and the staircases this is employed on a three-dimensional plane, producing an effect that is both astonishing and magnificent. One important point to be borne in mind is that the primitive features, although they cannot of course be ignored, do not set the tone of the building. They are combined with a most remarkable and specific concept of unity. We shall come across this dualism in other branches of art as well. At this point we can already say that it is symptomatic of the situation in which the Minoan world found itself, poised as it was on the border-line between prehistory and history, between the ancient East and the youthful West. Its art seems to express this situation. It was a bold attempt to realize an entity that had not yet fully taken shape.

The above enables us to understand the artistic effects we came across at Knossos. The striking treatment of light and shade in the design of the inner chambers suggests movement towards, or away from, a central point. In the view from the caravanserai we had a composite impression, formed by the merger of separate elements. This is the same impression one has on entering the central court, which creates a unity out of the various disparate buildings that surround it. In this way the Minoans anticipated the artists of the classical age, but without proceeding from the same premises as they did. This was their great achievement, and at the same time the limitation upon their greatness. Their style and mode of expression had a bold quality which nevertheless did not lead to disintegration. One must, however, be clear in one's mind that in saying this one is applying an external criterion. If one tries to comprehend Minoan art 'from within', i.e. to see its efforts at self-portrayal, one may appreciate that its lack of logical consistency, in the sense of subordination to natural laws, gives it a trait of spontaneity, a dream-like visionary quality, that is characteristic of this early stage of development. We shall have occasion to come back to this point again and again in discussing the representational and decorative art of the Palace period. Later on, after we have considered the religious background as well, we shall see that this quality in Minoan palace architecture expresses certain religious concepts. For to its builders a palace was a place for the epiphany of gods .

This interpretation is supported by the history of the construction of Knossos. *History of the Palace* The west forecourt and the central court were there from the beginning. But at first the various parts were just added on without any architectural design. Originally the two lower storeys on the eastern side of the slope were lacking, and the east wing seems to have been level with the central court. Furthermore, the various complexes of rooms arranged around the

FIG. 20 — *Steatite vessel from the island of Melos. Model of seven silos arranged around a court with a porch. Late 9th cent. B.C. National Museum, Athens. Height 10 cm. Cf. pp. 35, 49, 97.*

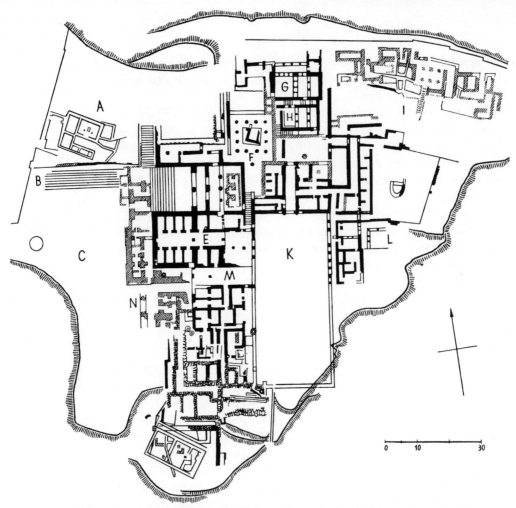

FIG. 21 — *Phaestos: Palace. First Palace (shown by hatched lines); Second Palace (area heavily shaded); Late Bronze Age buildings (area left blank). (The recently excavated south-west wing of the First Palace is not indicated.) A: Upper Terrace. B: Theatral Steps. C: West Court. D: Propylon and outside staircase. E: Magazine. F: Peristyle. G: Columnar Hall. H: Ante-room. I: North-east wing of First Palace. K: Central Court. L: Terrace. M: West Propylon of Second Palace. N: West Propylon of First Palace. Cf. p. 101.*

court were separated from one another by passageways that were open to the skies, giving the effect of a conglomeration of individual *insulae* around the court. This shows that the skilful use of the corridor as a means of linking the interior and exterior is the product of historical evolution. The practice of rounding off the corners of the walls, and the variations in the height of the different storeys (proved by the different thickness of the foundations) tended to hinder the integration of the structure.

At the end of the Palace period, so far as we know, only a few reconstructions took place. One of them was the so-called Little Throne Room, to the north of the staircase that leads down to the west side of the central court. It is basically nothing but a simplification of the pillar hall.

The palaces of Phaestos and Mallia were built shortly after Knossos. They *Phaestos* share with the latter such important features as the west forecourt with adjoining facade, the grouping of the buildings around a central court, store-rooms in the basement, and complexes of rooms with a pillar hall in the centre.

Phaestos towers high above the Messara and commands a fine view to the Fig. 21 south, east and north. As a result of excavations carried on there since the end of the second World War, we know more about the old palace (2000—1700 B.C.) than we do about early Knossos or Mallia. The west forecourt was in two sections, the northern one being about 6 metres higher than the southern one. They were joined by a ramp which curved around a bastion-like projection. In the lower west court a considerable part of the facade, which rested on an orthostat base, has been excavated. The rooms behind, which backed onto the slope, are long and narrow. They are divided by relatively thick walls such as we also find at Knossos in its early phase. These rooms show the perplexities that beset the early builders in the use of space. It is probably no coincidence that we have no evidence of pillar halls in this period. But columns were already known: they were arranged in rows to support a hall, and they also occurred individually to mark off different sections of a propylon. One can already see in this the new relationship between the inner room, extending outwards on all sides, and its exterior. The old palace at Phaestos was destroyed at least three times by earthquakes. When it was rebuilt the lower parts of the walls were left standing, a mortar-like substance (*astraki*) being poured on top to obtain the new level.

On the extreme right of the illustration on p. 85 one can see the upper west PLATE 20 court, viewed here from the north-west. In the foreground on the left is a terrace, which was built on later when the palace was destroyed for the last time. Below it, not visible in the picture, are some steps, which served to accommodate a crowd of spectators. From these steps a paved way led to a propylon, whence a corridor led due east to the central court, visible here in its entirety. One can also see the orthostat foundation of the old palace, which forms the eastern limit of the forecourt. When the new palace was built this open space was covered in up to the level of the orthostats. The west facade of the new building was set back about 8 metres. In the illustration this is viewed from the plinth wall south of the flight of steps and its continuation, most of which has been destroyed. When envisaging the palace in its later state, one has of course to remember that the west court was filled in up to the level of the old orthostats. The small rooms in the old basement contained objects used in the ritual performed in the court. Some of these can be seen in front of the steps. The steps belong to the new palace. They are 14 metres wide and lead up to the 'Piano Nobile'. The area above is generally held to be a propylon. The front is open, with a dividing column in the centre such as we often find in Minoan propyla. Behind it are two rooms that have the same width but are only about 3 metres deep. The wall between them has two great doors. The rear room opens upon a light-well, from which it is separated by an arrangement of two columns. A small door leads northwards into the royal apartments, while another, equally inconspicuous, leads to the ceremonial rooms above the magazines in the basement, which have been fairly well preserved. The paved central court was the same size, and was at the same level, in the old palace. Already at that time it was directly linked, by a corridor that ran from east to west, with a propylon on the east side of the forecourt. It has halls along its longer sides, and in the north a monumental facade

PLATE 21 of ashlar masonry, divided symmetrically (cf. Plate on p. 86-87). The gate leading to the north quarter was flanked by two half-columns and two niches. In the north-west corner of the court was a stepped altar which may still be seen there today. From the gate a corridor leads north to an inner court, whence one may take another corridor eastwards to the exit. This corridor, which has turnings in it, reproduces a motif that we noted on several occasions in the new palace at Knossos. Several rooms somewhat lower down the slope, in an isolated position, originated from the old palace and were utilized again in the new. The north wing also has pillar halls, peristyles, and flights

PLATE 17 of steps on many storeys. The Plate on p. 65 shows a small ante-room on the ground floor, level with the central court. The walls are covered with plaques of Cretan alabaster, and there are benches along the south and west sides. The room between the two groups of columns was covered in, whereas to the east there was a light-well. It is just visible in the foreground of the picture, on the left-hand side.

Most of the east and south of the central court has been lost as a result of landslides. At the north-eastern corner is a small pillar hall with adjoining bathroom, which is in a fairly good state of preservation. In front of it was a terrace with a small portico in the north and west. The terrace was open to the east and south, and commanded much the same view as may be

PLATE 20 seen in the Plate on p. 84. This photograph was taken from a point somewhat further to the west, outside the palace. This spot can be made out in front of the pine-trees, in the middle of the picture. It is important to the art historian, since it proves that the architects took the lay of the land into account.

The general character of Phaestos is one of greater splendour and serenity by comparison with Knossos. The domestic and administrative quarters are less important. The elevation above the plain is one of the main reasons why we obtain this impression. This elevation was not due to considerations of defence or ease of fortification — at least, not so far as the New Palace is concerned. This makes it all the more plain that its dominating situation was exploited for scenic effect.

The palace at Mallia, on the other hand, which is situated on flat coastland some 22 km. east of Knossos, appears severer, more tranquil and somewhat rustic in character. The basic features found at Knossos are repeated here: the west facade, built on top of an orthostat base with a forecourt to the west; magazines arranged along a corridor that runs from north to south in the west wing; a central court, with a staircase leading from its west side to the reception rooms; and an approach from the north by means of a path with several turnings. The entire east wing, however, consists of magazines. In addition there are eight circular silos in the south-west. In the south and east corridors lead directly into the court from the outside. Direct access in this way was necessary for the transport of supplies. In the west only a single side entrance leads into the magazines. There also existed a pillar hall in the north-west which was cut off from visual contact with the outside world. *Mallia*
FIG. 22

APPX. PL. 10

Little has survived of the building that dates from the Early Palace period. The old west facade was apparently incorporated into the structure that was erected later, of which only the foundation walls are extant.

The palace of Phaestos stands on the lowest and easternmost summit of a mountain with three peaks. Not for from Hagia Triada, at the foot of the western side of this mountain, a small royal residence has been excavated; it has been called the Royal Villa. The charm of its situation lies in the view it commands over the fertile plain, watered by the lower reaches of the Geropotamos, as well as the mountain ranges across the Gulf of Hagia Galene, which is only 3 km. away. It is built in an angle open to the south-east, since there is a low plateau, where the small church of Hagios Georgios stands today, that slopes down to the west and north, while in the east and south it is overshadowed by hills. The Plate on p. 83 shows the north wing only. The west wing is likewise situated on the slope and in the illustration is therefore hidden by the far edge of the plateau. From here one can see the court, with some of its pavement still intact, enclosed by the two wings, extending forwards to the left-hand side of the picture. A ramp, with several gentle *Hagia Triada*

FIG. 23
PLATE 19

PLATE 19

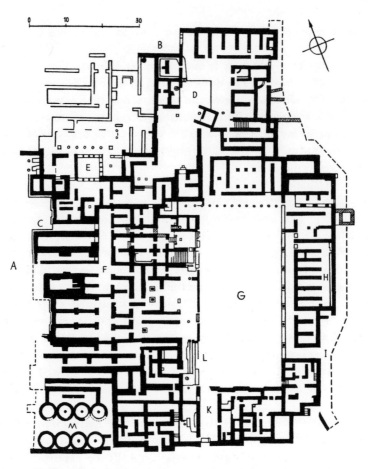

FIG. 22 — *Mallia: Palace. State in 16th cent. B.C. A: West Court. B: North Propylon. C: West Entrance. D: North Court. E: Columnar Hall. F: Corridor with West Magazines. G: Central Court. H: East Magazine. I: East Entrance. K: South Entrance. L: Staircase leading to State Apartments. M: Silos. Cf. p. 103.*

flights of steps, leads up from the bay to the outer wall of the palace on the north side. In the centre of the foreground it turns off southwards at a right angle and follows the east facade, in the form of a flight of steps, up to the court, where it once again makes a right-angled turn and finally leads to a propylon with a single column, which is open towards the east. The chambers in the basement of this wing — magazines, crypts, staircases and a columnar hall — are of a particularly labyrinth-like complexity, since imposing buildings were erected over them during the post-Palatial period. The latter include the large stone conduit, used for carrying off water to the north, shown in the centre of the illustration, and the foundation behind it, which rises above the level of the court. In the north-western corner (and for this reason not shown here), level with the floor of the basement, there used to be a pillar hall with a portico, which was rectangular in plan and led to a terrace with a fine view. In the portico the same remarkable motif can be found as was observed at Phaestos. There is the same grouping of internal pillars and of columns in front of them, and on the other side a narrow light-well which forms part of the same arrangement of rooms (although on a smaller scale) as existed in the vestibule in the north wing of the palace at Phaestos (cf. Plate on p. 65). The antechamber has a bench running along PLATE 17 three sides. Adjoining it is an alcove that faces south, used as a dormitory. On three of its walls were painted the finest landscape frescoes in Minoan art. During the Early Palace period the palace at Hagia Triada did not as yet exist. It was not built until the Late Palace period, probably as early as the first half of the 16th century. It was destroyed at the same time as Knossos, Phaestos and Mallia, at the end of the 15th century. The absence of so-called Palace style pottery (LM II) at sites other than Knossos was formerly interpreted as an indication that Knossos survived the other palaces. But it has now been discovered that the later type of pottery from the preceding period (LM Ib), which is also found at Knossos as well as that of the other group, is not absent from the other sites. The destruction thus affected the whole area of Minoan culture; but while there was stagnation at the other sites from the early 15th century onwards, Knossos can boast of remarkable new features.

At Knossos at least a dozen elegant dwelling-houses have been excavated. *Villas and* They were grouped around the palace, some of them being located in its *mansions* immediate vicinity and influenced by it so far as their orientation was concerned. The most gracious of them is the so-called 'Little Palace'. To *FIG. 13* approach it one has to follow a paved path some 200 metres long, which leads due west from the northern propylon. Its foundations were laid during the Late Palace period, as was the case with most of these houses, but after the destruction of the main building it may have served for some time as an administrative centre. It opens to the east; the rear, where the domestic quarters are situated, abuts upon a sloping hill side. Most of the other private houses are built along similar lines. There are no central courts. But here, too, there are ubiquitous traces of the fact that the buildings grew outwards from a central nucleus — not always identical with the main hall. There is a tendency to arrange the domestic and ceremonial rooms, most of which are pillar halls, nearer the outside walls. But the fact that the rooms project or recede in a haphazard manner, and the absence of a compact plan, are features just as characteristic of these buildings as they are of the palaces.

FIG. 23 — *Hagia Triada: Palace. 16th cent. B.C. (The blank areas of the walls denote buildings of the post-Palatial period.) A: Path along ramp. B: Court. C: Propylon. D: Columnar Hall. E: Ante-room and bedroom. F: Small church of Hagios Georgios. Cf. p. 103.*

It is from the latter that the motifs are derived: not merely the pillar halls and the columns tapering at the base, but also the stairways, pillar crypts, bathrooms and light-wells. This whole group of houses is interesting less from the architectural standpoint than on account of the information it provides as to the importance of the nobility during the Palace period. At Mallia conditions are much the same. Adjacent to the rear of the palace was an open square, with houses situated along paved streets running eastwards from the palace. These houses were built over the old fortifications at least as late as the 16th century. They are larger than those at Knossos,

PLATE 25 — *Above:* gold signet-ring from a tomb near Knossos. Ritual dance performed by four women, with a deity appearing in the background. Approx. 1500 B.C. *Iraklion. Diameter 2.6 cm. Cf. pp. 138, 204.* *Below:* gold pendant showing two bees and a honey-comb. Embossed work with granulation. From a tomb near Mallia. First quarter of 2nd millennium B.C. *Iraklion. Width 4.7 cm. Cf. p. 140.*

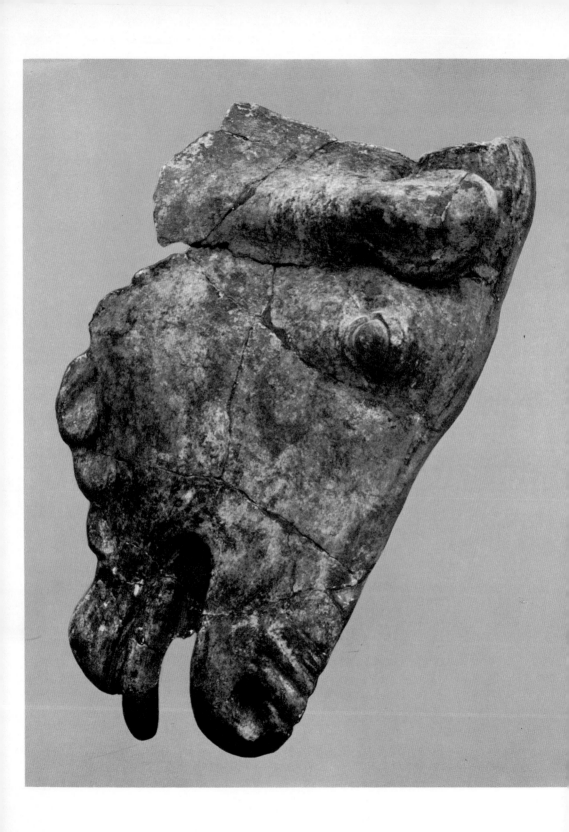

PLATE 27 — Faíence figure of a priestess holding snakes. From the Palace of Knossos. 17th cent. B.C. *Iraklion. Height 29.5 cm. Cf. pp. 125, 135, 141, 146.*

Opposite:
PLATE 26 — Fragment of painted stucco relief: head of a bull, larger than life. From the Palace of Knossos, 16th cent. B.C. *Iraklion. Height approx. 0.44 m. Cf. pp. 119, 125.*

PLATE 28 – Scene from the rear of a painted
limestone sarcophagus from Hagia Triada.
On the left: two women offering libations
and a lute-player. On the right: a man from
the adjoining scene, showing a sacrificial
offering. Approx. 1400 B.C. *Iraklion. Approx. height of figures 15 cm. Cf. p. 122.*

PLATE 29 — Vase covered with glaze paint. Palaikastro, eastern Crete. Early 15th cent. B.C. *Iraklion. Height 24.5 cm. Cf. p. 141.*

since more trade and agriculture was carried on. There are also some small inner courts. These buildings, too, like the palace itself, are less pretentious in their architecture.

Stately villas are to be found scattered over the whole country. One of the oldest known to us is situated not far from Amnisos, a coastal site some 4 km. north-east of Knossos. It was built as early as the 17th century, at the beginning of the Late Palace period, and was painted in a style that was still austere (MM III). A group of such houses has been studied near Tylissos, west of Knossos. They also occur individually — for example, near Achladia, Apodulu, Kannia, Korakies, Niru Chani, Sklavokampos, Vathypetros and Zou. Most of these houses were built during the 16th century (LM I). Generally speaking, all habitation ceased here at the time of the destruction of the palaces, in approx. 1400 B.C. Magazines and domestic quarters play a considerable part here as well. Whereas at Knossos the court nobility settled in the vicinity of the royal residence, these houses are the country seats of the landed aristocracy. The nature of the obligations owed by this class to the court is a subject for speculation. Inner courtyards are not lacking in these villas, but they do not perform a conjunctive function to the extent that they do in the palaces. The design of grouping the rooms around the central nucleus of the house also occurs here, and retains much of its earlier agglutinative character.

In eastern Crete small towns dating from the Late Palace period have been excavated at Gournia on the Gulf of Mirabello, on the small island of Pseira, and at Palaikastro. Characteristic features include narrow paved streets, some of which take the form of flights of steps, and a close network of small houses with interconnecting walls, in which the citizens of the town lived. Gournia is situated on a ridge running, in the main, from north to south, some 100 metres from the coast. There are two roads on top of the ridge, and one at the foot of the slope on the eastern side, all of which run from north to south and conform to the lay of the land. These roads are connected by narrow streets running crosswise. In the Plate on p. 90, which shows the view from the south looking north, we can see — in the middle distance, on the left — the westernmost of the three roads mentioned. The terraced walls above it support a small palace, situated approximately in the centre of the area that is built upon. The latter measures some 120 metres in length and 90 metres in width. The centre court may be seen higher up, further to the right. To the left of the tree-trunk in the foreground are the steps leading to the propylon on the south side of the palace. The area in front of it forms part of a large piazza south of the palace. The Plate on p. 89 illustrates one of the flights of steps leading up the eastern slope.

Small towns
PLATE 24

FIG. 24

PLATE 23

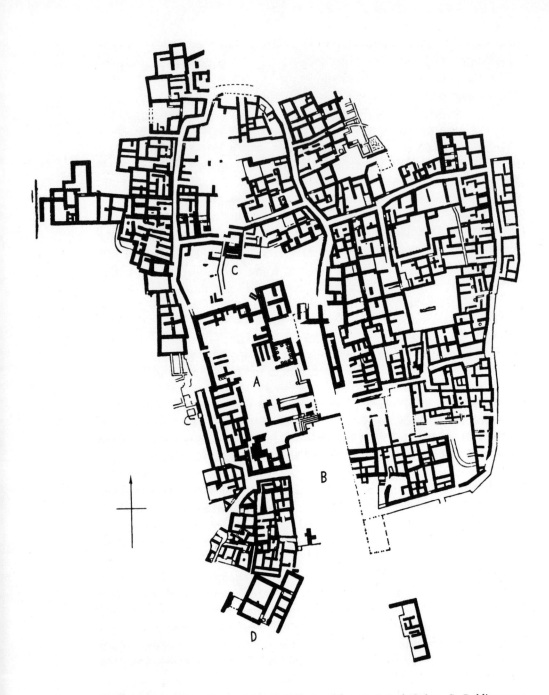

Fig. 24 — *Gournia, small town in eastern Crete. 16th cent. B.C. A: Palace. B: Public square. C: Chapel. D: Buildings of the Late period. Cf. p. 113.*

The walls of the houses that are visible in the picture consisted, up to quite a high level, of rubble, held together by clay. We must imagine that they were topped by sun-dried bricks and beams. To obtain a more vivid impression we may turn to a mosaic made of faience representing a whole town, which was discovered in one stratum of the Old Palace at Knossos, and depicts small houses of this kind as seen from the street. They consisted of one or two storeys over the ground floor. Daylight reached a light-well in the centre by a kind of lantern over the flat roof. At Gournia one of the transverse streets is a cul-de-sac which terminates in a small chapel, along the rear wall of which, on an elevation like a bench, there stood some terracotta idols. This complex seems to show that the town of Gournia survived the destruction of the palace; there is other evidence as well to this effect. So far as stylistic development is concerned, the arrangement of the buildings around the palace in the centre deserves to be noted as a Minoan feature, which in turn follows the design of the large palaces. This palace cannot have been anything but the residence of the governor. The small dwellings indicate that there was a fairly extensive class of citizens who made their living as farmers, craftsmen, fishermen or sailors. Below them there was undoubtedly a broad mass of slaves.

No royal tomb from the Early Palace period has as yet been discovered. *Tombs* The fact that the landed aristocracy continued at first to use the ancient family vaults, as well as building new ones, shows that it was developing into a court nobility. In the vicinity of the court sepulchral architecture also had a monumental quality similar to that of the palaces themselves. Not far from Mallia, between the palace and the sea-shore, in the meadow of Chrysolakkos, a sepulchral palace has been excavated which is nothing but an ossuary developed to the point of monumentality. The rectangular building (38 x 29 m.) with a wall consisting at the base of huge blocks has several burial chambers in addition to the one used for death rites; these chambers were accessible only from the top. There is a colonnade some 4 m. in depth before the whole frontage on the eastern longitudinal side, consisting of pillars and looking onto a paved piazza.

Approximately 1 km. south of Knossos, on the eastern slope of Gypsadhais Hill, is the so-called 'Temple Tomb', the only royal mausoleum known from the Late Palace period. The actual chamber tomb is a cavity (4 x 4 m.) hewn out of the rock. The vault, panelled with wood painted blue, is supported by a stone pillar. The walls are lined with slabs of alabaster, and the floor consists of flagstones. A wooden coffin must presumably once have stood here. A somewhat larger antechamber is reached from the east by way of a corridor 4 metres long. In front of the entrance is a small paved *FIG. 15* court, and on the opposite side a two-columned hallway, accessible from outside by means of a stepped street. A sanctuary chamber above the ante-chamber and a terrace in front of it, which faces the lower court and vestibule, indicate that the funerary rites performed here were designed to be observed from below. In this connection, as with the paintings featured on the Hagia Triada sarcophagus, we think of ceremonies performed to invoke the dead. In this case the ancient Mediterranean type of burial-cave has been embellished and monumentalized with the aid of architectonic motifs from the palaces. Rock-cut chamber tombs are to be found in large numbers not far from Knossos. The eastern side of the Kairatos valley, opposite the palace, can boast of a particularly impressive quantity. They must have belonged to the families who lived in the elegant houses situated there. Among the tombs at Knossos there are also domed ones which represent an intermediary stage between the *tholoi* of the Messara and the later vaulted tombs of the Greek mainland. A chamber tomb that was built (as distinct from being hewn out of the rock) has been excavated near Isopata, north of Knossos. It must be assigned to the latest part of the Palace period. The vault, the walls of which converge at the top, is constructed on the principle of the so-called false vault, i.e. by means of a series of overlapping horizontal courses. There are similar examples dating from the same period at Ras Shamra on the Syrian coast and at Mycenae.

The reason for the absence of sacred architecture other than tombs is to be sought in Minoan religion, which we shall be dealing with in due course. The Minoans, who believed in epiphany, regarded the palace itself as a place where the gods made themselves manifest. This is also apparent in the sacred facades known from pictorial representations. There is concrete evidence that these facades existed at the west end of the central court at Knossos, as well as at Vathypetros. The pillar crypts in the palaces must likewise be regarded as places of divine incarnation.

Fig. 28

Is Minoan architecture monumental?

The statement that Minoan architecture of the Palace period is characterized by its monumentality needs some explanation, especially in view of the undeniably monumental character of Egyptian and ancient Oriental build-ings. In the latter a sense of timelessness is engendered by the static style, whereas Cretan architecture is full of dynamism; instead of enormous size and massive proportions we have serenity and an eye for detail. The fact that this contrast is so obvious makes it difficult to get beyond it. If, on the other hand, we look back to the greatest achievements in the architecture of the preceding phase, citadels such as Troy II, and if we do not allow ourselves to be misled by the evident differences between the motifs of citadel and palace, it is clear that the Minoans took a decisive step towards artistic unity. This becomes even more evident when we consider the Mycenaean citadels. It is actually from them that we first learn how additive the building method still was in Troy II. What has been noted above concerning the central organization of Minoan palaces is also of importance in evaluating them, so long as one agrees in defining 'monumentality' as the interdependence between magnitude of expression and magnitude of form. Neither absolute magnitude nor the representation of tranquillity are in themselves decisive here, but only the relationship between the two aspects of formal structure. In this sense, despite the great difference between them, Minoan style is on a par with that of Egypt and the Near East. One gains the impression that it has lost the prehistoric quality of the Palace period and is now part of the world of the ancient civilizations. This is true both so far as the history of art is concerned and in a wider sense. The historian can speak of a 'twilight' between one culture and another. The art historian can call it a blending of the refined and the primitive. This differentiation enables us to be more precise in our definition. The replacement of an early phase that is still clumsy and awkward by the mature self-realization of the Late Palace period not only helps us to understand the course of historical development but also to clarify our conclusions. We shall state these once we have considered other branches of art besides architecture.

It is characteristic of Minoan style that it avoids monumentality in plastic FRESCOES art but does evidence it in painting. This style of painting is closely related to architecture, in that it puts the finishing touches to the treatment of three-dimensional space. But our understanding of it is limited by the fact that little of it has been preserved. What we have are in the main fragments of *State of* wall stucco painted *al fresco*. However, the artists were not actually at- *preservation* tempting to produce a picture in isolation but to decorate and interpret a certain space. Only occasionally can we obtain, by devious means, a general idea of their work. In addition to this the colours suffered severe damage during the fires that swept through the palaces, and it is the finest frescoes that suffered most. It is almost a miracle that despite these difficulties we should be in a position to trace, over a considerable length of time, not only the fine draughtsmanship, but also the unique skill in composition shown by these artists and their choice of colours. In this connection, although allowances naturally have to be made, the coloured reconstructions by E. Gilliéron Sr. and Jr. are an indispensable aid. These have been produced with painstaking care and a sure sense of style. In choosing the coloured plates for this volume the criterion was necessarily the freshness of colour. They therefore do not give a fully representative picture of the material.

Walls coated with stucco painted red were to be found already in the pre- *Early styles*

Palatial period. The earliest frescoes featuring figures known to us date from the first phase of the Late Palace period, which came to an end in approximately 1570 B.C. These were discovered at Amnisos and Knossos. The absence of frescoes at Mallia and the rare instances in which they occur at Phaestos are probably due to fortuitousness of excavation work. The affinities both in the technique employed and the manner of representing the human figure show distinctly that the painters were influenced by prototypes from Egypt and Asia Minor. These are, however, no longer available. The magnificent Egyptian frescoes from the Middle Kingdom were painted more than one hundred years before the later palaces were built. Although those from the palace at Mari on the upper reaches of the Euphrates are ascribed to the 18th century, they are of greater antiquity than the earliest Minoan ones known to us.

In the same way their decoration can only be considered the product of Cretan influence. We can but surmise that frescoes appear in Crete at the latest by the beginning of the Early Palace period. The fragmentary frescoes at Tell Atchana in Syria, which date from the 17th century, already show the influence of Minoan motifs.

In the early paintings from Amnisos and Knossos we encounter for the first time the naturalistic style of the Palace period, which has been the subject

APPX. PL. 4

of so much discussion and admiration. In the case of the wealth of glyptic objects it can be traced even further back in time. At Amnisos it has been possible to restore the decoration of one room from the first storey, which shows in a frieze 1.80 m. high a row of lilies and other plants growing in pots. The blossoms, which are captured vividly and stylized in an equally impressive manner, are inlaid with coloured paste on a ruby ground, by a method similar to that used for inlaying intarsia. This is a rare technical

FIG. 25

process. Dating is made possible by concurrence with vases originating from a Late MM IIIa level.

FIG. 26

This is also the case with the 'Saffron-gatherer' from Knossos. It is in fact an ape, painted in blue. The entire frieze, measuring some 0.25 m. in height, featured a number of these apes on a red ground gathering white crocus blossoms and putting them into baskets. The scene is set in a park and evidently depicted the preparation for some rite. The design and the naturalistic style of the flowers showed a sure touch on the part of the artist, in spite of the herbarium-like flatness and the absence of shading. More remarkable still is the composition. The flowers are shown growing in jagged tracts of land, like contours, running along the lower border of the frieze and hanging down into it from the upper border. An attempt to explain this can only be given if, after examining other branches of art, we can arrive at

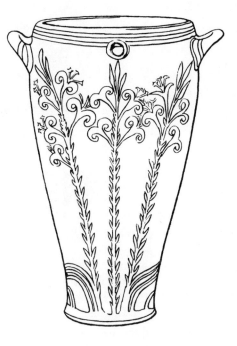

FIG. 25 — *Vase with lily design. Painted white on dark glaze. From Knossos, approx. 1600 B.C. Iraklion. Height 27 cm. Cf. above and p. 147.*

a definition of the specific qualities of Minoan pictorial art in general.

Most of the fragmentary frescoes may be assigned to the phase known as LM I. As a rule these are spread over a period of one hundred years, between 1570 and 1470 B.C. From the standpoint of subject-matter they are limited to the representation of scenes from nature and the typically Minoan combination of ritual and courtly scenes. The colours retain their simple unrefracted character. Apart from white and black the most prevalent are red, blue and yellow. Green occurs rarely; whether it was made from blue and yellow is uncertain, and it is possible that a special colouring substance may have been used. Some of these frescoes feature life-sized figures, or figures slightly larger than life, which are truly monumental in character. They also sometimes occur in combination with a flat stucco relief. They include the representation of a bull-game shown in the loggia of the north propylon (cf. p. 108). The head of a galloping PLATE 26 bull depicted in the Figure on p. 108 originates from the same source. The 'Prince with the Plumed Head-dress' from the grand vestibule in the west wing was also modelled in plaster on a painted ground. Male and female FIG. 27 donors, portrayed larger than life-size, adorned the walls of the processional corridor, and the well-known 'Cup-bearer' belongs to another such frieze. The men are shown wearing loin cloths of woven and embroidered material, sometimes with a network of beads hanging far down in front. There are also fine examples of the costume worn by women at court especially in the fragments called 'Ladies in Blue'. A gaily woven and embroidered bodice leaves the breasts free. The flowing skirt below the wasp-waisted corsage may be trimmed with gaily-coloured flounces. The hair, neck and wrists are lavishly embellished with jewellery.

The dancing-girl from the 'Queen's Megaron' is less than life-size. She seems to be wearing underneath her bodice a garment made of some thin and light material. From the way in which the eye is depicted as seen from the front when the head is in profile we can recognize that this style is of Egyptian

FIG. 26 — *Fragment of a fresco from Knossos: so-called 'Saffron-gatherer', in reality an ape painted in blue on a red ground. Approx. 1600 B.C. Iraklion. Height 25 cm. Cf. p. 118.*

origin, for here too the human figure was put together from several disjointed pieces.

The fragment showing the 'Little Parisienne' was found lying in one of the western magazines when excavation was carried out. When the palace was burned it dropped down there from the upper floor, together with other PLATE 30 fragments that had adorned the same wall. In the Plate on p. 129 it is reproduced as it looks today after expert cleaning. It belongs to one of the bands, 0.32 m. high, in what was probably a frieze consisting of four bands, portraying seated or standing men and women arranged facing one another. It is called, after the shape of the seats, the 'Camp-stool Fresco'.

With its juxtaposition of primitive and elaborate features this fragment represents Minoan woman in concentrated form. Just as the combination of the profile with the excessively large eye gives the impression of being naive and additive, so there is a sense of spontaneity and a superior air about the turned-up nose, the slender neck set over the well-developed breasts and the lock of hair in front, which has worked its way free and hangs down over the forehead. The deep blue colour of the elaborate costume, with the large knot at the nape of the neck, give the delicate figure a solemn and engagingly knowing look. The combination of the ivory-coloured skin, pitch-black hair and eye, and coral red, slightly pursed lips makes it particularly difficult to distinguish between what is naive and what is deliberately contrived. The candour and sureness with which it is treated suggest a sense of pulsating life, and thus another significant analogy to the flowing style of palace architecture.

Landscapes of the type illustrated by the 'Saffron-gatherer' fresco continue

FIG. 27 — *Painted stucco relief from Knossos: 'Prince with Plumed Head-dress'. A great deal has been added later. 16th cent. B.C. Iraklion. Height approx. 2.20 m. Cf. pp. 119, 170.*

to be produced in this phase of development. That in the famous dormitory at Hagia Triada has already been mentioned. In addition to this there are the fragments from the so-called 'House of Frescoes' in the western part of the palace at Knossos, the wall with the flying fish painted by a Cretan in the palace of Phylakopi on Melos, and the partridge fresco in the caravanserai at Knossos, dating from a relatively late period. The meaning of the subjects of these pictures has not yet been clarified. But we can clearly discern the artists' enthusiasm, reflecting their joy at the evident beauty of the world in which they lived.

Of the miniature frescoes there are two from Knossos which can most easily be evaluated, despite their fragmentary state: one portrays a sacred facade and ritual assembly, and the other a ritual dance performed on a lawn, with olive trees and a large number of spectators. These form part of a frieze measuring some 30—40 cm. in height which adorned some small rooms. In both cases the theme treated was probably the ceremony performed when the incarnation of a deity was anticipated. Crowds of men are suggested by painting the ground in a characteristic reddish-brown colour, white being applied to indicate — roughly but vividly — eyes, necklaces and loin-cloths, and black for hair. The women are rendered by the patches of white ground which break up these areas of the surface, their heads being perfunctorily suggested in a similarly animated manner. From an artistic point of view this foreshadows the introduction of integral motifs, still beyond men's grasp in this period, when the media available limited them to two-dimensional representation.

During the final phase of the Palace period (LM II, late 15th century) the direct appeal and sense of movement conveyed by these paintings are superseded by greater rigidity and monumentality of expression. The griffin fresco found in the Little Throne Room at Knossos already shows a tendency towards this new style by reason of the heraldic arrangement, the large proportions of the motifs, the solemn posture of the griffins, and their splendid decoration, consisting of spiral crests and a large curl containing a rosette.

Late styles

FIG. 29

PLATE 28

APPX. PL. 1-3

From the end of this period comes the limestone sarcophagus covered with a layer of stucco found in a tomb at Hagia Triada. The Plate on pp.110—11 represents, in approximately the same size as the original, much of the left half of the rear side of the frieze, which bears figures. Of the lavishly decorated frame only the inner parts are visible. On the right we can see the ends of two processions meeting almost in the centre of the longitudinal side. The one pointing to the left belongs to the larger of the two cycles, which occupies the adjoining small side and the front part of the opposite longitudinal side. It represents offerings of sacrifice, some bloody and others of a different character, and also portrays two goddesses arriving in response to the ceremony in a chariot drawn by griffins. The smaller composition, in which a man is shown carrying a small calf in his arms, is limited to the right-hand half of this longitudinal panel and the adjacent small side. This scene represents a ceremony for the invocation of the dead. The man, clad in a shaggy fleece, is sacrificing a calf, or possibly merely the substitute figure of one. At the end of the procession moving towards the left a lyre-player in a long red garment is depicted with his instrument. The vertical border is of course really in front. The composite view of the lower part thus corresponds to that of the head. A woman of similar appearance, but clad in blue and wearing a crown of flowers, carries on her shoulder a shaft from which two bucket-like receptacles are suspended. Another woman, wearing a ritual fleece kilt and bodice, is pouring the contents of a similar vessel into a larger one. The latter is placed between two shafts entwined with foliage, resting upon marble bases and topped by double axes with birds, in whose form the gods became incarnate. The tendencies towards consolidation during the late phase are expressed by dark contour lines, which occur even on coloured surfaces. Formerly only white surfaces were outlined in such a way. But by comparison with Egyptian, Near Eastern or Early Greek paintings this style on the whole still shows plenty of dynamism.

On the sarcophagus, curiously enough, no attempt is made to relate the painting to the corners of the object, and the compositions continue round them. Only one of them constitutes a major break, in that the ends of the two processions, which are moving in different directions, come together here. Another caesura of this kind is shown in the Plate on pp.110—11. In this case it is emphasized by a difference in the colour of the ground, which counteracts the tectonic arrangement and gives a sense of unity. That this was the artist's purpose is corroborated by observations made with regard to the relationship of the paintings to the rooms in the palace where they were found.

In Egyptian art it is an iron law that corners must be marked off. This *Decoration* applies both to decorated rooms and to objects, and goes so far that objects which in themselves are round become orthogonal as a result of their square decoration. In Minoan decoration, on the other hand, no attention is paid to corners. From this point of view there is no difference in treatment between the figure and the ornament. For purely decorative ornamentation also plays a part in fresco-painting. Instead of painting the bases of the walls black, or in strong colours, or incrusting them with slabs of alabaster, the Minoans preferred to make painted imitations of marble stones or coloured breccia. Elsewhere walls are embellished simply by orna- Appx. pl. 5 ments in the form of bands. The ceilings alone have surface designs, consisting of meanders and spirals in an *en rapport* pattern. These decorative bands usually continue beyond the corners. Scenes are invariably depicted in the form of a frieze. The viewer's eye is led in a particular direction, often that followed by a procession, by changes in the colour of the ground: the broad wavy bands are not broken at the corners and emphasize the movement of the figures. In the procession fresco there is a wavy blue band in the middle, at the level of the men's loin cloths, contrasting with the yellow colour above and below it. The loin cloths on this blue ground are alternately yellow with a blue pattern or blue with a yellow pattern, whereas the red fleshy tint of the upper part of the body and the legs stands out against the yellow ground above and below. This not only links the various elements of the frieze together but makes it an integral part of the room it serves to decorate, so that we can grasp the whole instead of seeing merely the detail. We noted the same effect in the painting of the caravanserai. We are now in a position to interpret landscapes such as those that formed the decoration of the small dormitory at Hagia Triada: they were not only compositions around a central nucleus but deliberately contrived views which gave an impression of the scenery on the other side of the wall. The underlying spatial concept is in both cases not the objective stereometric approach

FIG. 29 — *Knossos: 'Little Throne Room'. Detail of the reconstructed Griffin Fresco. The ground, segmented by wavy lines, is painted alternately in ruby and yellowish-brown colours. 15th cent. B.C. Cf. p. 122.*

that we ourselves adopt, but is one centred upon the human figure in relation to the space about him. This illustrates once again the extent to which the stylistic structure of Minoan paintings coincides with that of Minoan architecture.

SCULPTURE

Bull's head

PLATE 31

The small series of plastic works in the round dating from the Palace period must do duty here for this branch of art. Let us consider first a piece that is relatively large in size: the bull's head of black steatite shown in the Plate on p. 130. Characteristically enough, it is a vessel. The neck has at the rear a closely fitting lid. Liquid is introduced through an aperture at the top and is poured out between the lips. Only the right-hand half of the head, or a little more than this, can claim to be of real antiquity. The ears were made of steatite and the horns of gold plate; the latter were affixed subsequently. The nostrils are framed by a shell inlay. Another inlay of rock-crystal served for the eye, which has a pupil painted red, a black iris and a red border. This type of vessel, known as a rhyton, originates from the Orient. In Crete it was used to contain ritual offerings. This example was in fact also found at Knossos, in a chamber in the 'Little Palace' where rites were performed. It was made in the 16th century (LM I). Oriental bulls' heads tend to be more stylized. Those from Greece are more tectonic in character, great importance being attached to representation of the skeleton, although this may also be merely implicit. The bull's head from Knossos has a spontaneous naturalism in which the sense of the animal's vitality is blended with an element of myth and mystery. This is brought about by the absolutely confident three-dimensional plasticity, which has neither the rectangular system found in Egyptian art nor the Greek concept of organic wholeness. It will help us to gain a better understanding of the work if we recall that in Minoan pictorial representation the bull symbolizes a sacrificial animal and sacrifice as such. The view of some scholars that the Minoans worshipped a bull-god seems untenable. The underlying idea is rather that of an antithetic manifestation of divine force that triumphs in overcoming this symbol of power and fertility. The bull's head on the stucco relief of the North Propylon shown in the Plate on p. 108 is more PLATE 26 austere and expressive, and is hampered to a greater extent by the decoration. It is older, and a comparison between the two affords an insight into artistic development during the Late Palace period. With this rhyton Minoan 'naturalism' reached its apogee.

Also of greater antiquity is the female faience figure shown in the Plate on 'Snake Goddess' p. 109. It was buried during the destruction of the palace in approximately PLATE 27 1570 B.C. and therefore still belongs to the early phase of the Late Palace period. The snakes which she is holding up are manifestations of the Great Goddess, and the small lion on her head is an attendant. However, the term 'Snake Goddess' is not really appropriate. This is a votive, not a cult figure and probably represents a priestess — possibly the princess herself clad in the garb of the goddess, which corresponds to the costume worn at court. Only the kilt and the headgear are of ritual significance. Plasticity and dynamism are still hampered by the decorative element, especially by the flatness of the lower part and the symmetrical structure. But by comparison with figures from the pre-Palatial era the form is balanced and sure. The concentration of power expressed in the laced waist may be regarded as typically Minoan: in other words, even here we have concentration in a central point instead of in an organic or crystalline fashion!

The ivory figure representing an acrobat from Knossos shown in the Plate Acrobat on p. 132 illustrates once again the naturalistic style at the height of its PLATE 33 development. It dates from the late 16th century. The individual parts display particularly elaborate workmanship and are interlocked with one another. Curls of hair, made of gold wire, were inserted. The motif of vaulting over the back of a bull, which is a favourite in Minoan art, is not suggested in this case. The movement made by this slender youth can only be understood if one imagines that he is jumping from some high point on to the back of the bull in order to enrage the animal, which can then be chased and caught in a snare. This little masterpiece has been chosen to illustrate the Minoans' talent for the representation of movement. It was found together with fragments of faience bulls. The ivory figure must have been suspended over such a bull. This illustrates the indifference of this style towards the static element, which seems to be an integral part of plastic art.

The stone vessels in relief dating from this period are represented here by the steatite beaker from Hagia Triada depicted in the Plate on p. 133, approximately in its original size. An officer is introducing to a youth of high station, probably a prince, three men with long hair, carrying huge shields covered with skins. As in other Minoan paintings where the subject can be 'read' from left to right, the shields are shown on the right-hand side of their bearers for the sake of clarity. Perhaps this is an audience of ambassadors. The three men from the other part of the representation are not visible in our illustration. The officer is wearing high-laced boots of soft leather, a kilt, and rings on his neck and wrists. With his right hand he is shouldering his sword, and in his left hand he is holding a sheath, provided at the end with a tassel characteristic of Minoan and Mycenaean sword-sheaths. The prince, who is somewhat taller, is also wearing boots and a kilt, and holds a sceptre in his outstretched right hand with a commanding gesture. He is portrayed with long hair and an abundance of jewellery on his neck and arms. His torso is not shown in profile but his shoulders are viewed from the front. A pillar-like structure behind him separates the end of the procession from its goal. The figures featured as 'surface lines' in the frieze conform to the conical shape of the vessel. Particularly charming is the way in which the artist has overcome the difficulty inherent in the static heaviness of his subject. It was precisely from this unpromising starting-point that he was able to develop a sense of movement in his figures. The officer is portrayed with his back bent and with objects on his shoulders, leaning backwards, following the diverging lines of the cone. By these means the artist seeks to express military discipline and the respect due to rank. In a similar way the prince's authoritative self-confidence is shown by his posture, sitting back with his arm outstretched and holding a sceptre in his hand. This, too, results in a form that diverges upwards, in accordance with the shape of the surface area treated. An analogous blending of composition and decoration has already been noted in our examination of wall-paintings. It will be recalled that this combination was an essential feature of the earliest Minoan paintings already in the pre-Palatial period, in that emphasis was laid upon the decorative element rather than upon the figures themselves. We shall do well to bear this affinity in mind as we go along.

The two gold cups found in a vaulted tomb near Vapheio in Laconia, on the mainland, have been imported from Crete (cf. Plate on p. 152). This opinion is based, not upon the quality of the workmanship, but upon study of the style of glyptic art objects. For we are now able to distinguish between Minoan products and those from the mainland, and it is to the former group that these two cups belong. They may be assigned to the late 16th or early 15th century. There are no other Minoan pictures that can boast the same degree of perfection and living immediacy in expressing the world about them. Against the background of other works of their time they can only be termed classical.

Gold cups from Vapheio

PLATE 37
FIG. 30, APPX.
PL. 27, 17

These two cups are companion pieces. One depicts the taking of some wild bulls and the other the peaceful life of tame cattle. The pictorial friezes and the base are all embossed from a single piece of gold plate. The rim is bent over, thereby connecting the friezes with the inner surface of the cup. The handles are riveted on. Each of the two friezes consists of one central motif and two panels of equal size. On the cup showing the bull's capture the central scene is the bull caught in the snare. The two other bulls are charging off in opposite directions, not in a symmetrical arrangement but in a distinct formal correlation. A man has swung himself on to the back of the left-hand bull, but has been thrown off and is falling headlong to the ground. Another man is performing a feat of matchless daring: he has seized the bull by its horns before it started moving and is now swinging one knee over its left horn, with a swift turn to the front, so as to land on the back of its neck. The aim of the two catchers is to enrage the bull so that it may be chased blindly into a snare. Of crucial importance in the composition is the way the bull leaps from the lower right to the upper left. Its partner on the other side of the central section is depicted making an equally impressive leap from upper left to lower right, tossing its head into the air — whereas the first bull had its head lowered for the charge. The bull caught in the snare has the same spiral coil that we have noted on seals of the pre-Palatial period. From this we can observe that the other two bulls are also based on a spiral pattern. This gives the figures and the composition of the vessel as a whole a familiar decorative scheme, popular in Crete already before the Palace period. It is derived from a series of 'S' scrolls and may be described as a whorl in two parts. For example, on the vase from the Early Palace period depicted in the Plate on p. 176, it occurs three times, but vertically instead of horizontally. Similarly, the spiral design also forms the basis of the composition of the other cup. In this case,

PLATE 44

FIG. 30 — *Development of designs of two gold cups from the Vapheio tomb (Laconia): Capture of the bull' and 'Cattle pasturing'. Cretan. Approx. 1500 B.C. Diameter approx. 10.5 cm. National Museum, Athens. Cf. pp. 127, 138.*

however, it is not in the centre but runs like a frieze towards the left. This frieze is made up of three parts, of which that in the centre is particularly accentuated. This is the so-called wavy tendril, a design that was to play a role of great importance in later periods of ancient art; we know that it was created by Minoans during their age of efflorescence.

The naturalistic style of the scenes on the two cups is so obvious that it need not be discussed in detail. It now becomes evident that this style, even in the case of its most perfect specimens, has as much system as does the apparently unrestrained exuberance found in works of architecture. On closer examination we discover that it is actually related to a central point; but this is of less importance for our understanding of its structure than its basically decorative character. This was the case already with the steatite cup. It must suffice to point out that these are only selected symptomatic examples. But this relation between composition and decoration can be observed more or less distinctly in every Minoan painting. We have already pointed to its beginnings in the pre-Palatial period, when greater emphasis was laid on ornamentation than on the actual composition. In the efflorescent period both elements are correspondingly reinforced, resulting in a picture that is both convincing in form and rich in expressiveness.

These two cups also have a suggestion of scenery on the lower and upper border which we have already noted in some of the frescoes. Its origin and meaning may be similarly explained. This brings us back to the history and significance of Minoan pictorial art as such.

PLATE 30 — Fragment of fresco from the Palace of Knossos: 'La Petite Parisienne'. 16th cent. B.C. *Iraklion.*
Height of part preserved approx. 25 cm. pp. 203, 204.

PLATE 31 — Sacrificial vessel (rhyton) in the shape of a bull's head. Steatite, inlaid with limestone and rock-crystal. Found in the 'Little Palace' at Knossos. Approx. 1500 B.C. *Iraklion. Height 26 cm. Cf. pp. 124, 168.*

PLATE 32 — 'Pilgrim's flask' covered with glaze paint, showing an octopus. Palaikastro, eastern Crete. Close of 16th cent. B.C. *Iraklion. Height 28 cm. Cf. p. 142.*

PLATE 33 — Ivory figure of an acrobat. The long hair was of gold wire. From the Palace of Knossos, 16th cent. B.C. *Iraklion. Length 29 cm. Cf. p. 125.*

Opposite:
PLATE 34 — Steatite cup with reliefs showing an officer presenting foreign envoys to a prince. From the Palace of Hagia Triada. 16th cent. B.C. *Iraklion. Diameter of rim 9.9 cm. Cf. p. 126.*

PLATE 35 — Amphora with three handles, covered with glaze paint. Palace style. From the Palace of Knossos. Latter half of 15th cent. B.C. *Iraklion. Height 78 cm. Cf. p. 142.*

It can be followed almost without interruption in glytic art, where the traditions of the pre-Palatial period are carried on.

The immense amount of material available may be classified by reference to some finds that are from closed sites, and for which we have a good deal of information as regards their style, stratigraphy and chronological sequence. The oldest and most important do not have original seal- stones, but clay impressions. The evidence they provide is nevertheless fully valid.

The earliest of these groups is that from an archive at Phaestos, buried when the First Palace was destroyed towards the end of the 19th century B.C. No less than three thousand impressions have been collected, the number of different types used amounting to approx. 280. They overlap in part with later pieces from the *tholoi* of the Messara.

At Knossos the so-called 'Hieroglyphic Deposit' belongs to the transitional FIG. 31 epoch between the Early and Late Palace period. The individual lumps of clay used for sealing bear several impressions. The 150 impressions from Knossos discovered in a stone cist beneath a floor, which belong to the group of finds known as the 'Temple Repositories', may be dated from a horizon of the later palace, destroyed in or about 1570 B.C. The style of this phase is referred to as MM IIIa . The 'Snake Goddess' belongs to the same find. PLATE 27

Two large deposits of impressions, comprising some 400 to 500 pieces each, from Hagia Triada and Zakro in eastern Crete are representative of the naturalistic style of the 16th century (LM I).

Finally, the Late Palace period of the 15th century is documented by some seals from the so-called Warrior Graves at Knossos and by impressions found in the refuse of the final destruction. They are engraved with signs in Linear B script. Among approximately 40 seal-stones from the *tholos* tomb near Vapheio, which may also be dated to the 15th century, there are many that were imported from Crete. From a stylistic point of view they coincide with those found in the Warrior Graves at Knossos.

Steatite is only used for unpretentious work. Ivory disappears completely. Precious material is used to enhance the beauty of the object. In the case of precious stones such as agate,

FIG. 31 — *Clay impressions of seals from the so-called 'Hieroglyphic Deposit' at Knossos. Approx. 1700 B.C. Enlarged. Iraklion. Cf. pp. 136, 165 and above.*

amethyst, chalcedony, jasper, carnelian and rock-crystal, which are all now in use, an Oriental technique is adopted in which drills and a turning wheel are employed. Gold signet-rings with a convex shield, and likewise some bearing engraved designs, are favourites from the late 17th century onwards. On the other hand, the variety of motifs diminishes. The signet ceases to exist in the Early Palace period. The prism type is produced not later than the beginning of the Early Palace period. It serves special purposes and when used for hieroglyphs is elaborately worked. Cylinder seals are rare and must be seen as copies of Oriental prototypes. Most common is the lentoid gem. Also popular are the almond-shaped or amygdaloid designs, as well as the

PLATE 40   so-called flattened cylinders (cf. Plate on p. 155).

Amulets   The seal-stones bearing Minoan hieroglyphs perform a magic function such as was already associated with the glyptic products, in particular the steatite prism types, that appeared before the Palace period. In the Late Palace period we find a large group of gems featuring symbolic signs. There are no impressions of this kind and they must therefore be regarded as amulets rather than seals. These are of greater interest for cultural history generally than for the history of art.

Early styles   Attention has already been drawn (cf. p. 68) to the endeavours made during the pre-Palatial period to obtain a balance between pictorial motifs, derived from foreign sources, and ornament. The impressions from Phaestos show a more assured approach and greater artistic pretension in both directions. But ornamental designs still predominate, as is shown by the fact that more than two-thirds of the types found are purely decorative in character. They tally with the Kamares pottery of the same period. Among the subjects treated animals are more frequent and better represented than human beings. We already find the 'flying gallop', a characteristic new Minoan type that had an important effect on later development. It conveys an enhanced sense of dynamism. From this and other characteristic features as well one can note a more definite tendency towards naturalism. But on the whole this find is still archaic in style.

FIG. 31   In the Hieroglyphic Deposit the new style comes into its own. The symbolic human figures have disappeared, and instead there occur actual likenesses – the first known in Europe. The head of a man in profile probably represents a ruler, that of a boy a young prince. The same sureness of hand is shown in depicting racial features in the former instance and the age of the boy in the latter. Animals and landscape elements such as rocks and trees are rendered with a new sense of freedom and immediacy, and the composition exhibits a new power of concentration. It is often developed out of the round shape of the seal and in this way continues the efforts made in this direction by earlier glyptic art, when they were limited by the decorative element (cf. p. 68). A comparison of the earlier works with, for example, the impression of a predatory fish seizing a polyp against a background of coral reefs shows that in both cases, despite the disappearance of the decorative element, the pictorial arrangement is radial. This corroborates the assumption made above with regard to the spatial arrangement in the case of both the frescoes of the Saffron-gatherer type and the cups from Vapheio (cf. p. 152). To see this point in historical perspective, we have to consider the pictorial concepts current in Egypt and the Orient, which also form the basis — although with some characteristic modifications — of archaic Greek products. Here the picture is an existing *reality*. Its revolutionary transformation into a *representation*, which is fundamental to Western art, is one of the achievements of the Hellenes. The Minoan pictures we are dealing with are still a long way distant from this goal: they are still encumbered with far too many uncontrolled primitive features for them to be called representational pictures in our sense of the word. But from a structural point of view they are striving spontaneously towards this objective. Thus in this field, too, the Minoans are ahead of their time. In particular, their style is anything but lacking in structure. The element of inner unity is due to the way in which everything is related to a central point and determined by the decoration. This in itself explains why we can say that European pictorial art begins with the Minoans.

There is no doubt that this development came about from within. It seems as though the Hieroglyphic Deposit still belongs to the level of the ancient palace at the time of its destruction. If this is so, this process will have taken place during its very last years. But even if it coincides with the new impulses, of which there was no lack when the palaces were rebuilt at the beginning of the second phase, the links with the preceding period are so close that the appearance of a new creative generation must have been the really decisive factor.

The impressions from the Temple Repositories are for this reason even more intricate in structure, indicating a new wave of influences from the Orient. So far as subject-matter is concerned, this finds expression in the new interest in the human figure. There is still a predilection for the custom of distributing the figures over a two-dimensional surface, and not binding them by a baseline. The human figures in particular show the use of the decorative element and the relation to a central point. Indeed, one gains the impression that all the force is concentrated in the wasp-waists of these men and women, whose limbs and bodily contours swing outwards from the centre with a volute-like curve. The men featured on the vessels in relief (cf. Figures on

Flowering period

pp. 121, 128) or the 'Prince with the Plumed Head-dress' are characteristic in this respect.

This style reaches its apogee in the large finds of seal-impressions from Hagia Triada and Zakro, as well as in the originals associated with them. It is simply the reverse side of the freedom that pictorial art has now, obtained. There now also develops alongside it a category of heraldic compositions in which the decorative element is purposefully emphasized on a basis of figure motifs. It is also characteristic that the pictures representing action — cult scenes (including bull-games) as well as hunting and battle scenes — should show greater interest in general and typical situations than in the dramatic aspect or in 'individuation'. This is probably connected with the fact that the animal pictures are more exquisite, and occur more frequently, than those featuring human beings. Of matchless beauty are the pictures of lions, bulls, ibexes, birds and animals locked in combat. Griffins and sphinxes illustrate the influences exerted by the Orient, and fantastic compositions of demons bear witness to the Minoans' unique wealth of imagination.

PLATE 45 The two gold rings from Shaft Grave IV in the citadel of Mycenae may be helpful in illustrating this stage in the development of glyptic art (cf. Plate on p. 177). One of these represents a stag-hunt by chariot, and the other a fight between four men. They belong to works produced by artists on the mainland for Mycenaean princes. This inference is drawn not so much from the subject-matter as from a slight tendency towards rigidity in style. The composition of the picture is characterized as much by angularity and parallel lines as by curvilinear and spiral elements.

PLATE 40 The lentoid carnelian shown in the Plate on p. 155 originates from a Cretan grave dating from the post-Palatial period. It is a fine example of the engraving technique mentioned above — the design is deeply engraved and splendidly combined with the precious material — as well as of the peculiar heraldic pattern: two ibexes, shown running, one of them being attacked by a dog.

PLATE 25 The gold ring from Isopata, not far from Knossos (cf. Plate on p. 107) is on the whole an adequate example of this type of style, although it dates from a later period than the impressions from Hagia Triada and Zakro. Four women wearing Minoan head-dress, depicted in ecstatic movement as though performing a dance, are arranged freely upon a ground recognizable as a meadow strewn with flowers. The two women on the left-hand border are shown bending backwards with their arms raised, and looking up at a tiny figure wearing the same attire and whirling about — as is clearly evident from her skirt and flowing hair. The woman in the centre is turning to the right as though blinded by this scene. The fourth woman, on the right-hand border, is looking to the left and has both arms raised in a joyful gesture. The theme is the same as in one of the miniature frescoes from Knossos. The small figure is a goddess who appears in the distance, summoned by the ecstatic dance. Anyone who has been following the history of Minoan pictorial art cannot help noticing the blending of Aegean surface delineation with Oriental elements. However, unlike the beginning of this process, when particular emphasis was placed on the decorative element, it is now the other element which takes the lead. The most curious feature of the gold ring from Isopata, the figure in the distance, can now be interpreted from our knowledge of the representative character of Minoan pictorial art in general and the way in which the elements are arranged spatially about a central point. Once again this is evidence of the relationship between one of the most curious aspects of Minoan religion, the belief in the epiphany of their gods, and its expression in cults, on one hand, and Minoan formal structure on the other.

The final stage in the development of glyptic art is illustrated by the flattened cylinder of bright blue chalcedony, mounted on gold, in the Plate on p. 155. It was found in the same tomb as the gold ring, but belongs to a later burial, subsequent to the destruction of the palaces. The big dog with its massive collar is out of proportion to the two men standing next to it. This is probably because the animal is sacred to the gods and venerated as their companion. The coarse rendering of the forms is offset by a new assurance and firmness in the composition of the picture. As the curvilinear element is suppressed the composition is determined by the horizontal and vertical dividing lines. This small work is later in date than the sarcophagus from Hagia Triada on which this motif is already foreshadowed. To what extent and for what reason it is symptomatic of its period is a question we shall consider in the final chapter.

Late styles
PLATE 40

We may conclude this examination of Minoan pictorial art by emphasizing the fact that its character is best expressed in glyptic works, i.e. in miniatures. It is in this field that development is most distinct and consistent. This is evidently not only due to chance or the quantity of material preserved. Comparisons with the first beginnings of a tendency towards monumentality, such as we see in some frescoes and reliefs in stucco, lead to the assumption that there are probably profound reasons for this phenomenon. Without losing sight of the features connecting this culture with the great civilizations of antiquity — also in regard to its historical function — we may now appreciate how important the tendency in Minoan art towards miniature (and thus towards glyptic art) is, especially by comparison with the absolute monumentality found in Egypt and the Orient. So far as art history is concerned, we have here reached the limit of our enquiry.

It remains for us only to reconsider and supplement what has been said above with regard to decoration. This is necessary on account of the obvious interlocking of these two elements, if for no other reason.

GOLD
JEWELLERY

PLATE 25

The gold pendant from a burial at Chrysolakkos, not far from Mallia (cf. Plate on p. 107; width 0.047 m.) is at the same time a work of decorative art and a pictorial representation. Two queen bees are arranged around a honeycomb in heraldic fashion. The hesitation we feel about two queen bees being placed side by side may not matter in view of the unmistakable naturalistic rendering, for in the early history of art double or multiple symbols were thought to possess correspondingly greater effect. This little masterpiece, produced by means of embossing and granulation, may be ascribed to the beginning of the Palace period from evidence of its style and the circumstances of its discovery. Its *forte* is the deftness with which the living prototype is depicted, despite the emphasis given to decoration in rendering detail and in the composition as a whole.

POTTERY
Early styles:
Kamares ware

PLATE 44

The beak-spouted vase shown in the Plate on p. 176 was found in the First Palace at Phaestos. It is a characteristic example of the intricate Kamares pottery (MM II). The design is derived from four 'S' scrolls in an oblique position. The ends of two adjoining coils are connected to the whorl in two parts which we mentioned above. The oblique combinations have been enriched by an oval-shaped motif which features a red design resembling a double tongue, and enhanced by the fact that they direct the viewer's eye diagonally across the surface of the vessel. The spirals are thus made to serve the torsion in a unique and magnificent way. The surface of the vessel and the figures encompassed by it are thus expressed as a meaningful unit. Despite this, they are also related, in an equally characteristic and skilful manner, to the other extreme: lavishness and splendour of appearance. Everything about the design remains ornamental. It not only has a quality of movement about it but also has a curious inner affinity with the vegetable kingdom.

PLATE 38

From the same stylistic phase we have the cup shown in the Plate on p. 153. It was also found in an early horizon of the old palace at Phaestos. This is an example of 'egg-shell ware' which deserves our admiration on account of the perfection of the ceramic technique alone. The motif of scales, which probably originated in Egypt and is always popular in textile designs, is one of the favourite patterns in Minoan surface decoration because it conveys a sense of unity instead of dividing the surface into fields. On this cup it is combined with small buds emerging from two red calyx-leaves with white centres. These need not be regarded as a means of filling in the scales. In the curves one can also see chains of interconnected flowers similar to Late

Greek anthemia. It is in any case worth noting the way in which the ornamentation comes to adopt plant designs. This corresponds to the seals, where this tendency also occurs at this time. All Kamares pottery is distinguished by this linking and interlocking element.

APPX. PL. 12

So far as vase-painting in white, red, and orange on a chocolate-coloured 'glazed' ground is concerned, there are significant specimens of this still in the early phase of the Late Palace period. They include the vases with lily designs from Knossos, which are akin to the frescoes from Amnisos. The level from which they originate dates from the Late Middle Minoan phase; the Temple Repositories with the seal impressions mentioned above, and the faience Snake Goddess, also belong to this period (cf. Plate on p. 109). After the first Late Minoan phase, which begins approximately during the mid-16th century, the vessels are painted predominantly in dark colours on a light ground. Apart from ornamental patterns only plant motifs were at first used. Towards the close of the century designs taken from marine flora and fauna came to enjoy popularity: octopuses, nautili, Triton's shells, starfish and seaweed.

FIG. 25

PLATE 27

The vase from Palaikastro (eastern Crete) shown in the Plate on p. 112 is a late product of this phase and may have been made during the first third of the 15th century. The plant-like decoration consists of a triple repetition of a spiral-like involute twig terminating in a flower. Seen from the standpoint of decorative syntax, this magnificent combination of spiral pattern and naturalistic form directs the viewer's eye over the elegant and bold curvature of the vessel in all three dimensions. The design therefore fulfils the function which elsewhere is performed by torsion. The connection with the styles used in pictorial art lies not only in the common predilection for spirals but also in their systematic employment. The vessel narrows towards the base and flares outwards at the top, expressing the idea of a blossoming plant growing upwards from the centre. This means of conveying the impression of a plant is the product of an unusual combination of the shape of the vessel, the motif and the decoration. It throws light upon the structural background of the unity found in pictures, due to the use of the decorative element. In this connection, too, while we are dealing with the transitional period between the close of the age of efflorescence (LM Ib) and the last phase of the Palace style before the destruction (LM II), we may consider the large amphora with three handles, shown in the Plate on p. 198; although it was found in a *tholos* tomb on the mainland. The group of vessels to which it belongs was produced on the mainland during the first third of the 15th century, but Cretan painters were responsible for the ornamentation. The three decorated panels have coral-reef-like borders which project into the

Flowering period: naturalistic style

PLATE 29

PLATE 50

actual picture in the familiar way. Each of the surface planes has four floating nautili, arranged in two rows with a trefoil-like design and seaweed in the empty space in the centre. It probably represents a rock; viewed from above. These are sections of an *en rapport* pattern. We can see how the decorative design serves to give unity to the wealth of vigorous naturalistic forms, and at the same time ensures that the vessel and the decoration on it form a whole by virtue of the function the latter fulfils on the surface of the vessel.

PLATE 32   The pilgrim's flask found at Palaikastro and shown in the Plate on p. 131 is slightly older than the vase from the same site, although the marine motifs of later times are used. An octopus swimming in a direction diagonal to the axis of the vessel is surrounded by coral-like reefs with seaweed and Triton's shells. In this case the naturalistic form is combined with the whorl pattern, which established a unity of style in spite of the dynamism and the indifference towards a static and tectonic rendering. This naturalism is certainly startling, but it alone and its apparent freedom do not determine the character of this style: this role is played by the decoration. It is this that holds the key to its fate, so to speak.

Late style:
Palace style

PLATE 35
APPX. PL. 14

APPX. PL. 13

What is meant by this remark will become clearer after examining the large three-handled amphora from Knossos shown in the Plate on p. 134, which illustrates the final phase of pottery in the Palace period. The vessel is an example of the so-called Palace style, which only occurs at Knossos and is typical of the final 60 years or more before catastrophe struck the city (LM II). Round the vessel are six papyrus reeds. The three below the handles are smaller than the others, with wavy stems. The three large ones in the intermediate spaces have a design resembling a vertical stem. The light ground is marked off by free wavy lines from the intervening spaces, which are covered with thinned-down painted glaze. Free vigorous naturalism has been superseded here by a new kind of ornamentalism. It is associated with a pretension to splendid effect that borders upon monumentality. One can speak of a tendency towards rigidity. But does the biological analogy help us to comprehend the way in which the style developed? A vertical arrangement into parts begins to make itself felt, though it is still blurred by the numerous curves. This is also in contrast to the decorative syntax met with hitherto. In the pictorial and glyptic art of the final phase of the Palace period it is possible to observe a similar tendency.

The new disintegration of the elements enables us to understand why the decorative naturalism of the efflorescent period was so short-lived. Since this could only find realization in a transitory stage, in this milieu it can boast the charism of classicism. But in the new style of decoration there are not only resolved elements, as is evident from the systematic arrangement. The fact that this limitation is inherent in the structure can be inferred from its occurrence in other branches of art as well. The reasons for the appearance of this completely new phenomenon remain for the time being an enigma. Perhaps it will be possible to approach a solution of this problem after attempting, in the following chapter, to trace its function in the history of art during the Late Bronze Age.

The decoration of the Early and Late Palace period thus has as its elements *Minoan* spirals and wavy lines, and as its basic syntactical forms whorls, torsions and *decoration* *en rapport* patterns. Proceeding from this view we have been able to demon- *in general* strate, even in detail, the continuity that characterizes the development of Minoan design. This approach finds substantial corroboration in the fact that there is throughout a striking tendency to continue the 'individuation' of these motifs developed before the Palace period, which in turn were already encountered in embryonic form in the Neolithic material. We have been able to follow the two stages of development during the Palace period in architecture as well as in pictorial art and decoration. So far as palace architecture itself is concerned, the first stage was marked by a simple additive construction which imposed restraints and limitations upon the sense of monumental unity. In pictorial art and decoration, correspondingly, the dominant role was played by the ornamental element. The remodelling of figures of the type known in Egypt and Asia Minor under the inspiration of the Minoan ornamental style was but one particular expression of this tendency.

But our knowledge of the process of development is of advantage to us only in so far as it enables us to understand the style: its individuality, its purpose, its message. Some light seems to be thrown upon these problems by our conclusion, reached by employing a historical approach, that painting and decoration have a common syntactical basis. This brings us back once again to the question of 'inner form', or formal structure. We have seen that Minoan naturalism was inhibited by ornamentation. From the standpoint of structure this characteristic of being 'tethered to the decoration', so to speak, could also be placed on a common denominator with the basic syntactical forms that we have noted. It appears that the term 'central organization' comes closest to expressing the essence of the matter.

Here we seem to have reached a point in our analysis where, with 'inner BACKGROUND form', we find ourselves touching the limits of the finite material world, and the danger arises that our conclusions may be lacking in substance and isolated from reality, unless we also bear in mind the historical background in so far as this is relevant to our theme. The historian of Minoan art is thus faced with a particularly difficult problem. His subject-matter is no longer properly speaking prehistoric, yet he has no hope of finding it reflected in written sources. On the contrary, the very records which supply him with chronological evidence must also provide the material on which to base his interpretation. This is why we have frequently touched on the latter aspect when introducing to the reader various works of art. Nevertheless it will probably not have been superfluous, particularly where we seek to assess the significance of the Palace period in the history of art, to summarize the present state of our knowledge with regard to this background before going on to deal with the transition to Greek art.

Political factors The Greeks of later times thought of King Minos as a monarch who held sway over the seas. This was not, as some have assumed, simply a reflection of the fact that classical Athens was a maritime power. It has been corroborated by excavations. The stratigraphic evidence shows that after the palaces were destroyed they were time and again rebuilt on a more lavish and splendid scale. The more recent palaces no longer have any fortifications at all. The destructions can only have been caused by natural catastrophes. Under these circumstances it must also be presumed, from the fact that the palaces existed side by side with one another simultaneously, that conditions were peaceful and that the whole island recognized the authority of a central government. In view of the overseas trade that was carried on, of which evidence has been brought to light by excavation, this presupposes the existence of a Cretan fleet that must have been powerful enough to control the maritime routes.

Sociological factors So far as social structure is concerned, several points have already been made above in connection with architecture (cf. p. 113). The transformation of the landed nobility into a court aristocracy may also be seen from the development of seals. Representatives of this class of nobles must be imagined as spread out all over the country, acting as governors on behalf of the king. In the majority of cases they must have served in the central administration and have sustained the splendour of the court. Manual labour was performed by an extensive class of artisans and by bondsmen, who were by now clearly quite numerous. Both these groups are represented in the masses of onlookers portrayed in the miniature frescoes. Particularly noteworthy is the important part played by women in social life. This finds expression already in their court attire, which was both splendid and fanciful, with an ingeniously contrived emphasis on woman's eternal femininity. In ritual women have special functions to fulfil as spectators at festivals and as priestesses. In the bull-game they match the men in boldness. All this is combined in a characteristic way with the unwarlike, enthusiastic, vigorous and basically irrational nature of the Minoans, which is manifest in all their works.

In contrast to Egypt and the Near East, the person of the king or queen is hardly ever portrayed directly in works of art. This is due primarily to ritual considerations. Minoan religion originates with the Great Mother Goddess, the only deity in the whole of the ancient Aegean to assume tangible form. It appears that she originally lacked a male partner. This place cannot have been taken by the bull-god, as has often been suggested. The great part played by the bull in Minoan art, where it occurs in many different forms in major works, suggests rather that the bull had a *ritual* significance as a sacrificial animal. The bull-game, too, represents the taking of the sacrificial bull. The many pictures portraying bulls dying or being overwhelmed by lions are designed to show antithetically the triumph of the divine power over this quintessence of strength and procreative force. Since the bull sport has been documented already from the pre-Palatial period, this complex of ideas cannot be a product of the course of development in Crete, but must have taken shape at the very dawn of Minoan religion.

There was nothing in the nature of a Minoan pantheon prior to the Late Palace period. But now there are male deities as well as female ones in various guises. Their retinue comprises lions, griffins and sphinxes. In this process a decisive role is played by pictorial borrowing from neighbouring lands. We also have a group of characteristic demonic creatures, part animal and part human. There is a complete absence of images made for worship. This custom only began to appear after the destruction of the palaces, when extraneous influences combined with local trends to bring it about. Clay idols of no great artistic merit, which used to stand in unpretentious little rooms rather like chapels during this late period, provide evidence of the piety of the common people and the changes that had taken place in their social conditions.

Religion and ritual

The positive aspect of this non-pictorial cult during the efflorescent period is the belief in the epiphany of the gods. They are conjured up by means of ecstatic dances and prayers, coupled with sacrificial offerings. They often appear in pictures in the guise of birds and snakes. This seems to have been the original form of this religion, and we can imagine its rites being performed in mountain sanctuaries and caves already during early times. The pillar crypts in the palaces must be regarded as taking the place of the old caves. Gods in human form and the ecstatic cult phenomena which they presuppose may be seen in pictures on seals, some of which date from the Early Palace period, as well as in frescoes and in the most complete pictorial document we have relating to Minoan religion: the cyclic fresco decoration of the sarcophagus from Hagia Triada. This shows that some kind of cult symbol was

FIG. 28

FIG. 14

indispensible. It may be either a tree or an altar. This is of particular assistance in understanding the 'sacred facades'. This term is the most apposite one to describe such pictorial representations as occur in one of the miniature frescoes from Knossos (cf. p. 121), since real objects of this kind have been found in excavations at the western side of the central court at Knossos and also in the mansion at Vathypetros. They have no real spatial function to fulfil, and are in any case much too small for this. But in this reduced and concentrated form they are abbreviated copies of the palace, to the ritual significance of which they testify. Related to them are the votive figurines portraying

PLATE 27

men in the guise of gods. There is no doubt that the priestess at least would appear clad in the attire of the goddess she served. If she was identical with the queen it would be reasonable to assume that the same was also true of the king. We may accordingly venture the suggestion that the most magnificent of Minoan facades, the West Propylon with the outside staircase at Phaestos, was designed to serve as a background for his ritual appearances.

All this is as specifically Minoan as it is remote from the religious concepts of the neighbouring civilizations of the ancient world. In Egypt portraits of kings are an expression of the fact that they enjoy eternal life. In the ancient Orient their relation to the gods assumes a monumental form, and consequently pictures of them have a monumental quality as well. The belief of the Minoans of Crete in epiphany is a belief in the reality of the fleeting present. In the same way their pictorial art is characterized by an enchantment with transitory phenomena. They had no motive to portray their rulers. Similarly, their sepulchral architecture is also designed to express, not a sense of eternity, but the continual return of the dead.

Administration, economic factors, writing, seals

This makes it remarkable enough in its uniqueness, particularly in the ancient world to which it belongs. Equally astonishing is the many-faceted character of the Minoans, which helps to explain the role they played in the history of antiquity. For with their enthusiastic, irrational and to some degree feminine traits they combined a masculine sobriety and realism. We can gain an idea of this from the palace administration and economy as revealed in the development of writing and seals. The hieroglyphic system which evolved in the Early Palace period probably served first and foremost ritual requirements. Originating in the pictographic writing of the preceding period, it develops along independent lines and bears only a general affinity to Egyptian script. It is known to us mostly from seals, which are mainly still of a representative and ritual character in the Hieroglyphic Deposit at Knossos, during the transition to the Late Palace period, as well as in the original works that followed. Already in the early years of the old palace we also find a linear syllabic script. To distinguish it from the later script it is termed 'Linear A'. It is well known from small clay tablets, but it has not as yet been deciphered. All we can say is that the language is not Indo-European and that the content is exclusively of an administrative and economic character, as is also the case with the later group. At Knossos it is superseded by the 'Linear B' script during the final phase in the existence Fɪɢ. 32 of the palaces (LM II), when the Palace style of pottery, and a new style of frescoes and seals, also appeared. This system has also been authenticated on the mainland by considerable finds made since 1939. But these do not commence before the latter part of the 13th century, and are therefore two hundred years later than the ones from Crete. It may be mentioned in passing that an attempt has been made to eliminate this gap in historical continuity and to attach a late date also to the tablets bearing Linear B script from Knossos; but this hypothesis has not withstood critical examination. As a result of the discovery made by Michael Ventris in 1953, the Linear B script may now be regarded as deciphered. It came as a great surprise when the language in which it was written turned out to be an early pre-Homeric form of Greek. This corroborated a hypothesis that had been put forward from time to time earlier: that in the course of the 15th century the ancestors of the later Greeks, whom we, following Homer, call Achaeans, and who were responsible for the Mycenaean culture of the mainland, made themselves masters of the palace of Knossos. It would take us too far from our theme to deal with the content of these documents in detail, and a few remarks must suffice. The texts are for the most part short entries in account-books or similar lists. The information they provide relates directly to Achaean rather than to Minoan conditions. But it was precisely in administration and economic matters that the Achaeans were the disciples of the Minoans. In distinguishing between the contributions made by these two peoples scholars are still at the beginning of their task. Especially so far as data about ritual matters are concerned, the part played by the Minoans is problematical. On the other hand, there is no doubt that the data relating to administrative and economic questions which can be identified as Minoan were to a great extent based on Egyptian and Oriental models. There is, however, also a characteristic difference between Minoan palace organization and that in the lands from which it was derived. This is shown by the number and size of the magazines and the way in which they are accumulated in the basements. Minoan palaces are not only seats of government and administration and cult centres, but also centres where agricultural and industrial production are organized and trade in these products carried on. The evident lack of interest in military matters indicates the importance the rulers of these palaces attached to the development of trade and the economy. The remains of the archive from the old palace at Phaestos, which have been preserved in the seal impressions mentioned above, afford an insight into the beginnings of this development. These are clay lumps used to seal the cords securing the stoppers of vessels and other receptacles. Individual official seals were already common among landowners in the Messara before the Palace period, apparently also with the object of orderly management of their extensive estates. This was the point of departure for the royal administration. In the archives which the latter built up there seem to have been some documents written in ink on perishable material, in most cases probably Egyptian papyrus. This raises the question of the possible existence of written texts. There are no definite clues to go on, and in the present state of our knowledge it seems unlikely that any existed. The Late Palace period is the golden age of glyptic art, which reflects both the self-assertiveness of the court nobility and the high degree of organization achieved by the royal administration. Its history is also informative in that it shows how the central power succeeded in eliminating the former system under which the landowners enjoyed equality of status. This supports the sociological conclusions we arrived at above from the history of palace architecture. The seal impressions discovered at Lerna show that social and economic conditions on the mainland corresponded to those in Crete in the pre-Palatial era, which are most readily discernible in the Messara.

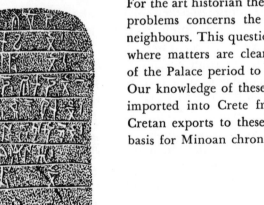

For the art historian the most important of these historical problems concerns the relations between Crete and its neighbours. This question leads us on to recorded history, where matters are clearer, and enables the Cretan style of the Palace period to emerge from prehistoric darkness. Our knowledge of these connections is based upon pieces imported into Crete from the ancient civilizations and Cretan exports to these countries. They also provide the basis for Minoan chronology. Since this is a complex and

FIG. 32 — *Clay tablet with Linear B script, from Pylos. Close of the 13th century B.C. National Museum, Athens. Cf. p. 147.*

highly specialized question, it can only be touched on briefly here. The absolute chronology of the Palace period may today be regarded in all essentials as solved. But of course we also have to consider the borrowing of motifs, in the broadest sense of the term, in both directions.

With Egypt indirect contact by way of Syrian ports seems to have been of greater importance than direct links. The stimulating effect this had upon Minoan production can be illustrated by many examples. Conversely, already during the period of the Middle Kingdom (*circa* 2050—1786 B.C.) Minoan textile designs containing the *en rapport* motif were copied in Egypt. The spiral ornamentation of Egyptian scarabs produced in this era was particularly subject to Minoan influence. And again, the naturalism of Amarna art, dating from a period approximately one generation later than the destruction of the Cretan palaces, can only be understood if we reckon with Minoan after-effects. An examination of ceramic imports from the Aegean into the Nile valley has shown that Cretan products were superseded by those from the mainland already during the 15th century. The same observation has been made along the western coast of Asia Minor from excavations at Miletus, and from others in the far west, on the Lipari Islands. In view of the part Achaeans from the mainland begin to play in Crete at this time, there are unmistakable signs here of the impending catastrophe.

The importance of the links with Syria lay ultimately in the metal trade. Copper from Cyprus was transported in the form of rectangular ingots with concave sides. Hagia Triada yielded a hoard of 19 such pieces weighing some 20 to 30 kg. One of the most important influences exerted in the reverse direction was the evolution of Mitannian art, in the area of the upper Euphrates, from the 15th century onwards, where we find an abundance of Minoan motifs.

Links with the interior of Asia Minor were not lacking, but they were less important than those with Egypt and Syria. This is understandable in view of the fact that both the first kingdom of the Hittites and the great empire founded in the 15th century had no outlet to the sea and were primarily oriented towards the east. It is only in the following period of Aegean history that contacts with the Hittites play a part, although even then they are still of an indirect character.

In the west definite evidence has not been found of links beyond Lipari. All the more intensive is Crete's orientation towards the north, to the Aegean. But here we have to distinguish between the Early and Late Palace era.

In the earlier period the rough cultural equilibrium that existed in the Aegean during the Early Bronze Age shifts finally and decisively in favour of Crete. From the finds it may be inferred that at that time this whole area came within the sphere of Cretan influence. The absence of any real rival in maritime trade naturally meant that the island had control of the sea routes, although this was doubtless not firm. The necessary conditions for this were provided by the consolidation of a central authority in Crete, which finds expression in the flourishing Palace culture, unparalleled elsewhere in the Aegean. Its rise was facilitated by the fall of Troy II, which occurred even before the close of the preceding epoch. But the principal cause was unquestionably the fact that during the first third of the second millennium B.C. the great powers were oriented towards the interior of the continent. The Egyptian Middle Kingdom maintained maritime trade only to the extent necessary to protect its interests in Syria, and perhaps also to ensure the supply of timber. The Syrian ports lacked a strong drive to expand since their hinterland was for the most part a zone of contention between the Pharaohs and their Asian antagonists.

Crete and the Aegean

This was the world in which Crete found itself in the Early Palace era. It avoided being drawn into the tumult politically and was able to consolidate its power in all fields. We have already sketched briefly the form this took in the political, social, economic and religious sphere. It now becomes clear that the consolidation of artistic styles, which as we have seen was the achievement of the Early Palace period so far as art was concerned, is nothing other than an expression of Crete's geographical and historical situation at the time. During the Late Palace period there is a further shift in the balance of power. From the 16th century onwards, if not earlier, the Cretans have their bases elsewhere in the Aegean. One could almost call them 'colonies'. Their presence has been authenticated on the islands of Melos, Rhodes and Thera, as well as along the coast of Asia Minor at Miletus. But even now we cannot speak of an Aegean empire ruled by King Minos. On the mainland, first of all at Mycenae, an independent centre of power emerges. The finds from the shaft graves at Mycenae commence at the very beginning of the 16th century B.C. In addition to imports from Crete and works in which the native tradition is continued, they include the products of Cretan craftsmen which were made either in or for Mycenae, as well as Mycenaean copies of Cretan works. They testify that this was materially an exceptionally flourishing period. Since the old idea that the Minoan empire extended to the mainland has been proved false, and since the hypothesis that these objects were looted from Crete has also failed to withstand criticism, we have no choice but to assume that during the 16th century, at least, conditions of peaceful coexistence generally prevailed. But there are plenty of signs pointing to an impending change for the worse. Much can be read into the introduction into the island of new improved types of arms, which are soon

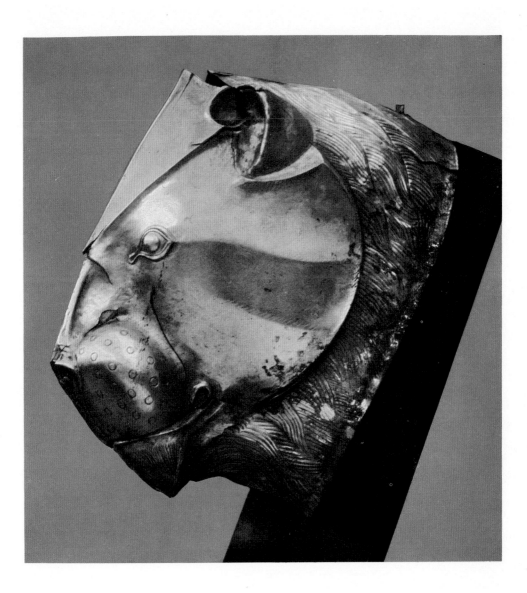

PLATE 36 — Sacrificial vessel in the shape of a lion's head. Embossed gold plate. From Shaft Grave IV, Mycenae. *National Museum, Athens. Height 20 cm. Cf. pp. 168, 172.*

PLATE 38 — Cup. Kamares ware. From the First Palace at Phaestos. Approx. 1800 B.C. *Iraklion. Diameter 12 cm. Cf. p. 140.*

Opposite:
PLATE 37 — Two gold cups from the *tholos* tomb near Vapheio, Laconia. *Above:* capture of wild bulls. *Below:* tame cattle pasturing. Minoan. Approx. 1500 B.C. *National Museum, Athens. Height approx. 8 cm. Cf. p. 127.*

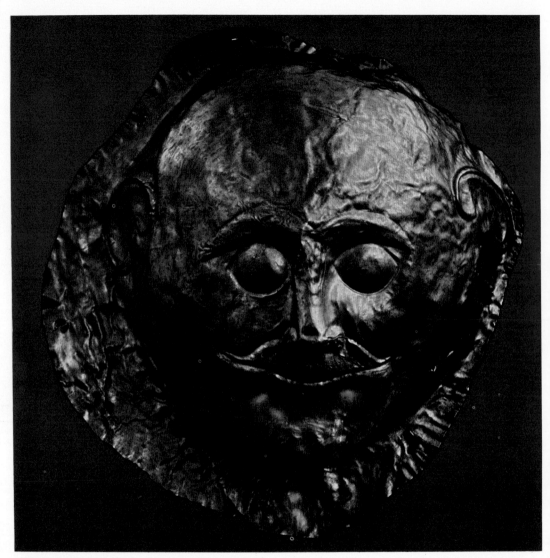

PLATE 39 — Gold mask of a prince. From Shaft Grave IV, Mycenae. 16th cent. B.C. *National Museum, Athens. Height 30.5 cm. Cf. pp. 165, 172.*

Opposite:
PLATE 40 — *Above:* seal of light blue chalcedony mounted in gold, in shape of a hollow flattened cylinder. Two men and a large mastiff are shown. From a tomb near Knossos. 14th—13th centuries B.C. *Iraklion. Length 27 cm. Cf. p. 139.*
Below: lenticular seal of red carnelian. Two ibexes and a dog. Crete. 14th—13th centuries B.C. *Iraklion. Diameter 25 cm. Cf. p. 138.*

PLATE 41 — Cup: so-called *kantharos*. Embossed gold plate, with handles riveted on. From Shaft Grave IV, Mycenae. 16th cent. B.C. *National Museum, Athens. Height without handles 9.2 cm. Cf. pp. 168, 172.*

adopted on the mainland as well. From the east come the horse and war-chariot. One Cretan invention of this period is the huge figure-of-eight shield, protecting the warrior from neck to feet, which can only have been used in conjunction with a chariot. In addition to this there are a helmet covered with boar's tusks and a new type of sword-blade, similar to a rapier, leather greaves and metal corselets.

PLATE 43, FIG. 47

FIG. 33

These are but the preparatory stages of a structural change which the whole of Minoan culture undergoes in the course of the 15th century. Mention has already been made of the texts in Linear B script at Knossos, which were written in Greek. Not only the language used points to the advent of new rulers: so also do the political and religious terms that they contain. One group of texts refers to stores of armour; elsewhere there is mention of horses, chariots, swords and cuirasses. Accounts are kept of their delivery, production and distribution for certain purposes. The 'Warrior Graves' already mentioned illustrate the same state of affairs. The use of weapons of this type and in such quantity as funerary gifts is an innovation in Minoan tombs. In addition to this there is the decidedly new and un-Minoan quality in the style of works of art, which we have noted with regard to frescoes, seals and pottery executed in the Palace style.

In all this the actual course of historical events can be traced only in general outline. It is surprising that the change of regime should have taken place without any accompanying vestiges of violent upheaval. It is of course merely a conjecture to explain this by reference to the unwarlike, Phaeacian, yet impetuous character of the Minoans, which is distinctly evident in their art. We have pointed out that this spirit was itself the product, in a sense, of Crete's international position. Even more puzzling is the actual catastrophe itself. All we know is that on a certain day in spring towards the close of the 15th century, when a strong south wind was blowing, the palace of Knossos went up in flames. The excavation of the Little Throne Room suggests that the inhabitants were taken by complete surprise. That this was not only a natural catastrophe may be deduced from the fact that this time the palace was not rebuilt, and that henceforward life ceased in the other palaces as well. According to clay tablets and seal impressions only the 'Little Palace' at Knossos survived for some time as an administrative centre of minor importance.

Wherever we have to depend upon archaeological sources alone, the imponderables are weightier and the course of events becomes even more nebulous than is otherwise the case. For the time being, therefore, we cannot do more than make conjectures, and this of course means giving rein to one's imagination. Nevertheless it appears possible that the destruction was

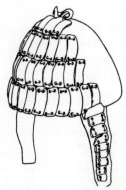

caused by dissension among the new rulers or insurrection on the part of the Minoans.

Conclusions It should, however, be borne in mind that despite this one historical fact of the utmost importance remains. A summary review of the Late Palace period shows that its actual content is no longer the interaction with the ancient civilizations but that with the neighbouring lands of the Aegean. We can now appreciate the way in which Minoan culture acted as a bridge between East and West. This process was closely connected with the flourishing classical period of Minoan style in art. This gave it a dynamic of its own, the effects of which will be dealt with in the next chapter. Thus we have fixed chronologically one terminal point at least of classical Minoan art.

IV. TRANSFORMATION AND RENAISSANCE
Mycenaean Style

With the destruction of Knossos in approximately 1400 B.C. the chain of historical events is interrupted. But this does not constitute the end of the first epoch in European history — an epoch that lasts up to the time when metals found their way into the Aegean. This is already evident from the fact that the Bronze Age continues in this area for another three hundred years at least. In art history, too, the Minoan style is still predominant in this phase. The centre of development has shifted from Crete to the Greek mainland. Thus production now spreads to the whole Aegean — whereas in the Palace period it was concentrated in Crete. From the time of Schliemann onwards the term 'Mycenaean culture' has been common usage in regard to the developments to be dealt with here. It would also be possible to speak of a Late Bronze Age in the Aegean. But the decisive factor in determining the different character of these three centuries is not the shift in area but the fact that a different people has now taken over the lead.

This new people emerges into the limelight of Minoan culture from a prehistoric darkness which is still very obscure. From a cursory view it seems as though Minoan styles have been adopted without restraint. But a change can be noted in what appears to the superficial observer as stagnation. For this reason Mycenaean art has often been interpreted as a degenerate form of Minoan art. But a more thorough examination reveals the existence of links with Greek art. The development of the geometric style begins several obscure centuries after the catastrophe that struck Mycenaean culture. The most remarkable fact is that the un-Minoan features of Mycenaean works, i.e. those that exhibit signs of the degeneration of Minoan style, should be the ones that determine the structure of Greek style.

The continuous upward course of Minoan development breaks off in or about the year 1400. Mycenaean art has an uneven character. But in view of the nature of the world that gave it birth it would be wrong to describe it as decadent. From the point of view of the history of art, and of thought generally, the situation is surprisingly similar to that a thousand years later, during the transition from Greece to Rome. The latter transition naturally has much wider implications than the former. For the same reason in both cases greater attention must be paid to historical events which the student of art cannot afford to overlook.

At first we must cast our thoughts back from the beginning of the Late

FIG. 34 — *Kantharos and pedestalled cup. So-called grey Minyan ware. Middle Helladic. First half of 2nd millennium B.C. From Korakou, near Corinth. Height of kantharos 12 cm.; height of cup 24 cm. Cf. p. 161.*

Bronze Age, which we reached in the last chapter, to the beginning of the Full Bronze Age on the mainland, since we have as yet to discuss the immediate circumstances in which Mycenaean art and culture emerged. From approximately the

MIDDLE HELLADIC PERIOD mid-20th century Early Helladic is superseded by the so-called Middle Helladic culture, which in turn gives way, in or about 1600 B.C., to the Early Mycenaean culture of the shaft-grave period.

The forms of settlement and architecture exhibit differences from the Early Helladic period, although there are many affinities between them as well. Even now megaron houses are still to be found. But oval-shaped houses, which may be of stately appearance, are also popular, as are apsidal buildings. The few residences known to us (Malthi in Messenia, Asine in Argolis) and fortifications (e.g. Aegina, Brauron in Attica, Malthi) are less pretentious than before. At Malthi an entire walled settlement has been uncovered. The fortification walls, which are more or less oval, are about 135 metres in diameter. There are no bastions. The five gateways are simply passages in the walls. The residence is situated in the centre. Many small rooms, of approximately the same size, are arranged radially around the inside of the wall. Most of the walled area is taken up by rooms with common walls. Everything is more primitive and rustic than in Early Helladic settlements of equivalent size.

Graves There are corresponding changes in the types of graves. It is usual for burial to take place in the houses and within the settled area. The typical Middle Helladic place of burial is a shaft grave, often in the form of a stone cist. It

160

generally contains one burial with unpretentious funerary gifts. The body is still placed in a recumbent crouching position, but burials with limbs extended are also found. Circular mounds, with earth filling, a stone crepis outside and cist tombs inside, have been discovered at Aphidna (Attica), Drachmani (Phocis) and Leukas. It will be noted that burials no longer take place in caves (cf. p. 115). The clay figures, bronze weapons and gold ornaments that have been found are of poor quality by comparison with Minoan work of this period, and even with objects of the Early Bronze Age. We can gain the clearest impression of Middle Helladic art from its pottery. *Pottery:* The so-called Minyan type derives its name from the Minyans, a vanished *Minyan* people who were believed by the Greeks to have once lived in Boeotia. Works of this kind were first discovered during excavations in this area. The largest group is termed grey Minyan ware. It continues to be produced well *Fig. 34* into the Mycenaean era. Black Minyan ware is also popular in the Peloponnese. Yellow Minyan ware only begins during this phase and finally merges into Mycenaean pottery, with its bright ground. All these three types are usually produced with the aid of a potter's wheel. A characteristic feature is the greasy surface. The vessels are modelled on those of metal. The principal forms are goblets or cups on a tall base, with fluting, and the so-called *Matt-painted* *kantharos,* a cup with two vertical handles. *pottery*

Fig. 35 — *Matt-painted storage vessel (pithos). Middle Helladic. First half of 2nd millennium B.C. Aegina. Height approx. 50 cm. Cf. p. 162.*

Another type of pottery is loosely termed Aegina ware. It is lavishly painted in matt colours. The workshops on this island produced a great deal for export, as did some of the other centres as well. In this case, too, the variety of types is not extensive. Most of them are bowls, beak-spouted vases and FIG. 35 medium-sized storage vessels known as *pithoi*. The painted designs on a dull yellow or greenish clay ground are black or brown in colour and are primarily geometric or rectilinear. Another favourite design is one of circles, each of them containing a cross. It is worth noting the tectonic syntax — the framing of the design within two horizontal lines, and a tendency towards right angles and diagonals. Despite some similarities these two types — the Minyan and the matt-painted type — are both easily distinguishable from Early Helladic ware.

The question of the origin of Middle Helladic culture is a crucial one, for it concerns the origins of the Hellenes — because Middle Helladic culture merges into Mycenaean culture without any interruption, or any archaeological evidence of connections with extraneous influences during the course of its evolution, and also because its producers were Achaeans, i.e. Greeks. We know this for certain, and not only from the fact that their documents were written in the Greek of Linear B. But at present we are unfortunately still very much in the dark about this most important problem.

Hitherto it was customary to think that Early Helladic culture terminated in a catastrophe horizon. This was because several Middle Helladic settlements were built, not over older settlements that had been destroyed, but at sites that had not previously been inhabited. Recent finds in the Peloponnese have shown that major destructions took place before the end of the last Early Helladic phase. These seem to have been followed by new features without any further intervening destruction. In Thessaly Middle Helladic objects are comparatively recent. It seems as if they were introduced here from the south. This has been explained as a movement in the reverse direction, on the assumption that the Middle Helladic people crossed Thessaly on their way to Hellas without leaving any traces of their presence behind. Nor, however, did they leave any such traces on the islands.

But in Troy VI Middle Helladic pottery is found from the very start and remains prominent until the destruction of this citadel. It was for the most part produced locally. But soon after the earliest specimens we find imports of matt-painted pottery from Greece, which is no longer evident in the last phase of Troy VI. Little is as yet known about the Antatolian pottery outside Troy that has been labelled proto-Minyan. It can only be said with certainty that both the Anatolian and the Greek type are closely related to metal vessels. The latter first appeared in Asia Minor, but became diffused through the medium of trade links rather than by migrating peoples. They have also left traces on Middle Minoan pottery in Crete. This means that the question of the origins of the Middle Helladic people is as yet unsolved. It is linked with the more far-reaching problem of the origin of the Indo-European peoples. From philological evidence it is known that they lived in Asia Minor from the early part of the 2nd millennium B.C. onwards. We shall show later why the people responsible for Mycenaean culture belonged to this group. The same of course also holds true with regard to their Middle Helladic ancestors. It only remains to be emphasized that there is not the slightest archaeological evidence of any change having taken place in the composition of the population on the Greek mainland between the beginning of Middle Helladic and the end of Mycenaean culture.

According to the evidence of Minoan parallel finds the transition to Early Mycenaean occurs in approximately 1600 B.C. This period is characterized first and foremost by two groups of shaft graves at Mycenae which extend up to the latter half of the 16th century. So far as chronological dating is concerned, the most important information is yielded by those vases recognizable as Minoan imports or copies of Minoan models. Despite the wealth contained in these graves our knowledge of this phase is limited. We have extremely little information about the palaces and defence works. The first group of royal shaft graves (A) was found by Schliemann in 1876 within the walls, just behind the Lion Gate. Six rectangular graves of varying size are cut out of the rock, which is here relatively soft. The largest of them (Grave IV) was 6.55 metres long and 4.10 metres wide. The bodies were interred upon an insulating layer of pebbles. The graves had walls of rubble masonry and a roof of wooden planks covered by stone slabs. They formed part of a necropolis outside the walls, which then must have run higher up and have enclosed a citadel (at that time still a fairly small one). It is not clear whether the graves were already then placed together to form a circular terrace and were enclosed. It was only when the citadel was enlarged, probably at the beginning of the 13th century, and the graves were enclosed within the circuit walls, that the terrace of graves (diameter approx. 28 m.) was filled up. At the same time the stelae that stood over them were removed to the new level.

The other grave circle (B) was not discovered until 1951. It is situated outside the walls, about 130 metres west of the Lion Gate, likewise in the middle of an older burial area. It is somewhat smaller in diameter (25 m.) and is surrounded by a low wall with inner and outer faces (width 1.55 m.; height 1.20 m.), which may have given the whole arrangement a terraced effect.

EARLY MYCENAEAN ART (SHAFT-GRAVE PERIOD)

Discovery
Fig. 36

Some 14 graves are assembled here. In general they are arranged in the same manner as those in Grave Circle A. In the 15th century a vaulted tomb of ashlar masonry was built inside the wall circuit, but it did not have any great effect upon the old graves. Most of them are smaller than in the other group. No traces of wooden coffins have been found. Stelae are again used to mark the spot above ground. The funerary gifts are on a more modest scale. It appears that the first of these graves were built some time before those of the other group, but in general they overlap. There is much to be said for the idea that this group belongs to a collateral line of the royal house.

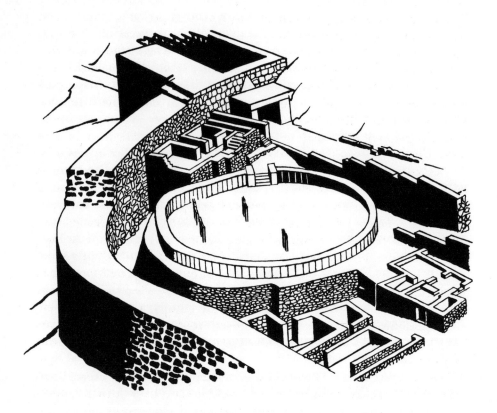

FIG. 36 — *Mycenae: grave-circle area in the citadel, after the reconstruction by Wace. Early 13th cent. B.C. Diameter of ring of standing slabs 28 m. Cf. p. 163.*

Of all these graves Grave IV in Grave Circle A is the largest and the richest. It contained seven bodies: three men, two women and two children. The Plates on pp. 151, 154, 156, 173-5, 177-8 illustrate some of the funerary gifts. An example of the three masks of embossed gold plate worn by the men is to be seen in the Plate on p. 154. The use of death masks is not a Minoan custom, and to judge by their features the dead are not Minoans either. The broad skull, the short nose with a prominent upper part, the thin lips, the bushy brows and protruding eyes — all these features suggest a different ethnic composition. The Minoans wore no beards, whereas on the mainland beards and side-whiskers were usual from this time onwards. Another point is that there is an unmistakable attempt at individual portraiture. But it is cruder than the old Minoan portraits, just as the subjects are of a rougher type. Of the four other gold masks in this grave circle, one of the two from Grave V, Schliemann's 'Agamemnon', has justly been seen as the forerunner of Greek physiognomy. Another mask from this grave, similar to the one illustrated, appears to represent a toothless old man. Least impressive as portraits are those of two other men in Grave IV. The eyebrows join; the lower part of the forehead bulges forth; the lips protrude. The same features are to be found on a less artistic bearded mask made of a silver and gold alloy (electrum), the only one from the other burial area. From the same grave we have the likeness of a bearded man on a gem — an amethyst cut by a Minoan craftsman.

Buried with the three men in Grave IV were a large number of weapons. They are exemplified by the well-known dagger-blade bearing a lion-hunting scene illustrated in the Plate on pp. 174–5 (shown slightly larger than life-size). This is of course a ceremonial weapon and not designed for ordinary use, but it can illustrate all the better the princes' passion for possessing and wearing weapons. The first of the five men has planted his lance in the jaws of the mightiest of the three lions, but has been mortally struck by a blow from its paw and thrown to the ground. The lion, however, cannot avoid the fate in store for it from the spears and arrows of the four other men. Two other lions may be seen bounding away in headlong flight.

The four gold-plated rivets affixed to the shoulder of the blade served to secure it to the hilt, which has been broken off. Other examples from the shaft graves include dagger- and sword-hilts made of costly material and with great artistry. The imaginative designs were modelled on those from Crete, as was the shape of the blade. A piece of bone or wood was encrusted with embossed gold plate, ivory or intarsia. Use was also made of gold, niello, glass, faience and rock-crystal. The pommels, most frequently of rock-crystal or ivory, were made separately.

Gold death masks

PLATES 36, 39, 41—3, 45—6

FIG. 31
APPX. PL. 20

Dagger bearing lion-hunt

PLATE 43

On the other side of the dagger-blade mentioned above is a lion pursuing four gazelles. Both these scenes are unexcelled in the technique of intarsia work on metal. The ornamental plaques made of a special alloy are inserted into the bronze blade. The designs themselves are cut out of differently-coloured sheets of electrum. An alloy consisting mainly of copper is used for the men, one of silver for their shields and loincloths, and one of gold for the lions. Without the metal being melted these designs were hammered into flat roughed-out spaces. As well as the engraved inner markings details such as the men's hair, their shield-straps, and the marking of the skin on one of the large shields, are hollowed out especially deeply and filled in with molten metal alloyed with sulphur (niello). This technique is met with at about the same time in Egypt as well and seems to have been the product of Cretan workshops.

In any case the style is Cretan. The type of lion represented, the full gallop, the slender build of the men and their posture, the shapes of the shields — all this has parallels in Minoan art of this period. But the theme of the 'lion-hunt' belongs to the mainland. The Cretans only knew lions in captivity or from representations. The short hair of the men is also Mycenaean rather than Minoan. In the composition there is a marked tension between the figures and the frame in the left-hand third of the picture. It is very expressive and differs, not only from the battle scenes on Minoan seals, but also from the truly Minoan swirling 'S' curves that dominate the other side of the blade. We have already noted something similar on gold rings and flattened cylinders from this grave, with pictorial themes resembling these. We may assume that the dagger was made by a Cretan craftsman and commissioned by someone from the mainland. The latter seems to have involuntarily transmitted something of his own character, and of his environment, to these craftsmen — as happened in the 15th century in the ceramic workshops at Knossos, where the so-called Palace style was first produced. The two gold signet-rings from the same grave illustrated in the Plate on p. 177 must have belonged to two women on account of their small diameter, although themes of masculine appeal such as a battle and stag-hunts are represented on them. For this reason they are mentioned here.

The purpose of the battle scene is to glorify a hero. In this case the hero is the warrior standing in the middle and preparing to stab his tottering enemy with his dagger. With his left hand he is seizing him by the neck, and one can see the vanquished warrior feebly and helplessly taking aim at the other man's head with his sword. If the hero were seeking to avenge on the two other men the defeated warrior crouching behind him on the ground, this would not explain the defensive posture of the man with the shield on the right-

hand side of the picture. His attitude is motivated by his feeling of horror at the violence being wrought on the two others. In this connection we may compare a seal impression from Hagia Triada with three warriors, showing the man in the centre as prominent. Thus this type of scene had a forerunner in Minoan art. In general the new element in the composition corresponds to that noted in the lion-hunt on the dagger. This is evident in the fact that parallel lines and acute angles are more prominent than curves and volutes. Here, too, we may suppose that a Minoan craftsman was carrying out a commission on behalf of some resident of the mainland. This ring has already been mentioned in connection with Minoan glyptic. It remains to be noted that, as may be seen from the battle scene, the actual representation is the negative of the original and not the positive of the sealing. A very few exceptions apart, this seems to be typical of the whole of Minoan and Mycenaean glyptic. Our illustration also shows the armour worn by the princes buried in the shaft graves. In all essential respects it is Minoan. This is true of the boar's-tusk helmet with cheek-flaps and horsehair plume, the dagger, the rapier-like sword, and the shield.

The other ring is of less artistic significance and was probably made by a different craftsman. It is doubtless no coincidence that there is no evidence in Crete of hunting from chariots with bow and arrow. The stag motif, which is unsuited to this composition, is taken from glyptic works of the heraldic type. More successful are the horses in the Minoan flying gallop. Horse and chariot appear at the same time, if not earlier, in Minoan pictures. Skeletons of horses of earlier date have been found in Troy VI. But the fondness for hunting scenes is typical of the mainland: they are rarely met with in Crete. The two sacrificial vessels (rhyta) from the same grave (Grave IV) are cult objects. One specimen of this type of vessel, from Knossos, has already been shown. The bull's head in the Plate on p. 178 is embossed out of a single piece of silver plate. Horns made of gold plate, which probably once had a wooden core, have been affixed. The bronze ears, plated with silver on the outside and gold on the inside, are worked separately and added later. The gold

Gold rhyta

PLATE 46

rosette on the forehead is affixed by means of a pin. The eyes originally had pupils of a different material, and the nostrils are plated with a thin layer of gold. The silver lid, which served to seal off the base of the neck, is missing. Between the horns is an aperture through which liquid was poured in, and the mouth forms another smaller aperture through which

PLATE 31

it ran out. Disregarding the incrustation, the head is treated with the same immediacy and plasticity as its companion-piece in stone from Knossos, which is probably of more recent date. The more decorative and archaic quality that it possesses is produced, not merely by the rosette, but also by the S-shaped curvature of the forelocks and the huge ornamental eye. Both its form and its ritual significance thus point to Minoan origin.

From the standpoint of decorative stylization this work is surpassed by the

PLATE 36

gold rhyton of a lion's head shown in the Plate on p. 151. This, too, is embossed in one piece and lacks the lid which formerly served to seal off the neck. The apertures used for pouring the fluid in and out of the vessel are to be found in identical places. Many of the plastically-treated forms are emphasized by being engraved afterwards with elaborate care. In spite of pronounced stylization the lion is Minoan in type — particularly in the ridges dividing the cheek from the neck, ears and forehead. The impressive naturalistic treatment of a basically decorative form also shows its ancient Minoan origin. It may be added that genuine Minoan rhyta of lions' heads and copies of them are to be found in Egyptian sepulchral paintings. In Minoan pictorial art the lion appears as an attendant of the Great Goddess from the Late Palace period onwards. This masterpiece, too, has thus been introduced from Crete.

Gold cups

The dead in Grave IV were buried with about three dozen drinking-vessels made of precious metal. In addition to imported pieces from Crete there are some native products. These include the gold *kantharos* with riveted

PLATE 41

handles illustrated in the Plate on p. 178. Its affinity with the clay *kantharoi* of Minyan pottery testifies to its origin. It has already been pointed out that the forms of Minyan vessels are derived from metal prototypes and were designed to be executed in metal. The noble and simple shape of this beaker gives it a classical appearance such as we find later in Greek vessels of this type. There are in fact a series of links which can be traced. This type survived for so long not only because of its connection with Dionysus, which we cannot go into here, but also because of its articulated functional clarity of expression.

Incrusted panels on chest

The influence of the shaft-grave art of the mainland is shown in more restrained form in some rectangular embossed sheets of gold plate, which originate from Grave V and are usually explained as two rows of incrusting panels on a

small hexagonal chest made of cypress wood (cf. Plate on p. 173, where it is PLATE 42
shown slightly enlarged). The decoration consists of several repetitions of
three types: a spiral *en rapport* pattern and the two pictures which appear
in the centre of the illustration: in one a lion is pursuing a stag, and in the
other a gazelle. The animal motifs and the plants used as space-filling are
Minoan. However, the forms are not only cruder but also un-Minoan in
the manner of their composition. Both the gazelle and the stag depicted on
the signet-ring in the Plate on p. 177 are taken from heraldic compositions. PLATE 45
The bucranium, which has no pictorial but only a formal function to fulfil,
shows the mouth opened in such a way as though it were viewed in profile.
It may also be noted that on account of the many vertical and horizontal
lines the full effect of the curvature produced by the motifs is not brought
out. Its decorative character is determined above all by the fact that no
limitations are imposed upon the space-filling, so that the borders give the
impression of being thrust outwards by their fillings. The same was true
of the lion-hunt depicted on the dagger-blade as well as of the battle scene
on the signet-ring. Thus it can no longer be doubted that there is a link with
the tectonic decoration on the matt-painted clay vessels. An essential stylistic
element from the mainland can be seen which is no longer ancient Aegean
in character but has been introduced by the people responsible for Middle
Helladic culture. The broken character of this form, shown in the reliefs
on the small chest, is undeniable. It is, however, worthy of note that these
alien and popular — but not fully comprehended — motifs are blended in a
new way that makes itself felt despite all obstacles. Only with further
development is it possible to show that this fermentation is the beginning
of a process of maturation. This leads to a conflict between a mode of
representation that is basically non-pictorial and one that is pictorial. *Jewellery*
In Grave Circle A the extravagance of the jewellery worn by the women
corresponds to the lavish weapons of the menfolk. It is not known whether
the costumes worn at the Minoan court were already found on the mainland.
When they were buried men and women were clad in long garments trimmed
with small pieces of gold plate, either sewn or stuck on. Some of these are FIG. 48
cut-out figures, and most are circular. The engraved or embossed designs
are characteristic of the transformation which Minoan motifs underwent on
the mainland. In the case of the ornamentation the result is less hampered
than in pictorial art, as we have seen in connection with the small chest
illustrated in the Plate on p. 173. The frequent use of the compass in
ornamental design stands in absolute contrast to the spirit of Minoan
decoration.
The gold crowns worn by the dead are modelled on Minoan headgear such FIG. 38

FIG. 27   as is worn, for example, by the 'Prince with the Plumed Head-dress'. The lilies on his diadem are replaced by funnel-shaped jagged ornaments. Minoan floral decoration has here struck deep root. But whereas syntactically Minoan style sought to express the volume or coherence of the surface, this composition tends towards thrust. This involves, or least aims at, a disintegration of the elements in the border and those enclosed within it, i.e. it performs a structural function by segmenting the surface. In other products of the shaft graves the same composition of scenes can be noted.

If one recalls the elegant manner in which Minoan ladies such as the 'Ladies in Blue' (in a fresco from Knossos dating from approximately the same period) used to entwine fine chains in their hair, the bronze hair-pins with their huge rock-crystal heads found in both burial-places must seem clumsy and primitive.

Minoan ear ornaments are more modest in size and of inferior workmanship as compared with those of ancient Aegean times, but the Mycenaean prin-

FIG. 38 — *Stamped gold funerary crown of a princess. From Shaft Grave III in the citadel at Mycenae. 16th cent. B.C. National Museum, Athens. Length 62.5 cm. Cf. p. 169.*

cesses preferred a more massive and elaborate style. Large ear-rings in the form of C-spirals with very thick gold wire in the middle are among the several types found in both groups of shaft graves. They originate from the southern Danubian lands: this is also the source of the necklaces and armlets of thin gold wire that have the shape of S- and C-spirals. Apart from these the most typical Minoan neck ornaments are those in which floral motifs and figures predominate. Most of these are pieces of cut gold leaf linked by threads, and are designed solely for funerary purposes. But the large number of heterogeneous motifs and their varying size suggest that these necklaces must have had a hybrid character. The necklace consisting of ten pairs of heraldically combined eagles, worn by one of the men in Grave V, is, in its subject alone, a typical mainland counterpart to the necklace with the lily-blossom design worn by the 'Prince with the Plumed Head-dress' at Knossos. *FIG. 27* Strings of beads made of coloured semi-precious stones, including pieces of rock-crystal, bronze, faience or gold, which have been found in both groups of graves, have parallels in Crete. It is worth noting the occurrence of Baltic amber.

In so far as it is possible to obtain by such indirect means a picture of the women who wore such jewellery, we cannot avoid the impression that they were less refined than the capricious and impetuous Cretan women, but that they were nevertheless women of power and passion. The image that emerges is one of women who were a match for their menfolk, with whom they shared the same grave, and whose funerary gifts show that they were also mighty warriors and hunters — not averse, incidentally, to joining in the carousing.

Ceramic ware from the shaft graves is of little interest to the art historian, *Clay vessels* but informative so far as the historical setting is concerned. Grave Circle B is dominated by Minyan groups and matt-painting. Among the matt-painted vessels there are some that are modelled upon prototypes of the Early Cretan LM I group. In the shaft graves of the citadel there occur, together with groups of the early type, imported Minoan objects that had already reached the advanced stage of the LM I type. Greater popularity is enjoyed by local imitations of the vessels painted with a dark glaze. In the earliest of these shaft graves (Grave VI) are also the so-called 'bird vases', produced on the island of Melos. Their date of origin must be close to that of those pieces found in the Temple Repositories at the palace of Knossos. For these the latest possible date is the destruction horizon, which may be assigned to the year 1570 B.C.

On the 'terrace of shaft graves' Schliemann found remains of 17 limestone *Grave stelae* stelae. They faced west, and a relationship existed between them and the

FIG. 37
APPX. PL. 19dead who were buried in the graves, with their heads pointing east; these stelae originally stood over the graves (but at a lower level). The largest of those that have been preserved is 1.86 m. high and 1.03 m. wide. Eleven of them bear engraved decoration or are carved in low relief. Over the graves in the other group are two plain stelae, as well as one that is engraved and one bearing reliefs. In its secondary function the latter had a depression, and served as the base for a plain slab. The scenes, inspired at least to some extent by Cretan designs, have themes that were also popular on the main

land: the capture of a wild bull, two men wrestling with two lions who have attacked a bull, and chariot-borne warriors fighting other warriors on foot. The clumsy treatment makes it difficult to interpret the meaning exactly. The principal ornamentation consists of wavy and spiral bands, which also derive from the Minoan repertoire. Most of the Cretan works bearing it are, however, not contemporaneous but relate to the preceding MM phase. They did, however, survive in textiles, so that these designs became known through fabrics in the workshops on the mainland where the stelae were produced. In spite of their lack of proportion and their unsophisticated character they are remarkable for their tendency towards monumentality, which finds a more satisfactory expression in the ornamentation than in the pictorial representations. This tendency received no stimulus from Crete.

The works of art found in the shaft graves are of a composite character. It is significant that the importation of objects produced by craftsmen plays a different role from that which it played earlier in Crete, since it gave a major stimulus to local production. Of the works mentioned above the two

gold and silver rhyta in the shape of animal heads (cf. Plates on pp. 151, 178) were definitely imported. This also applies to some of the vases, as well as to the weapons and other bronze implements. The alabaster vessels, works in faience, and ostrich eggs used to hold votive offerings have also justly been identified as imported objects.

The products of Cretan craftsmen made for patrons on the mainland form a separate group. Among them are such masterpieces as the dagger with the lion-hunt and the signet-ring featuring the battle scenes. Also mentioned above are a gem and a group of clay vessels which come into this category. It seems certain that these craftsmen moved to the mainland. We thus have here the first traces of the transformation which Minoan style underwent. Similar developments occurred in Crete during the century that followed, apparently stimulated by the same impulses.

However, it has been shown that the bulk of the finds on the mainland are the work of local craftsmen. This applies to the mask, *kantharos,* and incrustation of a small box, all in gold, illustrated in the Plates on pp. 154,

PLATE 42 — Embossed gold panels from an incrusted hexagonal wooden box. Shaft Grave V, Mycenae. 16th cent. B.C. *National Museum, Athens. Length 9.4 cm. Cf. pp. 169, 172.*

PLATE 43 — Bronze dagger-blade showing a lion-hunt. Intarsia work on metal. Four heavily-armed men and an archer are engaged in combat with a lion; one of them has been thrown to the ground by the animal, which has been pierced by a lance. Two other lions are shown fleeing to the right. The obverse

174

side of the blade (not shown) depicts a lion attacking a gazelle; two other gazelles are bounding away in flight. From Shaft Grave IV, Mycenae. 16th cent. B.C. *National Museum, Athens. Length 23.7 cm. Cf. pp. 157, 165.*

PLATE 45 — Two gold signet-rings, showing a stag-hunt and a combat between a hero and three enemies. From Shaft Grave IV, Mycenae. 16th cent. B.C. *National Museum, Athens. Diameter 3 cm., 3.5 cm. Cf. pp. 138, 166, 169.*

Opposite:

PLATE 44 — Beak-spouted vase. Kamares ware. From the First Palace at Phaestos. Approx. *1800 B.C. Iraklion. Height 27 cm. Cf. p. 127, 140.*

PLATE 46 — Sacrificial vessel (rhyton) in the shape of a bull's head. Embossed silver, with eyes and nostrils in gold plate; the horns and rosette affixed are also of gold plate. From Shaft Grave IV, Mycenae. 16th cent. B.C. *National Museum, Athens. Height without horns 15.5 cm. Cf. pp. 167, 172.*

156, and 173, as well as most of the women's jewellery, the pottery and the stelae.

It was for a long time thought that the inventory of the shaft graves consisted primarily of Cretan loot. The analysis given above shows why this cannot be the case.

Up to the golden age of the later Cretan palaces art developed under the stimulus of a creative imagination that obeyed laws of its own. The 'inner form', which remains constant throughout as the 'structure' of the style, may be traced with unusual clarity until the line of development is brusquely broken by a jolt from without and works of a different character appear. It is not just a matter of there being two groups of styles, one comprising the old structure but containing a new element, and the other a new structure with elements derived from the old one. The characteristic feature of the transitional period is that the second group is only beginning to grope its way forwards and is still quite indistinctly formulated. Another point is that we have to consider many factors that do not belong to the realm of art: e.g., the different ethnic background of the people responsible, and their different forms of political, social, economic and cultural life. This finds expression in material splendour and a hybrid style. Thus the further development of Mycenaean art depends upon the course of history — in other words, so far as the history of its structure is concerned, we have here a new dimension, since the structure hitherto prevailing no longer develops out of the contradictions within itself, but vies with a new structure.

As has already been mentioned, our knowledge is particularly deficient so far as the historical background of shaft-grave art is concerned. The occur- *Fig. 28* rence of Minoan idols and sacred facades can no more be taken as evidence of the actual adoption of their cult than can the existence of gold and silver votive vessels. On the other hand, if the interpretation of later documents in Linear B script can be relied upon, some Hellenic gods were worshipped already in Mycenaean times. But there is no pictorial evidence of this in the shaft graves.

The difference between the cult of the dead here and among the Minoans *Cult of* is apparent from the funerary gifts, and still more so from the fact that *the dead* whole families are interred in a common burial-place, as well as from the stelae and, lastly, from an altar found in the deposit on top of Grave Circle A, from which it is clear that the latter was not used subsequently. It does not appear to have been erected for the purpose of a sacrifice, designed to summon up the presence of the dead, but rather to keep alive in the family the memory of their ancestors, as men endowed during their lifetime with extraordinary power. It is their deeds that constitute the themes of the reliefs on the stelae. One cannot help being reminded of the hero cult of the later Greeks. It can no longer be ascertained whether, and to what extent, belief in survival after death, possibly in the bowels of the earth, was also influenced by ancient Aegean traditions.

There were no direct links with Egypt. The faiences, alabaster vessels and ostrich eggs — as their forms, and to some extent also their material, show — came from Crete, and not directly from the Nile valley. The latter route was blocked by the Minoans.

Contact with other areas On the other hand, the links with Asia Minor were closer than they were with Crete at this time. Those with Troy are evident from the parallels with Minyan pottery. One may mention in this connection a silver vessel in the form of a stag from Grave IV in the citadel. It is a typical specimen of the Anatolian art of the period prior to the Hittite empire.

Links with Europe are authenticated by amber beads, neck and ear ornaments from the Danubian lands, and the so-called bronze halberd from Grave VI, a type that was widely diffused during the Early Bronze Age in Europe. In any case there is no reason to suppose that in the battle scenes we have Minoans fighting Mycenaeans. We are dealing here primarily with rivalries among the noblemen of the mainland. A silver funnel-shaped vessel from Grave IV in the citadel, probably a Minoan work produced on the mainland, represents an episode from the siege of a city situated on the sea-coast. These scenes probably relate to campaigns undertaken by the princes buried in the shaft graves, together with Cretans, and perhaps even at their request, against the coasts of the Aegean lands.

To sum up: the interpretation of the shaft-grave finds confirms the observations made from study of contemporaneous finds on Crete, to the effect that the island's cultural and political predominance had not yet waned as a result of the rivalry of the mainland.

THE GOLDEN AGE OF MYCENAEAN CULTURE The golden age of Mycenaean culture begins after the era of the shaft graves, and reaches its apogee some two hundred years later, in the 13th century. It is no coincidence that its most important achievements are not, as in the preceding period, the products of craftsmen, but works of monumental architecture: citadels, palaces and *tholos* tombs.

Already in Early Helladic times the fertile Argive plain seems to have surpassed the other regions of Hellas in density of population and prosperity. One cannot say that it is lacking in hills whence, as from the Minoan palaces, one may command an impressive view over the fertile landscape. But Mycenae is hidden in the northernmost corner of this territory. The scenery here is dominated by barren mountains: the peaks of Arcadia rise in the

180

distance, and the sea is just visible 15 km. to the south. The citadel dominates the passes behind that lead across the mountains to the Isthmus of Corinth. The summit of Hagios Elias (807 m.) rises above it to the north like an enormous watch-tower. And there actually was a little fortified observation point on top. Its distance from the coast, and the development of the fortifications at Tiryns, made Mycenae safe against attack from the sea. The hilly terrain (altitude 278 m.) itself suggests a fortress. In the north and south-east there are gorges, in the south-west a precipitous glacis, and only in the north-west is there a gentle incline down to the nearby plateau. The two gorges are separated by a steep ridge to the east, which could easily be defended. From this point to the Lion Gate in the north-west the circuit wall stretches for 350 metres at its greatest extent. In general the wall follows the lie of the land. This means that its highest point is in the south-east, where it towers over the rocky face of the gorge. The northern stretch of wall was higher than the south-western part, shown in the Plate on p. 195 as it appears today after recent restoration. In several places it takes the form of a terraced wall and is higher on the outside than on the inside.

The Lion Gate is flanked to the east by the wall and to the west by a bastion which juts forwards for 14 metres, so that fire could be directed against an assailant from three sides (cf. p. 200).

The outer face of the wall and the wall with the gateway are built of blocks in ashlar work with rounded-off corners. The material used is not limestone, such as is generally employed for walls, but conglomerate. To make the blocks bronze saws and damp sand were used. In Mycenaean architecture this way of building the wall face is only found at ceremonial places, where it serves an artistic purpose. Elsewhere the walls are constructed in the so-called Cyclopean manner. Already the Hellenes used to say that they were built by primeval giants. Roughly-hewn blocks, often of considerable size, are dressed for the two faces, so as to give the general effect of a level exterior surface. They are covered with a layer of clay, the interstices being filled with small stones. The filling between the faces consists of stones packed with earth. The walls are on the average 6 metres thick. They were as much as 10 metres high and were formerly topped with clay bricks and timbers with a wooden parapet.

The gateway itself is composed of four massive blocks of conglomerate which serve as threshold, door-jambs and lintel. The largest one is the lintel (length 4.50; depth 2.10; height 1.00). Its weight has been put at 20 tons. The gate measures approximately 3 metres in all directions, in the clear. To take the weight off the lintel a 'relieving triangle', more than 3 metres high,

I. ARCHI-
TECTURE

*Citadel at
Mycenae*
PLATE 47

FIG. 39

PLATE 53

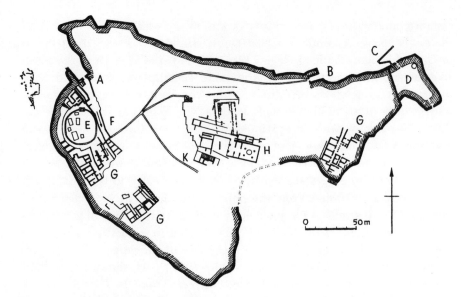

FIG. 39 — *Mycenae: the Citadel. 13th cent. B.C. A: Lion Gate. B: Side gate. C: Steps leading to well. D: Later extension of wall of citadel. E: Grave-circle area. F: Ramp. G: Dwelling-houses. H: Megaron. I: Forecourt. K: Stair-well. L: Greek temple. Cf. p. 18:1.*

has been constructed above it by setting forward some slabs. This empty area is blocked by a slab of limestone, some 0.70 metres thick, bearing the lions. On passing through the gateway into the interior of the citadel one finds oneself on a ramp leading directly upwards to the palace on the summit, which is approached by a winding path. To the west of the ramp lies the 'terrace of shaft graves' already mentioned. It is approximately at the same level as the path behind the Lion Gate. A banked-up supporting wall almost 5 metres high protects it from the west and south. It is bordered on top by a ring of slabs. Access is gained from the north.

The fortifications include another smaller gateway, a miniature copy of the Lion Gate, in the north wall. It was added subsequently. At the east end of the wall a tower-like extension was also built on later. Its purpose was to provide security against attack from the rocky ridge that begins at this point, and at the same time to ensure the supply of water. There are two tunnel-like sally-ports in the wall, one in the north and one in the south. Close to the northern one a narrow stepped path leads through the wall and continues outside below ground level, with many turnings. After 104 steps one reaches the place from which water was drawn. Clay pipes brought the water underground from a spring situated several hundred metres to the east.

In the west and east, behind the defensive wall, there are the residential and domestic quarters. These have been excavated. Immediately to the west of the Lion Gate is the so-called granary. To the south of the grave circle lies the Ramp House, Tsountas' House (so called after the Greek archaeologist), the House of the Warrior Vase, and the Citadel House. In addition, near the east end, is the most impressive building of all: the House of Columns. The palace occupied the summit of the hill. Most of it was destroyed during antiquity and replaced by other buildings. We have only parts of its southern section in the foundation walls. The megaron, which faces west, has a portico with two columns and *antae*, a transversely placed antechamber, and a rectangular principal chamber. The latter is 13 metres long, and had a low circular hearth in the middle; four columns support the roof. The rear of the megaron and its southern wall, which have now collapsed, once towered high over the precipitous rock face, on a supporting wall that was part of the circuit wall. The stuccoed court in front of the facade forms an approximate square (12 x 12 m.) and is enclosed in the north and west by Fig. 40 two-storey buildings. A corridor leading from east to west in the northernmost of them may be reached through a door in the north wall, in the antechamber of the megaron. In the west there is a small throne room, with a throne placed against the north wall. This room may be approached by means of a door in the south wall, to which access is gained through a small antechamber from the steps, which are here situated on a slope. There are two parallel flights of steps, which connect the palace with a terrace to the south-west, over 5 metres lower. The terrace could be reached by a path branching off from the main path through the citadel mentioned above. The main entrance to the palace lay at its north-western corner.

The history of the building of Mycenae begins with a small citadel on the hill, which must have existed at the time of the shaft graves. Unfortunately no remains have been preserved which could enable us to obtain an idea of its appearance. The oldest part of the citadel wall is that to the north of the Lion Gate, in which the smaller gateway was later inserted. At that time the path led in the opposite direction up to what was later to become the ramp. Later, when the wall by the Lion Gate was extended, the 'terrace with the shaft graves' was built, because the old royal tombs were located in the interior of the citadel at a higher level. The date can be ascertained from the pottery found in and under the walls. The *terminus post quem* is set by potsherds of the large middle group of Late Mycenaean ware (LH IIIB), about which little is unfortunately as yet known. It appears that these potsherds do not date from a later period. This would enable us to assign the Lion Gate, and the monumental buildings associated with it, to the first third of the 13th century. The wall on which the megaron stands is part of the wall of the citadel. This part of the palace therefore belongs to the same era, but the stair-well, which faces in a different direction, is probably of more recent date. The tower-like extension in the east was added not earlier than the end of the 13th century.

Other citadels

FIG. 41

FIG. 43

It is easier to judge the relationship between the fortifications and the palace at Tiryns than at Mycenae. Our knowledge of its history is assisted by study of remains of other Mycenaean citadels and palaces. The earliest of the palaces excavated, that at Iolkus (Thessaly), seems to belong to the shaft-grave period rather than to a later era. Excavations carried out since 1939 by an American team at Pylos in Messenia have uncovered the foundation walls of a palace visible in its final state prior to destruction. Among fortresses the best preserved is the great place of refuge at Gla, which may be the Homeric Arne, in the middle of the Kopais basin in Boeotia. There are ruins of a palace there as well. It is no accident that no comparable Middle Helladic works exist. The incipient monumentality of the Early Bronze Age has here been developed in a most splendid manner. In so far as we are cognizant of the architecture of the intervening period we may assume that in the construction of fortresses the old traditional techniques and styles were not abandoned, but only reduced to more modest proportions.

History of Mycenaean citadels

At this point the difficulties mentioned above in arriving at a history of Mycenaean art again come to the fore. There are no Cretan fortresses which could be compared with the Mycenaean ones and could throw light on their character. The reasons for this are historical rather than artistic. Another point is that fortress architecture as such, although monumental by nature, must in the first place be considered from the standpoint of its immediate function. On the other hand, it also gives expression to its milieu. We have already pointed to the monumental tendency of those parts of the walls at Mycenae that are built of ashlar masonry. We must therefore rely on comparisons with works from previous eras in the Aegean, and with contemporary works outside the Aegean, to understand the particular style of the fortifications at Mycenae.

On the first question it may be said that the Mycenaean citadels do not constitute a new type. They are a further development of those that went before. It is not without good reason that the Cyclopean walls have been thought to belong to the Megalithic architecture of the ancient Mediterranean. What is meant by this idea will by now be evident. After what has been said above about citadel walls in the Early Bronze Age, no further elaboration is needed to explain why the Mycenaean ones (in our illustrations represented by Mycenae itself, Tiryns and Athens) are their direct successors.

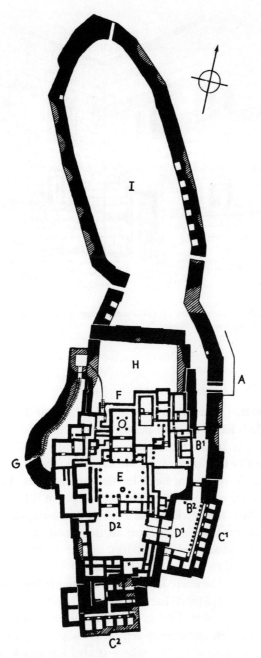

FIG. 41 — *Tiryns: the Citadel. 13th cent. B.C. A: Ramp. B¹, B²: Gateways. C¹, C²: Casemates. D¹, D²: Doorways leading to court. E: Court of palace, with altar. F: Megaron. G: Sally-port. H: Central citadel. I: Lower citadel (refuge). Cf. pp. 187 ff.*

Fig. 40 — *Mycenae: reconstruction of the Palace court (north-western corner). 13th cent.
B.C. Based upon data given by Wace. Cf. p. 183.*

We can thus see that in sepulchral architecture as well the traditional motifs
were not discontinued. The door-jambs, constructed from a few blocks with
a large slab on top, in the *tholoi* are to be found reproduced on a smaller
scale in the circular ossuaries of the Messara. The gateways at Mycenae and
the main gate at Tiryns were built in the same fashion. This development
cannot therefore have been inspired by archetypes of colossal size built prior
to the Bronze Age. Megalithic works reached their apogee later. But the
tendency in this direction is inherent in the trend of development, which
contrast with the mud-brick structures of the Orient — although such
works are also found in Anatolia and Syria.

The connection with the Early Bronze Age is also evident from the gateways.
We still find the propylon, characteristic of the final phase of Troy II.
Naturally it has been taken over in palace architecture (Tiryns, Pylos). The
radial gateway through the wall, noted previously at Dimini, Lerna, Malthi,
Thermi and Troy, occurs at Gla, where it also appears to show Anatolian
influence. The type with the flanking bastion, such as we find in simple
form in the Lion Gate at Mycenae, assumes a more artistic form at Tiryns

and Athens. At Tiryns attackers who succeeded in reaching the top of the PLATE 53
ramp visible in the Plate on p. 196, and turned left between the two ends FIG. 41
of the wall over it, had to pass a long narrow corridor before they could reach PLATE 48
the gate at the end, a copy of the Lion Gate; and after this there was another
passage with yet another gate at the end. At Athens in the Nike Bastion, as it
later became, there is a similar layout, with several turns around the projecting rock. Already in the days of the Hellenes the approach with the nine
passageways bore the name of 'the Pelasgian Nine Gates'. The East Gate VIh
at Troy, which is probably only slightly older, bears traces of this type of
architecture (cf. p. 199). The Early Helladic fortress at Aegina was already PLATE 51
furnished with a gate of this nature, but in this case it was derived from an
earlier form found at Troy I.

The city walls of Hattusas (Boghazköy), capital of the Hittite empire, provide
the nearest parallels, although there are noteworthy differences as well. These
walls also have a Cyclopean character.

We again find blocks more than two metres long — at Tiryns two to three
metres. The largest ones occur in the most recent parts of the fortress at Tiryns.
Gla, which can hardly be called a citadel on account of its odd size (maximum
length 700 metres), gives the impression of a smaller version of Hattusas (maximum length at least 2 km.). It is the same with the gates. They are radial
passageways through the wall and have guard-rooms and turrets. In their passion for building with huge blocks the rulers of Mycenae did not lag behind
the kings of Hatti. But none of the Mycenaean fortresses is as early in date
as the city wall of Hattusas. Its extension to the south was built in the first
half of the 14th century, if not earlier. Since the golden age of the Hittite
empire continues into the early 12th century, one cannot help concluding
that it exerted an influence upon the building of the Mycenaean citadels.
The ground had already been prepared by the similar conditions at both
places. The differences in the degree of monumentality are the result of the
layout. The individual motifs of the wall and the gate at Mycenae display
a similar articulating tendency. At Tiryns the bastions in the south and south-
east are furnished with vaulted chambers, corridors and internal stairways
(cf. Plate on p. 197). Furthermore, the gateway anticipates the winding of PLATE 49
the main path that leads to the centre of the complex, and in the ashlar
masonry of the gates and the adjoining wall may be seen the beginnings of
a more mature and articulated kind of Cyclopean naturalism.

The Mycenaean palace must be regarded as a development of and improve- *The Mycenaean*
ment upon the ancient Aegaean residences. This is already apparent in its cen- *palace*
tral nucleus, the megaron. Minoan motifs are adopted, as in other branches of
art. This had no consequences as regards the use of space or the composition

FIG. 41
FIG. 43

as such. At Tiryns the antechamber of the megaron opens upon a porch with two pillars *in antis,* in the manner of Cretan pillar halls. Porticos and propyla with Minoan columns tapering towards the base have the same origin, although we find antecedents in the palace forecourt of Late Troy II. A propylon at Pylos with one column *in antis* before and behind the doorjambs takes a Minoan archetype a stage further. The plastic ornamentation on the building is Minoan, too. A little bathroom at Tiryns has for a floor a single slab of limestone (3 x 4 x 0.7 m.), laid obliquely, over which the water was drained off from the terracotta bath-tub through an open passage in the wall and then through subterranean clay pipes. Here the luxury of the Minoans is achieved by primitive Megalithic means. The stairwell at Mycenae, too, copies Minoan designs. The winding approaches are in general reminiscent of Minoan palaces. At Tiryns the principal path from the point

PLATE 48

visible in the Plate on p. 196, between the two ends of the circuit wall leading to the facade of the megaron, has two almost right-angled turns. At Mycenae it rises up from the Lion Gate to the palace in serpentine windings. But there can be no question of one having been influenced by the other, since in Crete we only have covered-in corridors. More relevant is the feeling for space common to all the Aegean lands, in accordance with which buildings were frequently organized on the spiral principle instead of the radial peripheral system favoured in the Orient.

The really important architectonic feature of Mycenaean palaces is the

FIG. 41

build-up to a great climax. At Tiryns, on approaching from the north and passing the two corridors with their gates, one reaches the first of three forecourts. On its eastern side is a columnar hall, situated over the bastion with its casemates and in front of the superstructure of the circuit wall. Opposite it is a propylon leading into the second forecourt, which is larger. From here, after making another 90-degree turn to the north through a second propylon, one reaches the innermost court of the palace. The opposite side of this court is overshadowed by the facade of the megaron and there is a portico on the other three sides. The dominating character of the megaron is enhanced by the fact that it is the largest room in area and height (area 12 x 10 m.; height at least 6 m., or with the 'lantern' over the four central pillars, probably about 8 m.), and is also the highest point of the citadel. Even more magnificent was the layout at Mycenae, where the megaron, although situated about 4 metres below the summit, nevertheless dominates everything by virtue of its location over the precipitous rock face. Its south-east corner rests upon the circuit wall. At Pylos, Gla and

FIG. 43

Phylakopi on Melos it was surrounded by lower corridors and ancillary rooms to produce a similar effect.

The difference in design — in one case an enclosed citadel, in the other an open palace — rules out any comparison with Cretan architecture. But the excavations of the royal citadel on the rocky summit of Büyükkale, on the eastern outskirts of the city of Hattusas, provide further information as to the layout of Mycenaean citadels. The buildings, including the palace, are by and large arranged on a circular plan. In the north, east and west they back upon the wall, while in the south there is a low-lying part which can be considered as a sort of forecourt. This is the Oriental 'injunctive' type of court in less rigid form. It is repeated in stricter fashion in Hittite temples. At Büyükkale, too, the palace itself occupies the highest point. But the gradual accentuation is a secondary motif. The artist does not lead us up to the climax adequately. Mycenaean palaces are based upon the system of conjunctive courts, which was also used in the Minoan palaces, although with different motives in view. This was also a feature of Aegean citadels already at the time of Troy II, after the sub-Neolithic indeterminate form found, for example, at Dimini. The classical Greek temple is linked with the Mycenaean megaron not only typologically but also historically. The cult performed by royalty was continued in the Greek temple, but under new conditions. After the collapse of Mycenaean culture many of the royal megara that were still standing assumed an exclusively sacral function. Can we not say that the high elevation of the Greek temples — the Temple of Apollo at Corinth, the Temple of Aphaia at Aegina, the Parthenon at Athens — was anticipated by the Mycenaean palaces and that it thus had a particular significance?

Despite all the similarities with Hittite architecture, and even proven borrowings from it, the Mycenaean citadel may therefore be regarded as an essentially Aegean creation. As compared with Minoan architecture it introduces a new lapidary monumentality. Although one factor was the elementary need of its builders for fortresses, another factor of equal importance must have been its function as an expression of their architectural genius. At this point we may refer to the sepulchral architecture of this period, to which the same applies, although here there is no question of Anatolian prototypes. The naturalism and lack of sophistication that characterize these citadels also distinguish them from the mud-brick structures of the Orient and the stone ones of Egypt. This is another indication of the role played, also at this stage, by the Aegean lands as a transitional zone between Europe and the ancient civilizations. The same may be said of the Hittites, although it is worth noting some differences that now become apparent. Hittite works have a degree of affinity with those of the Orient unknown to Mycenaean works. This is evident both in their design and in the tendency to massive compositions. The Cyclopean walls, the introduction of ashlar masonry at points of emphasis, the functionally clear and orthogonal structure of the Lion Gate (and others like it), and finally the extensive use of 'false' or corbelled vaulting — all these features are evidence of a sense of the functional dynamism of stone architecture. This is lacking in Egyptian work in stone, where the emphasis lies upon timelessness and tranquillity, whereas the Hittites were unable to make any headway against the strong pressure for massive compositions.

Troy VI   Troy VI stands apart from Mycenaean architecture. The impressive remains of this citadel, uncovered by excavation from later deposits, date in the main

FIG. 5b   from a period at least one hundred years prior to the destruction of the city by earthquake, which is thought to have occurred shortly after the year 1300 B.C. The circuit wall extended much further to the east, south and south-west than it did in the Early Bronze Age. Its diameter, measured from east to west, was now almost double (approx. 200 m.). The interior of the citadel took the shape of concentric rings of terraces. Only some buildings in the southern half of the lower terraces are known to us. Those situated higher up were pulled down already in Hellenic or Roman times. The principal gateway was in the south. It was a simple radial opening in the wall, subsequently flanked by a tower to the west. A section of the paved road leading to the palace, which was apparently situated on top of the hill, has been preserved. The East Gate is formed by two overlapping walls. A

PLATE 51   smaller gate in the west is modelled upon it. The illustration on p. 199 shows the East Gate viewed from the south. One can also see that the tower in the foreground has been added on later, in front of the section of the east wall next to the gate. It is not connected with the wall, and its huge blocks lack the cushion-like bulges of its facing. The wall is for the most part terraced and may be dated to approximately 1400 B.C. The tower was probably built one hundred years or so later. Behind the girdle of the wall, upon which there formerly stood a superstructure of sun-dried brick and timbering, the foundations of some of the isolated buildings in the interior may be seen. The flat projections, which produce a jagged effect in the plan, and the shadows of which divide the face of the wall at regular intervals, are repeated on the interior. They are derived from walls built in sections such as we find in Early Anatolian architecture. At Troy, as also at Gla, for example, they only have a proportioning function. The horizontal joints run right through them.

The absence of the Cyclopean form may be explained by the fact that Troy did not survive to experience the great period of architectural activity that began in Greece shortly after 1300 B.C. At Troy the development of the

Middle Bronze Age style continued without interruption. This explains why the early vaulted tombs in Hellas, dating from the 15th and 14th centuries, are fairly similar to those of Troy VI so far as the construction of their walls is concerned. The importance given to concentric and radial motifs in their design is indicative of the increasing differentiation between the western Anatolian style and the Aegean style in the narrower sense of the term. Like Hattusas, the architecture of Troy follows the Oriental style. But the character of its relations with the Orient is different. We shall attempt to show below that in a certain sense Troy VI has a claim to be the Troy of Homer.

On the Greek mainland *tholos* tombs superseded shaft graves as royal burial- places in the later 16th century. Since vaulted tombs have been found at Pylos that are at least as early in date as those at Mycenae, the assumption that a change of dynasty occurred does not seem so certain as was hitherto thought. On the other hand, finds in Crete have shown that on the mainland the *tholos* tomb was derived from the Cretan type. This fits in with the adoption of Minoan motifs in mainland art at this time. The adoption of a new type is all the more illuminating.

Tholos tombs

The Plates on p. 199 and p. 218 complement one another. The former shows the exterior of the 'Treasury of Atreus' at Mycenae. The latter gives us a glimpse from above of the interior of the 'Lion Tomb', near the Lion Gate, which is a little smaller and older than the Treasury; the dome has collapsed. The approach (*dromos*) to the Treasury, which is cut out of the rock, is 35 metres long and 6 metres wide. The walls are built of ashlar conglomerate. The door was 5 metres high and tapered towards the top. A corridor some 5 metres long and 2.5 metres wide led into the vaulted interior. From the Plate on p. 218 it can be seen that the corridor was covered over by three large slabs. The largest of these is the one nearest the centre, the side of which adjoins the vaulting of the dome. In the 'Treasury of Atreus' only two slabs were used. The one nearer the outside is almost as wide as the *dromos,* and in front forms part of the door-frame. The interior is no less than 8 metres wide, 5 metres deep and 1.20 metres high. The relieving triangle on the top corresponds to that on the Lion Gate. Next to the doorway, against the facade, stood two slender half-columns of the Cretan type, made of green stone with ornamental relief. They were surmounted by a superstructure, or attic, with incrustation in red and green stone. Two small half-columns stood over the large ones. There is a striking contrast between the bold func- tionalism of the stone architecture, carried out with incomparable material and technical expertise, and the Minoan motifs decorating it, which were

PLATES 52, 55

APPX. PL. 16

PLATE 55

designed for spacious columnar halls of wood and sun-dried brick. The interior measures 14.50 metres in diameter and 13.20 metres in height. Whereas the 'Lion Tomb' only has ashlar masonry close to its entrance, and elsewhere walls consisting of small slabs over a base of such masonry, the 'Treasury of Atreus' is built throughout of large blocks. The structural device of corbelling is employed. The blocks are set in overlapping horizontal courses. The faces of the blocks are cut to enclose a dome-shaped space with a pointed top. The small rock-cut side-chamber in the 'Treasury of Atreus' is an unusual feature.

Apart from a few exceptions on the islands and along the western coast of Asia Minor, the distribution of Mycenaean *tholos* tombs is limited to the mainland, where they extend to the north as far as Thessaly. Mycenae itself can boast of 9 such specimens. A particularly large number are situated around Pylos in Messenia. Finally, there are the two most imposing representatives of this type of architecture: the 'Treasury of Atreus' at Mycenae and the 'Treasury of Minyas' at Orchomenos in Boeotia. There is a connection between them in that they have almost the same measurements, the same built-on side-chamber, and the same ashlar style. The architecture at Orchomenos is particularly ornate, since the ceiling in the side-chamber is panelled with green stone slabs decorated with ornaments in relief. In both cases their origin must be assigned to the first third of the 13th century. After this period the rock-cut tomb, which had existed for many centuries, was the only type used for royal tombs. The assumption that the Lion Gate and the 'Treasury of Atreus' were built simultaneously is based on a comparison between the style of the architecture and the technique of building, as well as on an examination of the potsherds found in the appropriate stratigraphic levels. It must be presumed that these two buildings were commissioned by the same person and also built by the same person. That this architect was also responsible for the construction of the 'Treasury of Minyas' is an attractive hypothesis. For the art historian the most important result obtained from the study of the vaulted tombs is the light thrown by them on the prehistory and development of Megalithic architecture. This evidence corroborates the observations made with reference to fortress architecture, where, as is shown by the rebuilding of the citadel walls at Tiryns two generations later, stones of an even larger size were used. The golden age of monumental architecture between 1300 and 1270 lead to the conclusion that Mycenae enjoyed a flourishing period of political power at this time.

Summary The *tholos* tombs are the largest unsupported chambers in antiquity prior to Emperor Hadrian's Pantheon. It is necessary to make this point for the very reason that it illustrates the contrast between this style and that of

Greece, as well as that of Egypt and the ancient Orient, and also because the same kind of naturalism finds expression here as in fortification works. In this respect these buildings supplement the evidence of the Mycenaean megara. This corresponds to their typological derivation from the ancient Aegean basis. The history of Megalithic architecture led to the same results, but for all the differences between them brings us closer to Greece with its monumental stone buildings. A similar maturity, with a tendency towards tectonic construction, can also be noted in the vaulted tombs. There is the same proportioning and accentuation in the relationship between the *dromos* and the vaulted chamber. These characteristics illustrate the differences between the Mycenaean palaces and those in Crete. But the way in which the tectonic beginnings are obscured by heterogeneous Minoan motifs, which will be dealt with later, is symptomatic of the broken and complex character of the transitional stage, with its quality of transformation and renaissance. It is therefore all the more surprising that such a sense of immediacy and forceful expressiveness should emanate from these tombs. The implication of this for the age when they were built can only be assessed if we consider some of the non-artistic aspects involved. But before we go on to deal with this question it is necessary to summarize briefly the results of Mycenaean architecture as expressed in fortresses, palaces and sepulchral monuments. It is in itself of some significance that stone buildings of functional and dynamic character should have existed already at this time on the same soil where the classical temple was to come into existence. This throws some light on the question raised in our introduction. But even if one regards these remarks as helping to clarify the problem, a certain reserve is necessary — for Mycenaean architects made some considerable headway towards solving problems of interior architecture as well. In addition to the *tholos* tombs there are the magnificent megara at Mycenae, Tiryns and Pylos, where four columns support a lantern-like structure over the hearth in the centre of the hall. At Büyükkale there is an enormous hall, almost square in plan, which measures approximately 39 metres in length and has some 25 wooden interior supports. These supplement the observations made at Troy II and in the Minoan palaces with regard to the tendencies towards an artistic arrangement of the interior of buildings during prehistoric times in the border region between the Orient and Europe. We know how reserved the later Greeks were in their attitude to this problem. If Mycenaean citadels are to be regarded as expressing one side of the Greek character, it must be borne in mind that they do so only in an embryonic latent fashion, if at all. How far removed they are from achieving an integrated form is shown by the fact that they co-exist with completely different forms of ancient Aegean

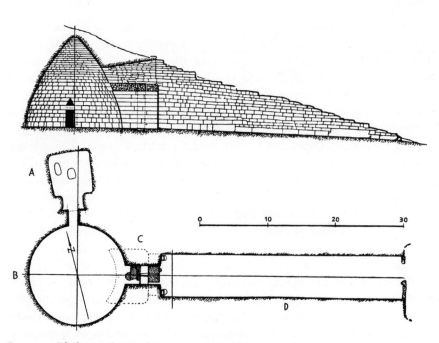

FIG. 42 — *Tholos tomb near Mycenae, so-called 'Treasury of Atreus'. Early 13th cent. B.C. A: Rock-cut burial chamber. B: Vaulted chamber. C: Colossal slab over entrance. D: Dromos (uncovered). Cf. p. 191.*

origin. Whether this makes for better understanding of classical works is a question we cannot go into here. But our view is that the dynamic forces in Greek art may emerge into our field of vision at this point. We have attempted to explain why Mycenaean architecture makes the great impression on us that it does. It will also now be evident that the new un-Minoan formal elements, found at first in Cretan products of the Late Palace era, and at a later stage in shaft-grave art, have been through a process of accentuation and are more compact. The convergence of earlier and later phenomena cannot be overlooked, in so far as attention is paid to the basic formal structure that exists despite the differences in motifs and subject matter. One's first impression is one of the modifications that have been made. Only now does it become clear in what sense this can be regarded as a positive development. For the style that has been superseded this signifies neither innovation nor decline. The allusion to the tectonic element in Mycenaean architecture — i.e. an element whose function in classical art is familiar enough — suggests that we have here something radically new. How far this is the historical purpose of Mycenaean art is a matter which we shall discuss in our concluding chapter.

PLATE 47 — Mycenae: the Citadel, seen from the south. 13th cent. B.C. In the background is Mt. Hagios Elias (807 m.). *Cf. p. 181.*

PLATE 48 — Tiryns: East entrance and Cyclopean wall of the citadel, with sloping path. Early 13th cent. B.C. *Thickness of wall approx. 6 m. Cf. pp. 187, 188.*

Opposite:

PLATE 49 — Tiryns: vaulted gallery and entrances to casemates in south-eastern bastion of the wall of the citadel. Late 13th cent. B.C. *Length approx. 30 m. Cf. p. 187.*

PLATE 50 — Amphora with three handles, covered with glaze paint, showing nautili, coral reefs and seaweed. From a *tholos* tomb near Kakovatos, Elis. 15th cent. B.C. *National Museum, Athens. Height 78 cm. Cf. pp. 141, 205.*

Opposite Top:
PLATE 51 — Troy VI: eastern side of fortifications. Foreground: remains of a projecting tower. In the rear, on the right: East Gate. 14th cent. B.C. *Height of part of wall preserved 3—4 m. Cf. pp. 187, 190.*

Opposite Bottom:
PLATE 52 — Doorway of the *tholos* tomb at Mycenae known as 'The Treasury of Atreus'. The facade and relieving triangle over the door were faced with slabs in relief and half-columns in coloured stone. Early 13th cent. B.C. *Height of door 5 m. Cf. p. 192.*

PLATE 53 — Lion Gate, in the citadel of Mycenae. Early 13th cent. B.C. *Width of passage 3 m. Cf. pp. 181, 201.*

For the moment it must suffice to illustrate the monumental relief and monumental painting of the golden age of Mycenaean art by two examples. The relief over the Lion Gate (cf. Plate on p. 200) is not an instance of a branch of art that is unknown to us elsewhere. Our survey of architecture has shown that it only offered rare opportunities to the sculptor. All the more astonishing is the character and perfection of this work, the product of a tradition of craftsmanship that was, to say the least, very weak. In addition to this, it will always have a special significance as the earliest monumental sculpture on Greek soil.

II. LATE
MYCENAEAN
SCULPTURE
AND PAINTING
Lion Gate relief

PLATE 53

The slab of sandstone bearing the relief is at least 3 metres high and about 0.70 metres thick. It is worked into the relieving triangle without a frame. The wall in which the gateway is situated was continued over the relief by at least one course of ashlar masonry. The relief is thus inserted into the wall without interrupting it. This is another instance of the tendency towards proportioning. The pair of lions are seated in a semi-erect position, their forepaws resting upon two bases placed side by side. Over the point where the latter touch, i.e. at a statically weak point in the architecture, there rises a column that serves to support an entablature. The lions have no heads. The mortises show that the figures were made of a different kind of stone or of bronze and faced forwards.

From glyptic works it is clear that the motif is Minoan, and Minoan scenes are also of assistance in elucidating their meaning: the lions are attendants upon the Great Goddess. For this reason the column with its altar-like bases and beams must be taken as a sign that this was a place of worship. When one considers the data mentioned above indicating that the palace was regarded as a place of divine epiphany, it becomes apparent that the column was intended to suggest the sacred facade, which fulfilled a ritual function. The old identification of the lion relief as a royal coat-of-arms misses the point. It is anything but an emblem or ornament. It is a powerful symbol which conjures up the protecting deity at the site.

FIG. 50

So far as style is concerned its actual size is not the most remarkable of its un-Minoan characteristics. The thrust of the lions' bodies, in conjunction with the vertical-horizontal parallelism of the composition within the triangle, expresses a non-organic tectonic interplay of forces, which characteristically enough is at once interrupted by the incongruous location of the column. Another inconsistency is the soft modelling and flowing contours of the lions, whose bones are not shown. This is a legacy of the Minoans. In the modification of style one may sense the new element more clearly than one can in Mycenaean architecture, because it contrasts with the essence of Minoan pictorial representation. Between Minoan decoration,

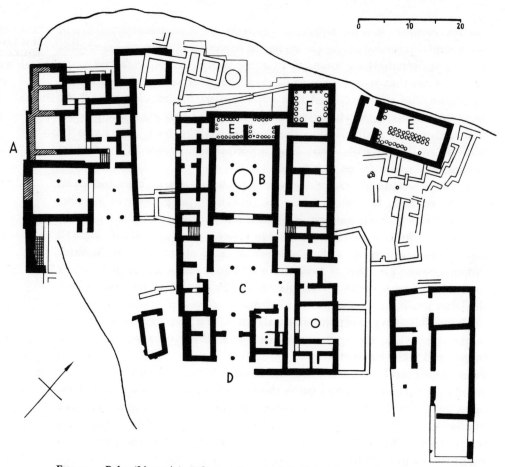

FIG. 43 — *Pylos (Messenia): Palace. 13th cent. B.C. State of excavations in 1959. A: Earlier complex of buildings. B: Megaron. C: Palace court. D: Propylon. E: Magazines. Cf. pp. 184, 188.*

with its radial composition, and a still primitive system of thrusting forces the gulf is so wide that from the structural point of view we have here a fresh start. We need only compare the spiral treatment of the lions' bodies on gems of this kind to comprehend the nature of this structural difference.

Frescoes The frescoes of the palaces are similar to those in Minoan palaces as regards technique and motifs. The murals are supplemented by painted and decorated stuccoed floors. Of the latter only one example has survived in Crete: at Hagia Triada. On the mainland ceilings treated in this manner
FIG. 47 have not as yet been found. The ornaments are identical. A favourite Minoan theme is that of the procession, which may be seen as an act of homage

to the king. Instead of the representation of ritual acts there is a predilection for battle and hunting scenes. The earliest remains are those from Thebes and Tiryns. The former constitute part of a procession of women. They are similar in style to Cretan works from the period of the destruction of the palaces (LM II), but must date already from the early 14th century. The fragments from Tiryns, which are approximately contemporaneous, form part of a procession of warriors and huntsmen on foot and in chariots. Noteworthy is the un-Minoan appearance of their clothing — a knee-length coat with short sleeves — and the short-cropped hair. The subsequent stylistic phase, which belongs to the later 13th century, is to be found at Mycenae, Pylos and Tiryns.

This group is illustrated by fragments which have been put together again, and are shown here (cf. Plate p. 88 and p. 217) as they can be seen at the National Museum in Athens. The places where new pieces have been added are indicated. This group forms part of a procession of women, almost life-size, from the palace at Tiryns. The women, who are carrying their offerings in front of them, are shown in motion against a blue ground. At the bottom the frame consists of a brown horizontal band suggesting grained wood, and on top are a number of decorative bands recalling the sarcophagus from Hagia Triada. Part of this ornamentation is repeated in the embroidered border of the red bodice. To find them clad in Minoan court-dress is a curious feature of Minoan art, which continued throughout the Mycenaean period, although it was not a dominant feature. It must be borne in mind that the Cretan palaces had already been destroyed approximately 150 years prior to this period without any others having been built subsequently in the island. This example, too, shows how great the differences are. A comparison between the 'Petite Parisienne' and the dancer from Knossos demonstrates this point (cf. pp. 88, 129). The pedantic accuracy of one work and the sketchiness of the other are the least important points of difference. These differences are evident even in minor details. One need only consider the small lock which has worked its way free of the forehead, the eyes, or the hair, which on the mainland are treated in an ornamental manner, whereas in Cretan art they are executed freely and dynamically. The most striking difference is to be found in the syntactic style. The Mycenaean woman is enclosed even more firmly between the lower and upper part of the frame than is the case with the figures on the sarcophagus. This can be seen plainly in the fragments illustrated. The curvature of the border of the bodice worn by the 'Petite Parisienne' merges with the contour lines of her bosom and neck. In the case of the woman from Tiryns the curve is interrupted. Together with the disproportionately large swelling breast there is a hori-

Women in procession (Tiryns)
PLATE 54

FIG. 46

PLATES 22, 30

zontal motif, which complements the vertical thrust. The motifs of the wasp waist and bent back are derived from the classical Minoan manner of representing the human figure. This could already be seen on the sarcophagus, where it was becoming more firmly established, and where it contrasts with its original form, consisting of spirals and whorls. Its introduction assists the articulation. That this was the purpose of this modification can also be seen from one of the Late Minoan seals (cf. p. 219).

Fig. 50

This formal basis produces a very different female type: of larger build, more austere, and more reserved. It is instructive to compare the slender neck of the 'Petite Parisienne' with that of the Mycenaean woman, which is thick-set. In one case the head is inclined, and the eyes are directed upwards, whereas in the other case the woman is holding her head upright and is looking straight ahead. In one instance the eyes are small and the eyebrows far apart, whereas in the other instance they are close together and the eyes are large. The similarity of physiognomy between the woman from Tiryns and the Greek woman of the 6th century B.C. is hardly accidental. Thus the outer and inner form, as well as the style and structure, complement one another, as was the case with the relief on the Lion Gate. The Minoan element is evident in the unique exterior aspect. It is, however, still far from giving full rein to the new element, which heralds the Hellenic style. But since it still only appears in pseudomorphosis, it is also impossible to regard Late Mycenaean as a stylistic phase of Minoan art. It can only be interpreted as a transitional stage. This fusion produces, especially in the finest works, something that hovers on the border between transformation and renaissance.

Plate 45
Plate 30

III. LATE MYCENAEAN CRAFTS The great variety of Late Mycenaean crafts will not be dealt with here. We shall only discuss their significance in terms of art history. Abundant finds from settlements and graves throw some light upon the question what life was like at the time and provide us with most valuable historical sources which, for example, prove useful in clarifying certain points regarding the area whence this culture drew its inspiration, its relationship with neighbouring areas, and its ultimate historical fate. Techniques, types and motifs remain Minoan in the case of women's jewellery in gold and glass, receptacles of gold, silver, bronze, stone, faience and clay, ivory implements, weapons and seals. This is also the case with miniature plastic works made of bronze, ivory or terracotta. The most remarkable point is that, although the technical level remained high during these two hundred years, genuinely creative impulses could not make themselves felt effectively within the framework of a self-assured style that had long since left behind it the crudities of shaft-grave art, as was the case with works from the golden age of Minoan art.

When some eighty years ago the Mycenaean ceramic ware of this epoch was discovered this style of pottery was regarded as undifferentiated and was labelled 'Mycenaean koine'. Nowadays this may be considered symptomatic of all the crafts practised. The insight into the dual character of this style, obtained from monumental architecture, plastic works and painting, may provide a key with which to unlock its secrets. It can thus be concluded that Late Mycenaean crafts hardly yield any results for the history of art that go beyond those already mentioned. The occurrence of new types of bronze weapons and implements — swords, daggers, knives, spear-heads, fibulae — during the latter half of the 13th century is an aspect too remote from art history to be considered here. These phenomena originate from Central Europe. They throw light upon a contemporary and subsequent historical process of great importance: the so-called Aegean migration. This was an extensive offshoot towards the south-east of a migration by the Urn-field culture people, who spread their culture over the whole of Europe. In the future scholars will doubtless discover more details concerning the date and style of Late Mycenaean crafts, once the painted pottery, which constitutes the largest and most difficult part of this complex, has been examined stratigraphically. We have to bear in mind that some of the essential data for the study of Mycenaean history have been provided by finds of very recent date. Our knowledge of history is also based upon seals whose classification always causes difficulties owing to their small size. Excavations carried out recently at Pylos and Mycenae have brought to light a large number of clay seal impressions in which the relation between the strata is clear. These will provide useful material for further study.

This also explains why we were able to discuss Late Mycenaean style without considering its development, without thereby leaving a real gap in art history. What can be said of this development on the basis of our present knowledge may be roughly indicated by three examples taken from pottery. The three-handled amphora (height 0.78 m.) from the *tholos* tomb at Kakovatos in Elis, shown in the Plate on p. 198, has already been mentioned in connection with the transition from LM Ib to the Palace style of Minoan ceramics (cf. p. 141). Slight differences in material, technique and style point to the fact that these were produced on the mainland. The painter will have been a Cretan. During the 15th century a complete Minoization continues, such as we already noted in some of the objects from the shaft graves.

The large fragment of a *krater* shown in the Plate on p. 218 was found at Mycenae. The portion preserved, of which part has been cut off at the top and bottom of the illustration, measures 0.32 m. in height. This group of

Amphora from Kakovatos

PLATE 50

'Levanto-Helladic' krater

PLATE 56

vessels, of which a particularly large number have been found in Cyprus, was probably produced in Mycenaean potteries on the coast of Asia Minor or on one of the islands. It is called Levanto-Helladic, and dates from the period between the late 14th century and the latter third of the 13th century (LH III A2 — IIIB). The object shown is an early example of this group. Two men are standing in a war-chariot moving to the left. A man with a lance is striding ahead. This motif of men riding in a chariot is derived from Minoan art. It is also authenticated, for example, by seal impressions from Hagia Triada dating from the 16th century. The decadent style cannot but catch our attention. The mannerism of this late period can be seen in the combination of the very thin legs of the horse with its elongated body; in the juxtaposition of the horse's head, viewed from the front, and the body, which is in profile; in the disintegration of the mane into bush-like ornamentation; in the inner contour lines of the horse; and, finally, in the dot-rosettes. On the other hand, there is a distinct tendency towards angularity of forms. This is offset in the most curious way by many 'S' curves, which do not however destroy the effect. On the whole one could say that transformation is the very purpose of such paintings. But the new element is more apparent than appears at first sight; it becomes evident as soon as we compare this scene with other products of the same period.

Bowl in 'metope style'

FIG. 44
The fine bowl reproduced in the Figure on p. 208, measuring 0.18 m. in height, was excavated on the citadel at Mycenae, close to the Lion Gate. It was located in a stratum that can be dated to the mid-13th century. In order to recognize the features that are still Minoan it is necessary to look at it closely. But the similarity with Greek bowls is much more pronounced, especially in their earliest form — the so-called geometric form. The zone around the handle has a broad band on top and two narrow dark bands below. It is filled in with four groups of vertical lines, between which are three rectangles of the same size. The one in the middle is decorated with horizontal wavy lines. Each of the other two has two groups of concentric semicircles. Thus a system is formed consisting of four triglyphs, corresponding to three metopes with a centre and symmetrical projections. Its segmentary character corresponds to the articulation of the vessel itself, in that it separates the lower undecorated part, which is enclosed within a convex surface, from the concave lip; its height is level with the base of the handles.

Its relationship to a point which has a real functional effect enables it to symbolize the forces manifest there, instead of serving simply as decorative filling. There is no need for us to explain why this is diametrically opposed to the classical Minoan style, which was concerned with filling in the surface in a uniform radial manner. On the other hand, it is not accidental that the end of Mycenaean development should be marked by a primarily tectonic, and at the same time largely Hellenistic, decorative system, consisting of triglyphs and metopes. Various attempts at tectonic and functional form could be noted from the time of shaft-grave art (and also from the end of the Minoan Palace period) onwards. They became more frequent in various branches of Late Mycenaean production, when, as is now evident, they began to go through a process of integration. During the Bronze Age this is as far as they could go. Only a certain gentle curvature of the surface of the vessel and its contour lines, and perfunctorily drawn tremulous lines to fill in the centre of the metope, have survived as relics of the ancient Aegean and Minoan heritage. Seen in retrospect, this corroborates our interpretation of its origins.

A comparison with a protogeometric vessel dating from the 11th or 10th FIG. 49 centuries B.C., which belongs already to the Iron Age, shows how close Late Mycenaean is to the Hellenic geometric style (cf. Figure on p. 215). The differences are apparent in the fact that in one case the decoration is executed by means of compass and ruler and in the other free-hand, and that the vessel itself has become articulated — as is particularly evident in the beginning of the neck above the wide belly. But it is not possible to speak of integration proper until the next phase. So far as we know at present, the intervening period was characterized by continuity in technique, the shape of the vessels, their ornamental motifs, and their style.

The Late Mycenaean vessel decorated with triglyphs and metopes which *'Granary style'* we have discussed is not a product of the final phase of the Mycenaean *and 'close style'* period. For more than two generations, from the closing years of the 13th century up to the destruction of Mycenaean culture in or about the mid-12th century, ceramic ware was in the main extremely simple. This type of pottery, known as the granary style, derives its name from the granary situated next to the Lion Gate at Mycenae, where it serves to identify the horizon of the final destruction of the citadel. Ornamentation, too, plays a smaller part: it now consists almost exclusively of horizontal painted bands. In addition there is a smaller type lavishly decorated with ornaments and figures which is called 'close style'. This type is characterized by the fact FIG. 45 that the motifs are contained within horizontal frames. The two groups form the IIIC stage. The preceding IIIB stage was represented by the bowl from Mycenae and the Levanto-Helladic *krater* (cf. Plate on p. 218 and Fig. on PL. 56, FIG. 44 p. 208). Shortly after the citadels were destroyed the IIIC types cease to appear, to be superseded by those of the so-called sub-Mycenaean type. With the latter Bronze Age production peters out in a system that is unpretentious both from the technical and artistic point of view.

FIG. 49

FIG. 44 — *Late Mycenaean bowl painted in 'metope style'. 13th cent. B.C. Found in a granary in the citadel at Mycenae, behind the Lion Gate. Diameter approx. 18 cm. Cf. pp. 206, 207.*

As regards the direct connection of this ceramic ware with that of the proto-geometric style, which appears in the 11th century, excavations carried out in the cemetery of Kerameikos in Athens have produced valuable clues. When the criteria already mentioned are applied, the protogeometric style is seen to be clearly distinguished by the fact that compass and ruler were used in painting, and by the articulation of the shape of the vessel. Thus we reach the beginning of the Iron Age, the Hellenic period and recorded history — and also the limits of our survey. We have here been looking ahead in order to show what we mean by referring to renaissance as well as transformation as the content of Mycenaean art history. The spectacle is a curious and paradoxical one, since it combines continuity, death and re-birth, as it were. The development of form alone is not of course sufficient to enable us to comprehend it fully. Many instances have shown how this process did not take place in isolation, but was determined to some extent by the pattern of historical events. In conclusion we shall therefore have to deal with the history of the closing phase of the Bronze Age.

HISTORICAL BACKGROUND For the three centuries of the Late Mycenaean period (1400—1100 B.C.) the sources provide a more closely-woven historical fabric than has hitherto been the case. Finds are now relatively numerous. This is partly due to the fact that they are distributed over a more extensive area, and that they are more easily accessible owing to their location in upper strata. But the main reason is that the period was in general a flourishing one, and its achievements were the work of a sizable element of the population. We also have the Linear B texts from the mainland which contain first-hand accounts of the

Epics and legends age when they were compiled, i.e. the late 13th century. Finally, there is the direct testimony of legend and epic saga. But the increase in the amount of material available raises new and complex problems. Ventris' deciphering of the Linear B script aroused a wave of tremendous optimism which was in turn followed by general disillusionment. Ten years' work on this problem has shown clearly how great a gap there is between deciphering these texts and interpreting them. The philologists are still discussing so many major questions that archaeologists are compelled to bide their time, unless, that is, they succumb to the temptation to construct broad hypotheses where they are competent to judge only one aspect. The greatest variety of opinions, including the most extreme, are still current with regard to the relationship between the monuments on one hand and the legends and epics on the other. There can be no doubt that the increase in the number of monuments has augmented the opportunities for linking them with mythical and epic tradition. The reason for this is probably that many scholars are now readier to take these traditions literally than they used to be. The mere fact that it is frequently possible to devise combinations seems to them sufficient proof of the historicity of mythical genealogical trees and events. A. J. B. Wace, the British scholar, whose excavations made a valuable contribution to the study of Mycenaean culture, proclaimed at the end of his life with considerable confidence that there were no further problems to be solved. We must free ourselves from the unsupported hypotheses of the past, he stated in 1956, and regard the culture, history and language of prehistoric and historic Greece as an indivisible entity.

Under the motto 'The Iliad is not a historical textbook' F. Hampl and others maintain that it is a hopeless endeavour to deduce useful data from the epic tradition with regard to the history of the 2nd millennium B.C. True, Homeric scholarship has in recent decades succeeded in throwing much light on the relationship of poetry to the Early Hellenic world, and in particular to its monuments of geometric art. Hitherto these sources had been insufficiently appreciated, overshadowed as they were by the colossal impression made by archaeological discoveries of Bronze Age monuments. Symptomatic of the continued conflict between these two points of view is the different interpretation given of the Catalogue of Ships in Book II of the Iliad. Some scholars see it as a Late Bronze Age document. Others refuse to regard it as historical evidence at all, because it cannot plausibly be linked to any Bronze Age or Early Greek situation of which we have knowledge. It has also been pronounced an invention of the early Greeks. The truth probably lies somewhere in the middle between these two extremes, where it was sought by the pioneers in this field: Furtwaengler, Ed. Meyer, Nilsson and Wilamowitz, and where nowadays, too, if we take a general synoptic view, archaeologists, philologists and historians appear to be directing their principal efforts. In order to understand what this means, i.e. what may be regarded as definite and essential, we shall give an outline sketch here, emphasizing the archaeological aspects. The archaeologist may

claim the right to do this in view of the present state of our knowledge and the semi-historical nature of the situation that confronts us.

Political and social life in Mycenaean Greece

The structure of state and society in Mycenaean Greece may be deduced in its essentials from the evidence of its citadels, the most important monuments of the time. A comparison with the unfortified Minoan palaces and villas scattered over the countryside shows that the power of the rulers of these citadels was based upon their armed might, and only to a lesser extent upon their wealth. It is only possible to understand the existence of neighbouring citadels (e.g., in the Argolis, Tiryns, Midea and Argos close to Mycenae) if we assume that there was a state of peaceful co-existence between the various petty states, either under the rule of a local overlord or by means of a firm or loose federation. In contrast to most of the citadels, which only fell into decay at the end of the period, at the time of the great migrations, the palace of Thebes was destroyed already during the early 14th century. This can only have been due to a feud between Mycenaean princes. This fact explains the general purpose of erecting such citadels. It is in this connection that we must consider the legend of the destruction of Thebes. After the seven heroes had made an unsuccessful raid against Eteocles, son of Oedipus, who had seized power after the death of his father, the city was conquered by their sons, the 'epigoni'. This is supposed to have happened before the Trojan War. There is in this case a relationship between the legend and a Mycenaean palace. The same may be true of other local feuds of which an account is given in the saga. We have to examine in each individual case whether the description of these feuds is based upon recollection of events that took place prior to the migrations, during the 'Dark Ages' between the end of Mycenaean culture and the 8th century.

Of equal importance is the testimony of Homeric geography. To ignore places which played such an important part in Homer's day as Corinth and

FIG. 46 — *Fresco showing a woman, from Tiryns. Reconstruction. White, red, blue and yellow on a blue ground. Almost life-size. 13th cent. B.C. Cf. p. 203.*

Miletus is just as characteristic as to ignore the Dorians. The geographical content of the epic is determined by its theme. But the remains of Mycenaean culture do substantiate its historical features by the mere fact of their geographical setting. During the Homeric age Mycenae and Pylos played an insignificant part by comparison with the main centres of Greek life at this time: Corinth, the Aegean islands, the cities on the coast of Asia Minor — all of which are of no interest, or only of passing interest, to the poet. The functions of the commanding general, as portrayed by Homer, cannot throw any light upon those of the Mycenaean king, even leaving out of account the fact that the tablets from Pylos seem to contain some information about landed property, from which it would seem possible to draw conclusions about his kingdom. Conditions in Ithaca and among the Phaeacians can only be comprehended if they are seen as reflections of the life of the early Greek nobility. But even the heroes of the Iliad are assisted by an army council. This seems to be excluded in the case of the princes buried in the shaft graves, and definitely so in the case of the builders of the citadels, who must have had vast numbers of unfree dependants at their disposal. Pictures of battle scenes and funerary gifts in necropolises, especially in Late Mycenaean chamber tombs, permit the assumption that there also existed nobles skilled in the use of arms who in times of peace were indispensable in administration. The lords of the shaft graves had themselves glorified as heroes. Hence, in addition to the weapons in the graves, we find the gold ring from Grave IV worn by one of the princesses. The heroic deed it represents must have served to extol the king.

How the Mycenaeans of this period consolidated their position by armed force, and how their treasures were collected, can be seen, at least in general outline, from archaeological finds. The funerary gifts in more recent graves, too, have a warlike character. This is particularly true of the pictures, and tallies with the fact that the women shared their menfolk's fondness for the chase. In a fresco from Tiryns, part of a rendering of a boar-hunt, it is just possible to see how the wild boar, pursued by the hounds, is struck by a spear held by some lady's gentle hand. The character of Mycenaean pictorial art is not such as to enable us to identify any particular event. But there can be no doubt that Atalanta, a figure taken from the Greek legend of the Calydonian Hunt, comes into being in this milieu.

A certain weakening and toning down of the heroic and militant note can, it is true, be noted when one compares this phase with the shaft-grave period. But the battle and hunting scenes of the later period also reflect the concerns of the age: first there are the long sea voyages which, although they served trade purposes, demanded a continual readiness to risk one's life; then there are contacts with the powers of Anatolia, of which traces can be seen in the legend of the Trojan War and in the traditions of the Hittites; and finally there are the defensive campaigns fought against the new invaders.

With the conquest of Crete in the course of the 15th century this loose community of large and small principalities, the activity of which had hitherto been limited to its immediate neighbourhood (apart from commercial contacts with Europe and Asia Minor), became a great power. It inherited the full legacy of the Minoans. A study of the ceramics imported from the Aegean into Egypt and the Levant has shown that from the 15th century onwards products from the mainland superseded those from Crete. It looks as though the Minoan traders were edged out just before the conquest of the island. This is also shown by the adoption of Minoan forms of administration, and can be followed as well in the emergence of Linear B script and in the texts on the tablets. Apparently the Linear A system was not suited to the language spoken by the Achaeans. From the finds in Linear B script on the mainland we may conclude that with the new extensive forms of economy and the development of communications the Minoan pattern of palace administration was introduced as well, and that it continued to develop there. It is true that the inscriptions that have survived from sites on the mainland are later in date than those from Knossos. The former belong to the destruction horizons, which are approximately two hundred years later. But this is due to the fact that they were produced of dried clay and were only preserved as a result of the fire that broke out when the building was destroyed, whereas the bulk of the earlier tablets were destroyed once they had fulfilled their purpose. For reasons given above we shall not enter into the question of their content. Here it is sufficient to point to the very unheroic — but for that reason all the more realistic — administrative and commercial character of these documents. It is noteworthy that the economic transformation which took place — the political and social implications of which are not yet fully clear — is only initially and temporarily linked to an increase in Minoan stylistic features. Subsequently the Late

F<small>IG</small>. 47 — *Painted decorative frieze from Tiryns. Figure-of-eight shields covered with ox-hide. Reconstruction. Black, white, red, blue and green. 13th cent. B.C. Height 64.5 cm. Cf. pp. 157, 202.*

Mycenaean renaissance makes itself felt all the more plainly. It reflects the real consolidation of Mycenaean Greek culture. It is accompanied, not only in artistic style, but also in the social structure, by the process of levelling already noted. Very little is known about urban settlements of this period. But much can be deduced from renderings of warriors dating from the most recent period (12th century). The famous 'Warrior Vase' found in the citadel A<small>PPX</small>. P<small>L</small>. 24 at Mycenae, and a painted funerary stele, also from Mycenae, feature files of soldiers marching or swinging their lances. In the shaft graves, however, we only find men locked in individual combat. From this it is clear that the old military ways were inadequate to meet the dangers of the catastrophe period. There must always have been masses of infantry as well as nobles on horseback, but now it is thought worth while to depict them. This is linked with a sense of anxiety. On the vase the warriors setting forth are watched by a woman wearing, not the gaily-coloured Minoan court attire, but a simple dark woollen garment, and raising her right hand to her head in mournful despair. We can already feel the proximity of the Homeric military system.

From these scenes it can be concluded that the courts on the mainland knew and practised the Minoan types of religious cult. Even after the shaft-grave period the same themes continue to be portrayed in abundance. In this connection we may recall the sacred scenes on seals and a little stucco painting from Mycenae showing two women worshipping the epiphany of the Shield Goddess. We know little about the changes that took place. There was already too little space in the citadels for the great epiphany services to be held. The belligerent nature of the Mycenaean princes prevented them from considering themselves, in the Minoan fashion, as priests in whose person a deity may become incarnate. But this does not exclude the possibility that they performed the function of priests in the palace ritual. For this ritual special chambers were erected, which differ from Minoan crypts in that venerated objects were arranged upon a bench against the wall. These objects are no longer confined simply to ritual symbols, but include clay portraits of the gods themselves. Ritual chambers of this type have been found at Asine and at Berbati near Mycenae. Several of them have been found in Crete, dating from the period after the destruction of the palaces. One is from the palace of Knossos, which was then largely in ruins. The raised arms of the idols are taken from Minoan renderings of the epiphany.

A circular altar in the innermost court in the palace of Tiryns was taken over by the early Greeks and after some adaptation continued to serve as a place of sacrifice to Hera. In her cult use was made of an edifice built in part on the foundations and walls of the

FIG. 48 — *Small embossed and engraved gold discs for trimming garments worn by the dead, from Shaft Grave III in the citadel at Mycenae. The designs are produced with the aid of a pair of compasses. 16th cent. B.C. National Museum, Athens. Diameter 5—6 cm. Cf. p. 169.*

FIG. 49 — *Protogeometric amphora from Kerameikos cemetery, Athens. Painted with dark glaze. 11th—10th cent. B.C. Kerameikos Museum, Athens. Height 44 cm. Cf. pp. 207, 208.*

Mycenaean megaron. It it not clear to what extent the goddess, whom we can here identify as the protectress of the old palace, was in the 13th century still regarded as the Great Mother of ancient Aegean times or already as the Greek Hera. But the existence of the Greek form of cult already in Mycenaean times (an altar before the facade of a megaron) is as deserving of our attention as the fact of its continuity. In the same way continuity was observed in the cult of Demeter at Eleusis. Beneath the most ancient Greek initiatory temples to be brought to light by excavation was a Late Mycenaean building within a rectangular enclosure — the only temple definitely known to us from the Aegean Bronze Age. The philologists who have deciphered the Linear B texts, on the other hand, are in general agreed that specific traces of Zeus do not as yet exist, whereas the Earth Goddess and her spouse seem to have been mentioned.

Chthonic beliefs seem to determine also the cult of the dead. This was already apparent in the shaft-grave era, so that this is another sign of the transformation of Minoan concepts. The original chthonic character of the Minoan cult of the dead is evident. But during the Palace period the latter was combined with the belief in a blessed Elysium as well as in the possibility of being able to revive the dead for a time. The Mycenaean *tholos* tombs and their less pretentious copies, the chamber tombs, are only to a secondary extent places for commemorating and conjuring up the dead. In some cases the entrances were walled up after burial took place. The pretentious facades of the classical *tholos* tombs are thus not the background to religious rituals, but instead serve to express entry into the underworld, represented by these impressive and seemingly eternal vaults. The dead obtain their power from their burial in the bowels of the earth. The extravagance lavished on these monuments, and the stress on the individual it implies, constitute the essential difference between the Mycenaean and Minoan cult of the dead. With the Minoans this takes second place to the cult of the gods, whereas on the other hand the Mycenaean Greeks emphasized rather the former aspect of their beliefs. One cannot help regarding this as something in the nature of a prelude to Greek hero-worship.

Cult of the dead

215

The area of Late Mycenaean culture extends southwards from Thessaly over the entire mainland, including the Ionian Islands in the west. On Melos, Thera, Rhodes and Kos Minoan settlements are superseded by Mycenaean ones. On Delos a *tholos* tomb continued to play a significant part in Greek religion. In general the Aegean islands seem to have been simply isolated outposts of Mycenaean culture, while Crete is merely a Mycenaean province. Its craft products, especially painted vases, do not follow the common trend, but develop a related individual style. At Miletus the original Minoan colony was taken over by the Mycenaeans. At the beginning of the 13th century a circuit wall was built to protect the city on the landward side. Apart from Miletus only isolated Mycenaean remains are known on the west coast of Asia Minor — among them a *tholos* tomb near Colophon. Miletus will not have been the only site of its kind (a sepulchral mound with a built chamber inside and a section of the city wall on the site of the later Heraeum on Samos may be mentioned), but we cannot yet speak of connected settlement. There were colonies in the narrower sense of the term, i.e. settlements of merchants and artisans, in Cyprus, in Cilicia, and at Ugarit (Ras Shamra) on the Syrian coast. At the latter site Mycenaean products were more than mere occasional imports, but did not overshadow the local works. We have already dealt with the extent of Mycenaean trade, which was carried on with the western Mediterranean lands as well as with Syria and Egypt. In this region new markets had already been opened up during the Late Palace period by the Minoans. Mycenaean remains are to be found on Ischia, in the Lipari Islands, in Sicily, and near Taranto.

Troy VI retains its cultural individuality within the general framework of Anatolian civilization. But imports of pottery indicate the existence of vigorous commercial relations with the Mycenaean world. It is not yet quite clear whether the Ahhijawa of the cuneiform texts from Hattusas (Boğazköy) are akin to the Achaeans. Their home must have been in the west of Asia Minor, close to the coast. From the texts it may be inferred that they occasionally came into conflict with the King of the Hattians.

The political history of the area can only to a limited extent be reconstructed from archaeological and mythological evidence. It must not be seen in isolation.

The expression 'Late Mycenaean', relating to the period 1400—1100, does not correspond precisely to the term 'Early Mycenaean' for the 16th century. This is clear already from the fact that the term 'Middle Mycenaean' only applies to the culture of the mainland during the 15th century, whereas in Crete the culture of this period is still Minoan (LM II). Scholars have

PLATE 54 — Fragment of fresco from Palace of Tiryns. Part of a scene showing a procession of women, almost life-size. 13th cent. B.C. *National Museum, Athens. Cf. p. 203.*

PLATE 55 — 'Lion Tomb' at Mycenae, viewed from above. The cupola has fallen in. 14th cent. B.C. *Cf. pp. 191, 192.*

PLATE 56 — Fragments of krater covered with glaze paint. Levanto-Helladic type. Mycenae. 14th—13th centuries B.C. *National Museum, Athens. Height of part preserved 32 cm. Cf. pp. 206, 207.*

adopted the practice of referring to the last three centuries of the Bronze Age in Crete as 'Late Minoan'. In fact this final phase (LM III) is only a local breach in the continuity of Late Mycenaean culture, which had by and large replaced Minoan culture over the whole area. The occurrence of several kinds of shaft-grave art objects must be seen in this light. They anticipate Mycenaean works. In the rest of Greece, with few exceptions, the Middle Helladic style continues. The pre-eminence of Mycenae in all realms of art during the subsequent period is thus based upon its particular relationship with Crete, probably due to the fact that the two areas had interests in common. In the ensuing 15th century the most important events are the extension of *The 15th century* Mycenaean power to Crete and the flourishing of Mycenaean centres throughout the Aegean. At the courts of many of the minor dynasties Middle Helladic styles are superseded and Minoan influences become predominant. This is evident from their pottery. In the case of the *tholos* tombs Minoan style spreads to the mainland. As well as the early ones in Mycenae, from this period mention may be made of those near Pylos, that near Vapheio in Laconia, and those near Kakovatos in Elis. Among the later ones is a chamber tomb at Athens, in the area that was to become the Agora, which belonged to the princely family then resident upon the Acropolis. The 'Warrior Graves' near Knossos contain the bodies of Achaeans who played their part in this acceptance of Minoan power and culture. The process of edging the Minoans out from their positions in Mediterranean trade led to control of the sea routes falling into the hands of the Mycenaeans. At the same time they occupied their outposts in the Aegean islands and on the coast of Asia Minor. All this took place at a time when the great powers of the Orient had for centuries lost interest, both politically and commercially, in the Aegean border area. The principal route whereby metals from Cyprus reached the West along the south coast of Asia Minor was now in Mycenaean hands. Until the end of the Bronze Age copper was transported along this route in the form of ingots, as it had been in olden times. Quite recently pieces of copper from the cargo of a sunken ship were retrieved from the sea-bed off the Carian coast. Meanwhile the land route by which metals were brought to Europe *via* the Dardanelles was still blocked by non-Mycenaean Troy. But by this time the Bronze Age had begun in central Europe, which enhanced the importance of this route.

FIG. 50 — *Lenticular seal of dark red steatite (impression): two lions with their forelegs resting upon a base. 15th—14th cent. B.C. Found in Crete. Enlarged. National Museums, Berlin. Cf. pp. 201, 204.*

This was a century of consolidation. It was now that Mycenaean culture attained its ultimate geographic limits.

The 14th century

The oldest remains yet known of citadels and palaces date, with a few exceptions, from the ensuing 14th century: Mycenae, Tiryns, Thebes, Pylos and the second city of Iolkus. Pylos had a circuit wall, with a gateway in the north-east, which seems to have fallen into neglect. It may have been built already towards the end of the 15th century. The earlier group of mainland frescoes belong to the palaces of this period. The struggles for power that took place are evidenced by the destruction of Thebes.

Finds of Mycenaean pottery in the palace of Akhenaten at Tell-el-Amarna testify to commercial links with this area and provide a welcome chronological clue. Equally important is the influence on the Amarna style of the art of Crete and Mycenae. In Asia Minor the same phenomenon may be observed in the emergence of Mitannian art, in which many Mycenaean motifs are adopted. In the area ruled by the Hittites the monumental sphinxes at the south gate of Boğazköy, from the beginning of the 14th century, display Aegean influence in their enormous head-dresses. Cultural exchanges took place as well as the exchange of material goods, and in this the Aegean of Mycenaean times played a role equal to that of the great powers. Thus the 14th century is an age of stability and efflorescence.

The 13th century

Of the relatively small citadel dating from the shaft-grave period at Mycenae only its existence can be authenticated: no remains have been preserved. The extensive Late Mycenaean additions began already at the close of the 14th century with the north wall. The age of the major work was the first third of the next century. It is still debatable whether the old wall continued to the south from the site of the Lion Gate east of the final west wall — this stretch having since been destroyed — or whether it extended to the north as far as the Lion Gate at the time when building began on the Lion Gate and the extension enclosing the burial-ground. In any case it was then that the 'Treasury of Atreus' was erected, as was the major part of the fortress still extant at Tiryns. Because the palace at Pylos was at this time still virtually unfortified, the building of the great wall at Mycenae can be attributed to the desire of its rulers to maintain their domination over the Peloponnese. Can the extension have been the result primarily of a desire to make the building more imposing, or of the architectural passion of an important prince? We can only answer this question after taking into account certain other events that occurred during the 13th century.

First migrations

Shortly after the middle of this century unrest again made itself felt. It reached its peak at least a hundred years or more later, in the catastrophe that struck the palaces. An early destruction horizon shows that Mycenaean culture was nipped in the bud between 1240 and 1230. During the next two or three generations, up to the end of this period, only remnants of it survived. The evidence of pottery finds indicates that at about the same time the destruction occurred of the palace of Pylos, the settlements near Zygouries in northern Argolis, other settlements near Argive Heraion (Heraeum) and five luxurious residences outside the citadel of Mycenae. At the same time a well with steps was dug on the northern slope of the Acropolis to provide water during a siege. In all these cases the ceramic ware in the destruction strata belongs to the last phase of LH IIIB, with some additions from early IIIC. One cannot therefore explain this as evidence of internal feuds among the Mycenaean Greeks, because already at an earlier date (i.e. approximately from the middle of the 13th century onwards) a group of bronze finds of new types appear which originate from the central European culture of the Full Bronze Age. They include, in addition to the tanged-hilted sword and fiddle-bow fibula, 'flame-shaped' lance-points, knives with 'S'-shaped edges, and the so-called Peschiera daggers. These types belong to the central European urn-field culture, which at that time was spread throughout much of Europe by the Illyrians in the so-called Urn-field migrations. But the first wave of this great migration to reach Greece ebbed again. It prepared the way for the second and final wave to which the citadels themselves fell victim.

When Dörpfeld discovered that Troy VI was destroyed during the period *Trojan War* of Mycenaean culture, he declared it to be Homer's Ilion. In the 1930s Blegen established, in the course of his follow-up excavations, that this citadel was laid low by an earthquake in or shortly after the year 1300. The following stratum, VIIA, a rather inadequate restoration of the older structures, survived for two generations at the most, so far as can be ascertained. It was destroyed by human hands. American scholars have taken this to be the scene of the Iliad, and have dated its fall, on the basis of pottery, to the period 1250—1240. These were the years when the invasions were beginning. This fact excludes the possibility of a Mycenaean expedition to the Dardanelles between 1250 and 1240. We thus seem to have cause for doubt here. But in reality this is only so if legend is taken as historical fact. It is all too often overlooked that the question of the Wooden Horse and its function in the destruction of Troy cannot be solved by archaeological means. It is pure myth. The philologist E. Bickel and the historian Schachermeyr already saw in it the figure of Poseidon, who himself originally appeared in the guise of a horse and to whom the horse was later sacred. This legendary motif thus leads to the realm of the Earth-shaker who in the Iliad is the bitter enemy of the Trojans. In addition leading philologists, by analyzing

Homer and studying the legends, have identified 'the memory of a fruitless raid into the Scamander valley' as the historical basis of the legend of the Trojan War. That at least was the view of Wilamowitz and Eduard Schwarz. It opens the way once again to the old theory, albeit in a new form: Troy VI is Homer's Troy, but its destruction by the Greeks is not an established historical fact. "The tales of the Iliupersis bear the stamp of later origin," writes Wilamowitz. The conquest of Troy VIIA, on the other hand, took place at about the same time as the destructions in Greece. It was the work of the same first wave of the Great Migration.

The expedition to Troy and the building of the great fortifications at Mycenae are thus approximately contemporaneous. The means currently at the disposal of archaeologists do not permit either to be identified as earlier than the other. The only fairly definite thing is that the works at Mycenae must have been undertaken by an important ruler who disposed of great power built up during a long period of peace. In any case the monumental extension of the citadel at Mycenae testifies to an age that was subjected to tensions hitherto unknown in the Aegean lands. The same picture emerges from the walls built simultaneously at Miletus. Until now this outpost had not been fortified. But the Hittite empire had now arisen and we can assume that the two events were connected — although we cannot yet decide the most interesting question of whether the relationship between them was a direct or an indirect one, or whether the Ahhijawa were involved. A few decades later these tensions reached breaking-point, as is indicated by the first catastrophe horizon. Hitherto the citadel on the Dardanelles had not only controlled the metal trade with Europe but had also been a bulwark situated at the most important point on the route between Europe and Asia Minor, where it crossed the Straits. The fact that it was no longer under firm control had fearful consequences. After the first catastrophe a number of major fortresses appeared in Greece itself. Among them was the place of refuge at Gla. Tiryns, too, was enlarged to include a place of refuge: the so-called lower citadel in the north of the palace. To this same period belong the casemates in the south-east and south walls at Tiryns and the steps and postern-gate built in the west wall, which gave access to a spring close by. Measures on an equally ambitious scale were taken to ensure supplies of water at Athens and Mycenae. In the latter city the additions made to the east wall of the citadel served to give added security at an exposed spot. The walls of the Acropolis at Athens were also strengthened. A Cyclopean barrier wall was built to protect the Isthmus of Corinth. This was a massive structure at least 6 km. long which served the interests of all concerned. It provides valuable confirmation of the political character of another enterprise taken in common by the Mycenaean Greeks not long before: the campaign against Troy. It can no longer be ascertained precisely whether these fortifications were erected shortly before the invasion in the hope of averting it or whether they were built somewhat later and incorporated the lessons learnt from the disaster. The accompanying ceramic finds belong for the most part to the phase LH IIIB, which was now coming to a close.

We know little about the course of events in the Mycenaean realm between *The catastrophe* the receding of the first wave of the Great Migration and the eventual fall of the citadels at the beginning of the latter half of the 12th century. We can only see that the period of cultural efflorescence was over. Apart from types of pottery (LH IIIC) we have no significant source material. The 'granary style', the 'close style', and painted vessels featuring figures, such as the 'Warrior Vase', are among the late forms. They are severe and realistic in tone. They too contain a new element, but it can only be perceived on close examination. In comparison with the first catastrophe, however, the general historical framework within which the final one took place is clearer. The 'Peoples of the Sea' annihilated by King Merneptah of Egypt in 1225 in the Nile delta belong to the first wave. The area under Mycenaean rule was temporarily spared, but the migration as such probably continued without any interruption. In 1190 Rameses III beat off an immigrant attack on the waters of the Nile and at the same time turned back large hordes of invaders on dry land. He celebrated his victory by carving gigantic reliefs, featuring masses of figures, on the walls of his temple at Medinet Habu (Thebes) in Upper Egypt. The ox-carts loaded with women and children give a vivid impression of the nature of this migration. The Philistines, who settled at that time on the coast of Palestine, had probably remained for a fairly long time in the realm of Mycenaean culture — or so we can conclude from the affinities between their pottery and Late Mycenaean ware. Even the Hittite empire succumbed to the storm. Boğazköy was destroyed in the first quarter of the 12th century. At Troy, which had been reconstructed in a somewhat makeshift fashion — Troy VIIB, as it is known — traces of the migrations are apparent. At the beginning of the 12th century the town was seized by people who came across from Thrace. The embossed and fluted pottery they brought with them originates in central Europe.

In Greek tradition that part of the migration that affected Greece itself is referred to as the 'Dorian Invasion' or as the 'Return of the Heraclidae'. Classical scholarship has dated this to the year 1104, which comes close to historical truth. Archaeological investigation has yielded a date a few decades further back, but in the circumstances this is not important. What the semi-mythical tradition does not bring out sufficiently is the fact that the people responsible for Mycenaean culture were brought into movement as well, and that this resulted in a complete upheaval for the Greek tribes. The Dorians were only one group of those Greeks who, living in the north-western Balkans, had remained outside the sphere of influence of Mycenaean culture. The so-called north-western Greeks — the Aetolians, Phocians, Locrians and kindred tribes — now took over possession of the lands to which they had given their name and ousted the Mycenaean population, while the Dorians won control of Argolis, Laconia and Messenia in the Peloponnese. In Arcadia, in the interior, the ancient population survived, as is clear from the language spoken by its inhabitants during Hellenic times. The same is true of Attica. The legend of the retreat of the invading Dorians, in which Kodros, king of Attica, met a hero's death, has a kernel of historical truth. The expulsion of the Mycenaean Achaeans from the mainland led to the settlement of the Aegean islands and the west coast of Asia Minor by the Aeolians and Ionians. The legend of the descendants of Nestor, the Neleidae, who are said to have moved from Pylos to Miletus by way of Athens, also reflects these events. It is worth noting that the fortifications at Miletus were destroyed at about the same time as the citadels in Hellas. The dialect spoken by Greeks in Cyprus in historical times, known from inscriptions, is closely related to Arcadian. In Cyprus there had previously been settlements of Mycenaean merchants and artisans. Now people of Mycenaean culture who had been driven from their homes founded compact settlements there. Finds show that this occurred in or about the year 1100.

The 'Dark Ages' This leads us to the post-Mycenaean 'Dark Ages', which end only in the 8th century, the age of Homer and the foundation of Greek colonies in Italy and Sicily. With this we reach the limits of our survey. It only remains for us to emphasize the point that this is the border-line between two eras. With the petering out of Mycenaean style in sub-Mycenaean the Bronze Age disappears from view. With the integration of Greek style, manifest in protogeometric pottery, a new age begins. On account of its organic transition to Hellenic forms, even its early phase, despite the absence of contemporary written sources, can no longer be regarded as prehistoric.

Mycenaean and Hellenic art We may now return to the question we posed in our introduction: Is there a concrete and evident link between pre-Hellenic and Greek style? We have attempted to answer this question without paying regard to the exciting and dynamic events that followed, but simply analyzing the interplay of creative forces that occurred. This was a story that was dramatic enough in its own right. In conclusion we found that it merged into Greek art. Nevertheless the

224.

breach in continuity was an essential one. The Greek element that was beginning to make itself felt remained bound up with the prehistoric past, which had called it into being but was now proving a troublesome burden. He who is so fascinated by this spectacle of its integration into Greek art that he seeks to trace its further course in history will now be aware that the ancient re-appears because integration is simply transition. But with the creative developments of Greek art the relationship between the two forces, the pre-Hellenic and the Greek, is reversed. Hence the significance of the breach in continuity and hence the significance of pre-Hellenic art in Greece.

ILLUSTRATED APPENDIX

1—3. Sarcophagus from Hagia Triada. Limestone with fresco painting on a coating of stucco. 1 (centre of rear side): sacrifice at the tomb. 2, 3 (shorter sides): two goddesses in a chariot. Close of 15th or early 14th cent. B.C. *Iraklion. Height of scenes approx. 15 cm. Cf. p. 119.*

4. Detail from a fresco of lilies. From the wall of a villa near Amnisos. Painted in white, red and green. Approx. 1600 B.C. *Iraklion. Height 1.89 m. Cf. p. 114.*

5. Fragments of a mural fresco from Knossos. Representation of a columnar hall with so-called 'Horns of Consecration' between the columns, over an ornamental frieze. Painted in white, black, blue, red and brown. 16th cent. B.C. *Iraklion. Height 24 cm. Cf. p. 114.*

6. Bronze statuette of a man praying. Tylissos. 16th cent. B.C. *Iraklion. Height 15 cm. Cf. pp. 127, 152.*

7. Fragments of a fresco from Knossos showing a Minoan officer leading a file of Negro soldiers, marching in quick time. Close of 16th cent. B.C. *Original height of figures approx. 15 cm. Cf. p. 114.*

8. Terracotta bull (sacrificial vessel). Pseira. Latter half of 16th cent. B.C. *Iraklion. Length approx. 25 cm.*

9. Knossos: one of the magazines in the west wing of the Palace. These were subterranean chambers faced and sealed with slabs of stone, over which stood clay vessels (*pithoi*) used for storage. 16th cent. B.C. *Cf. p. 82.*

10. Mallia: clay vessel (*pithos*), almost as tall as a man, used for storage. Early 16th cent. B.C. Near the north entrance to the Palace. *Cf. p. 100.*

11—12. Clay jugs. Middle Minoan II (Kamares ware). Painted in white and red on a dark ground. 19th cent. B.C. From the First Palace at Phaestos. *Iraklion. 11: height 69 cm.; 12: height 45 cm. Cf. p. 142.*

13. Clay vessel, painted and decorated in relief, showing papyrus reeds. Palace style. From one of the private houses at Knossos. 15th cent. B.C. *Iraklion. Height 97 cm. Cf. p. 145.*

14. Painted clay jug with design of lilies and shell-fish. Palace style. 15th cent. B.C. *Iraklion. Height 49 cm. Cf. p. 145.*

15—16. Upper part of a dark steatite sacrificial vessel. So-called 'Harvesters' Vase': scene of departure for the olive harvest. The leader is wearing a garment with scales. Behind him is a file of men carrying on their shoulders poles resembling pitchforks with knife-blades on them. Among them are four singers: their leader is swinging a jingling instrument (sistrum), while the three others have their chests puffed out as though singing. From Hagia Triada. 16th cent. B.C. *Iraklion. Diameter 11.5 cm. Cf. p. 127.*

17. Mycenae: 'Treasury of Atreus', looking into the vaulted chamber. Early 13th cent. B.C. *Cf. p. 200.*

18. Gold mask of a prince. Shaft-grave V, in the citadel at Mycenae. 16th cent. B.C. *National Museum, Athens. Height 31.5 cm. Cf. p. 166.*

19—20. Detail of scenes showing the capture of a bull, from one of the two gold cups from Vapheio. Enlarged. Approx. 1500 B.C. *National Museum, Athens. Cf. p. 129.*

21. Limestone funerary stele, showing battle scene. Formerly stood upon Shaft-grave V in the citadel at Mycenae. 16th cent. B.C. *National Museum, Athens. Width 106 cm. Cf. p. 178.*

22. Painted clay vessel (mixing bowl), showing warriors leaving home, with weeping women behind them. From the citadel at Mycenae. *National Museum, Athens. Height approx. 36 cm. Cf. p. 217.*

11

12

13

14

17

.18

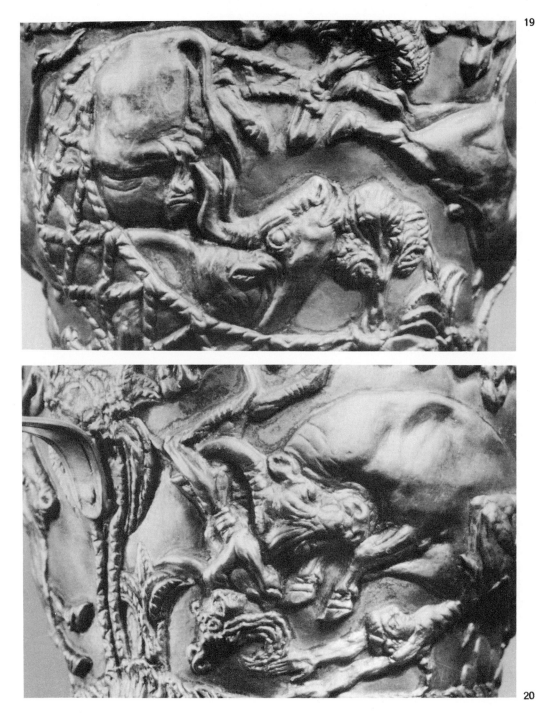

APPENDICES

	Egypt	Crete	Hellas	Cyclades	Troy
B.C.	Ist Dynasty 3100—2890				
2900					
2800	IInd Dynasty 2890—2686	Neolithic and sub-Neolithic	Neolithic and sub-Neolithic	Neolithic and sub-Neolithic	Neolithic and sub-Neolithic
2700	IIIrd Dynasty 2686—2613				
2600					I
2500	IVth—Vth Dyn. 2613—2345	EM I			
2400				Pelos group	II
2300	VIth Dynasty 2345—2181		I		
2200			EH		
2100	XIth Dynasty 2133—1991	EM II—III			
2000			II	Syros group	
1900	XIIth Dynasty 1991—1786	MM I	III		III—V
1800					
1700	IInd Inter-Dyn. period (Hyksos)	MM II	MH		A
1600		MM III			
1500	XVIIIth Dyn. 1567—1320	LM I	LH I		VI B
1400		LM II	LH II		
1300	XIXth Dynasty 1320—1200	LM III	LH III A	LH III	C
1200			B		VII A
1100	XXth Dynasty 1200—1085		C		VII B
1000		sub-Minoan Protogeometric	sub-Mycenaean Protogeometric	sub-Mycenaean Protogeometric	

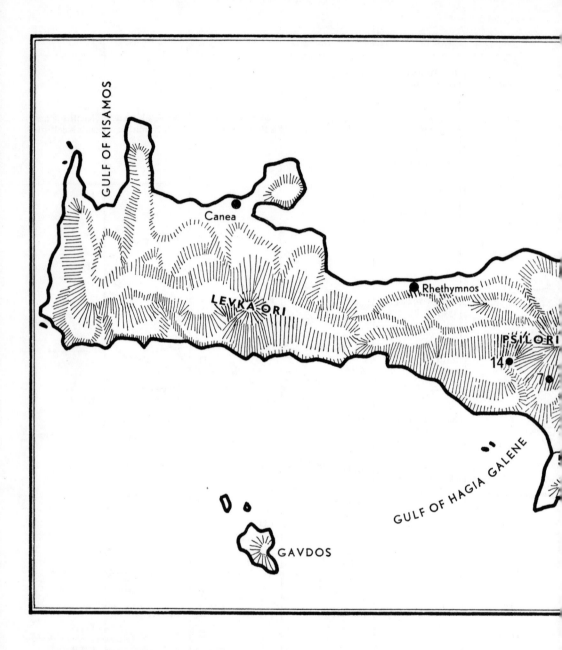

CRETE SHOWING PRINCIPAL SITES

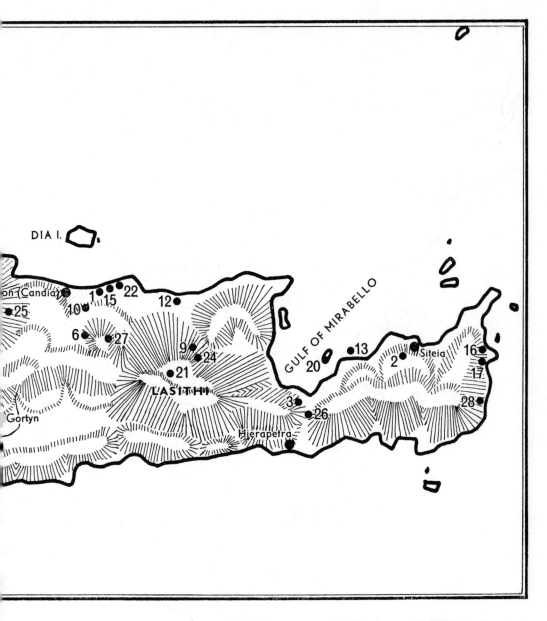

DIA I.

on (Candia)

GULF OF MIRABELLO

Siteia

LASITHI

Gortyn

Hierapetra

1 Amnisos	7 Kamares	15 Nirou Chani	23 Sklavokampos
2 Chamaizi	8 Kannia	16 Palaikastro	24 Trapeza
Eileithyia Cave:	9 Karphi	17 Petsofa	25 Tylissos
see Amnisos	10 Knossos	18 Phaestos	26 Vasiliki
3 Gournia	11 Lebena	19 Platanos	27 Vathypetros
4 Hagios Onouphrios	12 Mallia	20 Pseira	28 Zakro
5 Hagia Triada	13 Mochlos	21 Psychro	
6 Juktas	14 Monastiraki	22 Pyrgos	

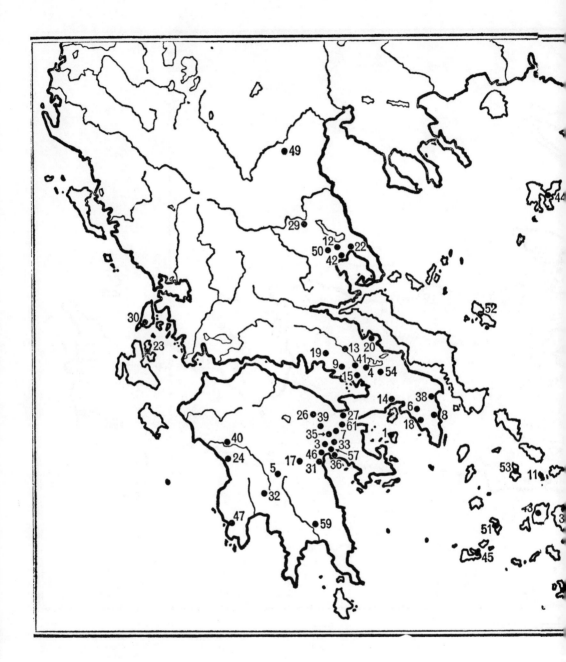

GREECE, AEGEAN ISLANDS AND WESTERN PART OF ASIA MINOR

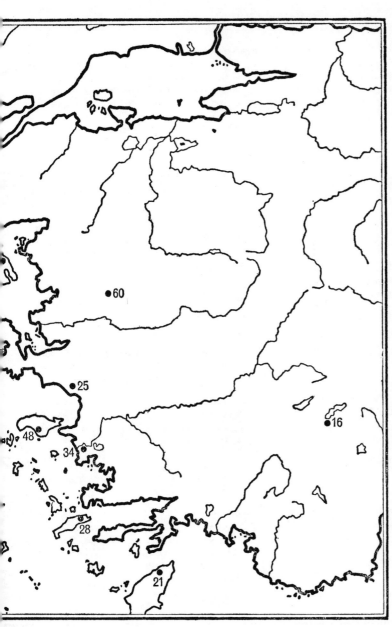

1 Aegina
2 Amorgos
3 Argos
4 Arne
5 Asea
6 Athens
7 Berbati
8 Brauron
9 Chaeronea
10 Chios
11 Delos
12 Dimini
13 Drachmani
14 Eleusis
15 Eutresis
16 Haçilar
17 Hagiorgitika
18 Hagios Kosmas
19 Hagia Marina
20 Halae
21 Ialysos
22 Iolkus
23 Ithaca
24 Kakovatos
25 Colophon
26 Korakou
27 Corinth
28 Kos
29 Larissa
30 Leukas
  Lemnos: *see* Poliochni
31 Lerna
  Lesbos: *see* Thermi
32 Malthi
33 Midea
34 Miletus
35 Mycenae
36 Nauplia
37 Naxos
38 Nea Makri
39 Nemea
40 Olympia
41 Orchomenos
42 Pagasae
43 Paros
  Phocis: *see* Drachmani
44 Poliochni
45 Phylakopi
46 Prosymna
47 Pylos
48 Samos
49 Servia
50 Sesklo
51 Siphnos
52 Skyros
53 Syros
  Tegea: *see*
  Hagiorgitika
54 Thebes
55 Thera
56 Thermi
57 Tiryns
58 Troy
59 Vapheio
  Volo: *see* Iolkus
60 Yortan
61 Zygouries

GLOSSARY

agglutinative construction
Layout of buildings without strict adherence to a plan, and according to spatial requirements alone. Rooms are joined together by common walls.

agora
In Greece, the market-place where the people used to assemble and all public events took place.

alcove
Small room without windows.

alloy
Mixture of various kinds of 'pure' metals.

Amarna art
Egyptian art of the New Kingdom during the so-called Amarna period, when King Amenhotep IV transferred his capital from Thebes to Tell-el-Amarna (14th cent. B.C.).

amphora
Two-handled vessel.

antae
Lateral walls of a building, carried out to form a portico, the thickened ends serving as pilasters.

anthemion
Ornamental frieze of palmettes and lotus-buds.

apse
Semi-circular recess in a building, often on the shorter side of a rectangular area.

ashlar masonry style
Architectural style employing large blocks of stone, which form an obvious and effective feature of the style.

astraki
Mortar-like substance (modern Greek, Cretan dialect).

attic
Low enclosed storey above the main cornice of a building.

banded ware
Type of pottery from the Neolithic culture of the Danubian lands, decorated with ornamental bands (mainly consisting of spirals and meanders).

bucranium
Representation of the head of an ox, viewed frontally.

Calydonian boar-hunt
According to Greek legend the Calydonian boar was sent by the goddess Artemis to ravage the gardens and meadows of Anatolia because she had been offended by King Oeneus. Meleager, the king's son, succeeded in killing the boar; Atalanta, Meleager's beloved, took part in the hunt.

carnelian
Reddish semi-precious stone, suitable for carving gems.

casemates
Chambers protected by specially strong fortifications, used for quartering troops and storing military supplies.

chalcedony
Opaque or scarcely transparent semi-precious stone, usually red in colour (quartz), especially suited for engraving gems.

clear, in the
Measurement to denote the interior diameter, height or width of an aperture.

conglomerate
Term used for pieces of rock cemented together by a natural binding material. Conglomerate is not the result of organic growth but of certain natural phenomena (volcanic eruptions, rock folds, etc.).

crepis, crepidoma
Stepped outer edge of the platform of a temple.

crypt
Underground ritual chamber.

Cyclops
In Greek legend, giant-like people who lived

in primeval times. They are said to have built the 'Cyclopean' walls, which consist of huge crudely-hewn stones piled on top of one another.

depas
Cf. Trojan depas.

dromos
Uncovered passageway.

epiphany
Manifestation of a deity.

faience
Earthenware made from a mixture of various kinds of clay, cleaned and tempered with water, and then glazed, thereby making the porous clay impermeable.

false arch
Type of arch constructed by carrying the walls inward by means of overlapping courses — as distinct from the true arch, built of conical stones or of stones held together by mortar.

fibula
Clasp or buckle used for fastening a loose garment.

flattened cylinder
Type of Minoan or Mycenaean gem consisting of a rectangular plate with convex sides separated by a kind of ridge, which is perforated lengthwise to take the cord on which it is strung.

fresco
Painting executed in casein paint on plaster while still damp. The colour permeated the plaster and was thus able to survive for a long period of time.

glyptic
Art of carving designs on precious stones, used in the production of gems and cameos.

granulation
Technique employed by goldsmiths to decorate pieces of jewellery, by soldering on small globules of gold and silver.

Hammurabi
King of Babylonia during the 18th cent. B.C.,
in his time the most important ruler of the Ancient Orient. His defeat of King Rim-Sin of Larsa enabled him to bring about the re-unification of his kingdom, which had disintegrated into petty states. His government was based upon a comprehensive reform of the laws, contained in the Code of Hammurabi.

Heraeum
Sanctuary dedicated to the worship of Hera, sister and consort of Zeus.

hip-roof
Roof with ridge in the centre and inclined sides.

Hittites, Hatti
Indo-European people who founded a great empire in Anatolia, in what is now Turkey, in the 2nd millennium B.C. Their capital was at Hattusas, now Boğazköy.

horizon
In prehistory and archaeology, a term used to denote excavated strata which may be assigned to the same period or culture.

Illyrians
Indo-European people who in prehistoric times migrated from central Europe to the north-western Balkans and the coast of the Adriatic.

incrustation
In stone-work, a method of decorating surfaces with inlaid coloured stones (corresponding to intarsia in wood-work).

ingot
Plate into which molten metal is poured for transport or storage.

injunction, conjunction
Terms used to indicate two diametrically different types of courtyard. In the injunctive type (Ancient Orient, Egypt) a space is left for the court in the centre of the building complex. In the conjunctive type (Crete) rooms are arranged around the sides of the court.

kantharos
Drinking-vessel with two tall vertical curved handles.

krater
Vessel used for mixing wine.

light-well
Uncovered court enclosed on all sides by a building.

magula
(= hump): In Thessaly, a mound that was once a prehistoric settlement.

meander
Rectilinear ornamental band winding in and out at right angles. The term was taken from the name of the small River Meander in Asia Minor, on account of its winding course.

megalith
Huge block of unworked or crudely-hewn stone.

megaron
Type of dwelling with porch and main chamber, with a hearth in the centre.

metope
Square or rectangular tablet placed over the architrave of a temple, alternating with triglyphs (*q.v.*). In the Early Greek period metopes were painted, but later they were decorated with reliefs.

Mitanni
Indo-European kingdom of the 15th cent. B.C., situated between Asia Minor, Syria and Mesopotamia.

necropolis
Prehistoric burial-place.

niello technique
Technique of decorating metal: a black substance consisting of lead, copper, silver, borax and sulphur is rubbed into the engraved design and then burned in by heating the metal. After the final polishing the black design stands out against the metallic colour of the ground.

nuraghe
In Sardinia, fortified dwellings dating from pre-Roman times, built in the form of towers measuring from 10 to 36 metres in diameter and from 12 to 20 metres in height. The walls consist of large unworked or crudely-hewn stones, constructed without the use of any binder. It is not as yet known who built them or why.

obsidian
Vitreous lava.

orthostat
Upright block of stone in the lowest course of a wall.

ossuary
Burial-place for bones of the dead.

pantheon
Idea of the existence of several deities, whose functions are universal and complement one another.

papyrus
Plant of the sedge family from the Nile, used in Ancient Egypt to prepare a writing material similar to paper.

peristyle
Covered court enclosed on all sides by a colonnade.

Phaeacians
In Homer, a legendary seafaring people.

Philistines
People of unknown origin who invaded the south-western coastal plain of Palestine shortly after 1200 B.C.

pithos
Large clay vessel used for storage purposes.

prolegomena
Introductory remarks.

propylon
Entrance to a large architectural complex.

rapport
Term referring to the section of a pattern that is repeated. If repetition is continued indefinitely in all directions, the term 'infinite rapport' is used.

relieving triangle
A triangular empty space left over a door-

jamb (lintel) to relieve the pressure on it, the sides of the triangle being formed by slabs that are set forward.

rhyton
Drinking-vessel, or vessel used for sacrificial purposes, having in most cases the form of a horn or an animal head.

scarab
Dung-beetle (pill-chafer). A sacred animal in Egyptian religion, in the shape of which seals and amulets were fashioned.

silo
Granary.

stalactite
Deposit of carbonate of lime, usually resembling large icicle, hanging from roof of cave, etc., formed by trickling water.

steatite
Talc: a soft mineral, generally dark green in colour.

stratigraphy
Science of distinguishing different cultures from strata uncovered by excavation.

stucco
Glutinous plaster consisting of gypsum, lime and sand, which must be applied by the carver to wood quickly, before it hardens.

tholos
circular structure (tomb).

torsion
Spiral twist.

triglyph
Grooved tablet: a tectonic ornament alternating with metopes (*q.v.*) in a frieze over an architrave.

Trojan depas
Funnel-shaped beaker without a base, furnished with two large handles. The type occurring in the Troy II—III stage of western Asia Minor culture was given the Homeric name by Schliemann.

BIBLIOGRAPHY

This bibliography is confined to books and some of the more essential articles that have recently appeared in periodicals. A list of the most important works that were published prior to 1950 is contained in the author's contribution *Ägäis* ('The Aegean') in: *Handbuch der Archäologie*, II, 4 (Munich, 1954). Publications that appeared between 1951 and 1956 are listed by F. Schachermeyr in *Anzeiger für Altertumswissenschaft*, VI, VII (Innsbruck, 1953, 1957). Literature on Mycenaean culture alone since 1955 may be found in the two lists compiled by Brenda E. Moon (University of London, Institute of Classical Studies *Bulletin*, Supplement, 1957, nos. 3 and 12). The second of these covers the period up to 1960.

Awaiting publication is a report by F. Schachermeyr on excavations and new finds relating to the Early Aegean period in the *Archäologischer Anzeiger* for 1962 (*Beiblatt zum Jahrbuch des Deutschen Archäologischen Instituts*), which will also contain a list of works that have appeared during the years 1957—1960.

I. HISTORY OF DISCOVERY

Evans, Joan: Time and Chance. The Story of Arthur Evans and his Forbears. London, 1943.

Goessler, P.: Wilhelm Dörpfeld. Ein Leben im Dienst der Antike. Berlin, 1951.

Schliemann, Heinrich: Briefe von Heinrich Schliemann in Auswahl. Edited by E. Meyer. Berlin, 1936.

Schliemann, Heinrich: Heinrich Schliemanns Briefwechsel. Aus dem Nachlass in Auswahl. Edited by E. Meyer. 2 vols. Berlin, 1953, 1958.

Schliemann, Heinrich: Selbstbiographie. Edited by Sophie Schliemann. 9th ed., edited by E. Meyer. Wiesbaden, 1955.

II. GENERAL WORKS

A. ARCHAEOLOGY

Bossert, H. Th.: Altkreta. 3rd ed. Berlin, 1937.

Fimmen, D.: Die kretisch-mykenische Kultur. 2nd ed., ed. by G. Karo. Leipzig, 1924.

Hutchinson, R. W.: Prehistoric Crete. Harmondsworth, 1962.

Kaschnitz-Weinberg, G. von: Die mittelmeerischen Grundlagen der antiken Kunst. Frankfurt-on-Main, 1944.

Marinatos, Sp.: Crete and Mycenae. London, 1960.

Matz, F.: Ägäis, in: Handbuch der Archäologie, vol. II. Munich (1950), 1954.

Matz, F.: Kreta, Mykene, Troja. Die minoische und die homerische Welt. Stuttgart, 1956.

B. HISTORY

Bengtson, H.: Griechische Geschichte. Handbuch der Altertumswissenschaft, III, 4. 2nd ed. Munich, 1960.

Berve, H.: Griechische Geschichte, vol. I. 2nd ed. Freiburg im Breisgau, 1951.

Schachermeyr, F.: Griechische Geschichte. Stuttgart, 1960.

C. OTHER WORKS

Lawrence, A. W.: Greek Architecture. Harmondsworth, 1958.

Nilsson, M. P.: The Minoan-Mycenaean Religion and its Survival in Greek Religion. Lund, 1950.

Nilsson, M. P.: Geschichte der griechischen Religion, I, in: Handbuch der Altertumswissenschaft, vol. V. 2nd ed. Munich, 1955.

Pendlebury, J. D. S.: Aegyptiaca. A Catalogue of Egyptian Objects in the Aegean Area. Cambridge, 1930.

Persson, A. W.: The Religion of Greece in Prehistoric Times. Berkeley-Los Angeles, 1942.

Picard, Ch.: Les religions préhelléniques (Crète et Mycènes). Paris, 1948.

Robinson, D. M.: Haus. Realenzyklopädie der klassischen Altertumswissenschaft, Supplement 7. Stuttgart, 1940.

Wiesner, J.: Grab und Jenseits. Berlin, 1938.

III. STONE AGE

Heurtley, W. A.: Prehistoric Macedonia. Cambridge, 1939.

Holmberg, E. J.: The Swedish Excavations at Asea in Arcadia. Stockholm, 1944.

Kunze, E.: Orchomenos II. Die neolithische Keramik. Munich, 1931.

Milojcic, V.: Ausgrabungen in Thessalien. Neue Deutsche Ausgrabungen im Mittelmeergebiet und im Vorderen Orient. Berlin, 1959.

Milojcic, V.: Chronologie der Jüngeren Steinzeit in Mittel- und Südosteuropa. Berlin, 1949.

Milojcic, V.: Zur Chronologie der Jüngeren Steinzeit in Griechenland. Jahrbuch des Deutschen Archäologischen Instituts, vol. 65-6, 1950-1.

Schachermeyr, F.: Die ältesten Kulturen Griechenlands. Stuttgart, 1955.

Schachermeyr, F.: Prähistorische Kulturen Griechenlands. Realenzyklopädie der klassischen Altertumswissenschaft, Supplement 9. Stuttgart, 1959.

Theocharis, D. R.: Nea Makri, eine grosse neolithische Siedlung in der Nähe von Marathon, in: Mitteilungen des Deutschen Archäologischen Instituts, vol. 71. Athens, 1956.

Tsountas, Chr.: The Prehistoric Citadels of Dimini and Sesklo. (In Greek.) Athens, 1908.

Wace, A. J. B. and Thompson, M. S.: Prehistoric Thessaly. Cambridge, 1912.

Walker-Kosmopoulos, L.: The Prehistoric Inhabitation of Corinth. Munich, 1948.

IV. EARLY BRONZE AGE

A. CRETE

Chapouthier, F., Demargne, P. and others: Mallia. Antiquités crétoises. Paris. vol. 1, 1928. vol. 2, 1930. vol. 4, 1936. vol. 5, 1938. vol. 6, 1942. vol. 7, 1945. vol. 9, 1953.

Evans, A. J.: The Palace of Minos at Knossos. 7 vols. London, 1921-36.

Matz, F.: Die frühkretischen Siegel. Berlin, 1928.

Pendlebury, J. D. S.: The Archaeology of Crete. London, 1939.

Seager, R.: Excavations on the Island of Mochlos. Boston, Mass., 1912.

Xanthoudides, St.: The Vaulted Tombs of Mesara. London, 1924.

Zervos, Chr.: L'art de la Crète néolithique et minoenne. Paris, 1956.

B. MAINLAND GREECE AND CYCLADES

Blegen, C. W.: Korakou. Boston-New York, 1921.

Dörpfeld, W.: Alt-Ithaka. Munich, 1927.

Goldman, H.: Excavations at Eutresis in Boeotia. Cambridge, Mass., 1931.

Kunze, E.: Orchomenos III. Die Keramik der frühen Bronzezeit. Munich, 1934.

Müller, K.: Tiryns. Die Ergebnisse der Ausgrabungen des Instituts, IV. Die Urfirniskeramik. Munich, 1944.

Mylonas, G.: Aghios Kosmas. Princeton, N.J., 1950.

Valmin, N.: The Swedish Messenia Expedition, 1933. Lund, 1938.

C. TROY AND WESTERN ASIA MINOR

Bittel, K.: Grundzüge der Vor- und Frühgeschichte Kleinasiens. 2nd ed. Tübingen, 1950.

Blegen, C. W.: Troy I-IV. Princeton, N.J., 1950-8.

Bossert, H. Th.: Altanatolien. Berlin, 1942.

Brea, L. Bernabò: Recenti Scavi a Poliochni nell' Isola di Lemnos, in: Bollettino d'Arte, 1957, pp. 193 et seq.

Dörpfeld, W.: Troja und Ilion. 2 vols. Berlin, 1902.

Lamb, W.: Excavations at Thermi. Cambridge, 1936.

Schliemann, H.: Ilios. Stadt und Land der Trojaner. Leipzig, 1881.

Schmidt, H.: Heinrich Schliemanns Sammlung trojanischer Altertümer. Berlin, 1902.

V. MINOAN PALACE PERIOD

Alexiou, St.: The Minoan Goddess with Raised Hands. (In Greek.) Athens, 1958.

Biesantz, H.: Kretisch-mykenische Siegelbilder. Marburg-on-Lahn, 1954.

Boyd Hawes, H.: Gournia. Philadelphia, 1908.

Kenna, V. E. G., Cretan Seals. Oxford, 1960.

Levi, D.: Festos, in: Bollettino d'Arte, vols. 51, 53. 1955, 1956. Annuario della Scuola Archeologica Italiana, vols. 30-32, 1955, vols. 35-6, 1958.

Matz, F.: Göttererscheinung und Kultbild im minoischen Kreta. Wiesbaden, 1958.

Pendlebury, J. D. S.: A Handbook of the Palace of Minos at Knossos. 2nd ed. London, 1955.

Pernier, L. and Banti, L.: Festos, 2 vols. Rome, 1935, 1951.

Snijder, G. A. S.: Kretische Kunst. Berlin, 1936.

IV. MYCENAEAN CULTURE

Blegen, C. W.: Prosymna. Cambridge, 1937.

Blegen, C. W.: Pylos. (Excavation reports). In: American Journal of Archaeology, 1939 and 1953 ff.

Blegen, C. W.: Zygouries. Cambridge, Mass., 1928.

Furumark, A.: The Chronology of Mycenaean Pottery. Copenhagen, 1941.

Furumark, A.: Mycenaean Pottery. Analysis and Classification. Copenhagen, 1941.

Kantor, H.: The Aegean and the Orient in the 2nd Millennium B.C. Bloomington, Ind., 1947.

Karo, G.: Die Schachtgräber von Mykenae. Munich, 1930-33.

Mylonas, G.: Ancient Mycenae. London, 1957.

Persson, A. W.: New Tombs at Dendra. Lund, 1942.

Persson, A. W.: The Royal Tombs at Dendra near Midea. Lund, 1931.

Rodenwaldt, G.: Der Fries des Megaron von Mykenae. Halle, 1921.

Rodenwaldt, G. and Müller, K.: Tiryns. vols. 2, 3. Athens-Munich, 1912, 1930.

Schliemann, H.: Mykenae. Leipzig, 1878.

Stubbings, F. H.: Mycenaean Pottery from the Levant. Cambridge, 1951.

Taylour, Lord W.: Mycenaean Pottery in Italy and Adjacent Areas. Cambridge, 1958.

Wace, A. J. B.: The Chamber Tombs of Mycenae. Cambridge, 1932.

Wace, A. J. B.: Mycenae. An Archaeological History and Guide. Princeton, N.J., 1949.

VII. WRITTEN RECORDS

Bennett, E. L., Jr.: A Minoan Linear B Index. Princeton, N.J., 1953.

Bennett, E. L., Jr.: The Pylos Tablets. A Preliminary Transcription. Princeton, N.J., 1951.

Brice, W. C.: Inscriptions in the Minoan Linear Script of Class A. Oxford, 1961.

Chadwick, J.: The Decipherment of Linear B. Cambridge, 1958.

Evans, A. J.: Scripta Minoa. 2 vols. (vol. 2 ed. by J. L. Myres). Oxford, 1909, 1951.

Palmer, L. R.: Mycenaeans and Minoans. London, 1961.

Ventris, M. and Chadwick, J.: Documents in Mycenaean Greek. Cambridge, 1956.

VIII. HOMER AND THE MONUMENTS

Lorimer, H. L.: Homer and the Monuments. London, 1950.

Nilsson, M. P.: Homer and Mycenae. London, 1933.

Page, D.: History and the Homeric Iliad. Berkeley-Los Angeles, 1959.

Starr, C. G.: The Origins of Greek Civilization. 1100-650 B.C. New York, 1961.

Webster, T. B. L.: From Mycenae to Homer. London, 1958.